The
Handbook of
PAINTED
DECORATION

The Handbook of PAINTED DECORATION

The tools,
materials,
and step-by-step
techniques
of trompe l'œil
painting

Yannick Guégan
& Roger Le Puil

W.W. Norton & Company
New York • London

A NORTON PROFESSIONAL BOOK

English translation by Josh Heuman
English translation copyright © 1996 by W. W. Norton
& Company, Inc.
Originally published in French as:

Imitation des Marbres
Yannick Guégan
With the collaboration of Claudine Guégan
Copyright © Dessain & Tolra, Paris, 1989
© Dessain & Tolra / H.E.R., 2000

Imitation des Bois
Yannick Guégan
With the collaboration of Claudine Guégan
Photography by Jean-François Farouault and Pierre Mannu
Copyright © Dessain & Tolra, Paris, 1991

Patines et Matières
Roger Le Puil
Copyright © Dessain & Tolra, Paris, 1992

Frises et Ornements
Yannick Guégan
Copyright © Desain & Tolra, Paris, 1993

Drapés en Trompe-l'œil
Yannick Guégan
With the collaboration of Claudine Guégan
Copyright © Dessain & Tolra, Paris, 1995

Peinture Décoratives
Roger Le Puil
Copyright © Dessain & Tolra, Paris, 1995

The text of this book is composed in Bembo with the
display set in Bembo.

Composition and production by Ken Gross.

Library of Congress Cataloging-in-Publication Data

Guégan, Yannick, 1947–
    Handbook of painted decoration / Yannick Guégan and Roger Le
Puil.
        p.   cm.
        "A Norton professional book."
    Originally published in French as 6 books with titles: Imitation des
marbres; Imitation des bois; Patines et matières; Frises et ornements;
Drapés en trompe-l'œil; Peintures décoratives.
    Includes index.
    ISBN 0-393-73001-8
    1. Painting—Technique.   2. Decoration and ornament.   I. Le Puil,
Roger. II. Title.
TT385.G84   1996
698'. 14—dc20   95-38006
                                                                CIP

ISBN 0-393-73001-8

W. W. Norton & Company, Inc., 500 Fifth Avenue, New York NY 10110
W. W. Norton & Company Ltd., 10 Coptic Street, London WC1A 1PU

0 9 8 7 6 5

PREFACE

As president of the professional society *Meilleurs Ouvriers de France* (Best Craftsmen of France), it is a pleasure and an honor for me to introduce this remarkable handbook by two laureates of our Best Craftsman competition. A prestigious award that recognizes both tradition and modernism in French artisanry, the title *Meilleur Ouvrier de France* is the premier honor for artisanal work in France, as the Oscars are for American film or the Olympics for international athletics.

Both in their work and in their writing, Yannick Guégan and Roger Le Puil demonstrate that the ideals of excellence, put into practice by the hands of masters, are an enduring necessity. Distinguished teachers and impassioned professionals, Guégan and Le Puil are serious about their craft, and they reveal its "secrets" in this book with great ardor. *The Handbook of Painted Decoration* is a tool that will help artists to develop their creative sensibilities, to express their talents, and to create greater harmony in their corner of the world.

Realizing any sort of artistic project represents the highest expression of the natural capacities of humankind. We have always felt the need to beautify our surroundings, from places of worship to our homes and objects of everyday use. Interior decoration, always evolving, holds a constant attraction for both the general public and professionals—interior designers, painters, decorators, upholsterers, experienced amateurs, enthusiastic neophytes. To all of these readers, this accessible manual offers a clear and thorough explanation of decorative painting, from preliminary layout to step-by-step execution of the designs, including the play of light and shadow and the subtlety and harmony of colors.

As Alfred de Vigny so aptly wrote, "Work is good and noble. It gives pride and confidence in oneself that inherited wealth cannot bestow." The craftsmanship, quality, and beauty of projects like those presented by Yannick Guégan and Roger Le Puil in these pages resonate as a source of satisfaction and fulfillment for the artist. The artistic and professional values they impart confer balance in the quest for the absolute form of the artistic object, a quest representing an immutable twofold virtue: love of the well-wrought work, and of life itself.

The Handbook of Painted Decoration, with its typically French methods, will be of great interest to those who appreciate our culture and traditions, but also to those who seek freedom and innovation. The book is a synthesis of the theory and practical methods and materials of decorative painting by two uniquely qualified painters who combine the spirit of tradition with projects that are completely contemporary. We sincerely hope that the *Handbook* will meet with great success, and that many professionals and able amateurs will beautify their living spaces, discover their artistic sensibilities and talents, and learn to share our passion for these artisanal crafts.

Madame Olga Saurat
National President, *Societé des Meilleurs Ouvriers de France*

FOREWORD

I am pleased to present to you the English translation of the books, previously published only in French, of Yannick Gué-gan and Roger Le Puil. This volume brings to you the highest level of traditional French decorative painting. It is unique in offering a broad repertoire of decorative painting, including not only exceptional patinas and faux marbles, woods, and masonry that are subjects familiar to every trompe l'œil painter, but also many unusual and exciting subjects, such as drapery, mosaics, and marquetry. In addition, it offers a host of rare and almost forgotten techniques, such as painting under glass, marouflage, and imitation stained glass and laquerware, that are little known here.

The Handbook of Painted Decoration is a significant contribution to the theory and application of the traditional techniques of European masters of decorative painting, but more important, it shows how we can interpret these techniques with contemporary materials, especially water-based paints and acrylic products. These materials allow us to perform in a matter of hours the many steps that formerly required several days to achieve. This is of particular interest to those who seek convenient and safe products and increased productivity.

Decorative painters, both professional and amateur, interior designers, and architects who want a deeper knowledge and appreciation of techniques relatively new to the English-speaking world will find this book an essential addition to their personal library. It provides an invaluable source of high-quality examples and detailed explanations that will assist them with the often difficult task of communicating these fascinating decorative ideas to clients and contractors. Students of art history, too, will find an authoritative reference of decorative technique to enrich their understanding of decorative art.

I first met Yannick Guégan in 1985 when I was a student of this distinguished master of painted illusion. I was immediately impressed by his artistic talent and his ability to communicate his art and passion in understandable terms. Thanks to this ability and to his great know-how, he founded his own institute in Mesquer-Quimiac in Brittany, where he teaches his techniques.

The book reflects my own experience as a student. In these pages, the authors, masters of their art, generously share the unique knowledge that they acquired from years of study and practice. This professional and practical manual will lead you through the steps that lead to successful execution of fine trompe l'œil work and the personal satisfaction that comes from it.

Nicola Vigini
Seattle, Washington

CONTENTS

INTRODUCTION

The recent return of neoclassicism has led us to rediscover the legacy not only of our recent forebears but also of those millennia distant. From a perpetual cycle comes a return to classical and ancient art, and to their well-established ornamental foundations.

Painted decoration has existed since the dawn of time. Whether in caves, on easel canvases, wall frescos, or furnishings, it ceaselessly evolves, from cave art to ancient Egypt to the Middle Ages, by way of classical antiquity, the zenith that constitutes the basis of decorative craft. After the Middle Ages, the Renaissance and the Empire style again took up the ancient models. After the neoclassical revival of the nineteenth century came the floral and naturalistic forms of the Modern and Art Deco, which recalled, with their volutes and other motifs, the pure Egyptian style. Artists improved their craft, as much in materials and techniques as in form, passing from flat and simple representations to elaborately detailed renderings, with shadows and highlights accompanying intricate perspective. The most skillfully rendered paintings deceive the viewer, giving an illusionary appearance of reality. Hence the name *trompe l'œil,* fool the eye, and the term *faux,* false.

We abandon the practices of the previous generation in the name of "evolution"; curiously, this evolution takes up (wholly or partially) older themes that have fallen out of currency. Even the Greek and Roman masters practiced thus. We invent nothing; we only appropriate. Furniture and fashion are good examples. It would of course be difficult, in the twentieth century, to dress in Louis XIV style—impractical for the modern way of life. But in painted decoration, in trompe l'œil, we do not hesitate to raid the storehouse of the ages.

Imagine the anonymous painter decorating Pompeii's Villa of the Mysteries. With such an expert hand, such concern for perfection, he painted everyday lives. Imagine him preparing his brushes, his colors, his parchment sketches. Those wall paintings, with their delicate strokes, presage impressionism—in the age of the fourth Pompeiian style, at the beginning of the Christian era. And the imitation marble dado, with paneling and molding to mark off the furnished area in the villa of Lucretius Fronto, recalls the entrances to French buildings of the last century, and the salons of Versailles. These heights of trompe l'œil, are they ancient or modern?

With the shifting winds of fashion, the art of trompe l'œil fell gently into obscurity for nearly half a century. Interest was rekindled in the 1980s, by the taste for "retro" and the classical, and continues unabated to the present.

Contemporary painted decoration has little in common with that of the nineteenth century; modern methods allow soundness, neatness, and, thanks to photography, perfect imitation.

After a period variously termed decadent, modern, different, and transitional, the contemporary eye has rediscovered frescos, balustrades, columns, perspectives, harmonious drapes, cloudy skies, wondrous gardens. . . . The goal of the decorative painter today is not to render imitation wood or marble as Grandpa did, but to imitate the noble materials perfectly, and above all to integrate them with their surroundings, in a composition in which landscape, character, ornament, and perspective are the key players. Paint five hundred square yards of gray breccia or oak paneling and, even if the imitations are good, they will always announce themselves as imitations. Execute the same material effects with the same level of skill, but arrange them in sculpted panels, cornices, columns in an ornamental composition, all in light and shadow—that is trompe l'œil.

Trompe l'œil painting stems from the union of an art—painting—and a passion—that of the decorative painter. The name "painter" comprises different occupations: the house painter, the sign painter, the painter of trompe l'œil, the decorative painter working large-scale, and the fine artist or easel painter. The decorative painter brings together all the specialized techniques of each discipline and melds them into one. The decorative painter can create an ancient world or an illusionistic Escher world, causing us to forget the everyday for a moment. What can be more stunning to a visitor than to reach out for an object on a bookcase . . . and find only flat wall? What is more marvelous than enlarging a tiny, dark room with a verdant terrace? What is more amusing for the renderer than to follow the astonished gaze of the cabinetmaker or mason who encounters a piece of false marquetry or marble that is more real than nature?

What satisfaction, too, to be able to ornament a workpiece with ivory or tortoiseshell without endangering the species! It is a privilege for the impassioned initiate. For this is all about passion, coupled with technique. And what a range of techniques: the preparation of supports, the properties of paints and solvents, the battery of tools, the mastery of ornament and edging, the ability to render perspective, architectural and landscape detail, the subtlety and harmony of color, the play of light and shadow, not to mention the rendering of the indispensable materials and subjects: wood, marble, stonework, brick, gilding, glass, drapery, moldings, paneling, ornament, landscape, people, animals, and so forth.

And that is not all. The decorative painter must also be able to integrate these techniques within a time period and style, with the skill of a master mason, cabinetmaker, landscaper, architect, and artist.

This book therefore covers numerous distinct aspects of decorative painting. It was conceived as a practical manual explaining the process from the preparation of supports, equipment and supplies to the detailed steps of imitating various materials and the tricks of a successful studio. The explanations come from professional practice. They can be considered a useful foundation for the amateur or beginning decorator, or as helpful complements to an already existing foundation for a more accomplished interior painter. The demonstrations in the following chapters are accessible to anyone interested: most of the methods used are simple, the equipment readily available.

The projects can be realized on all the usual surfaces: walls, paneling, floors, ceilings, and furniture, as well as on objects of all sizes: moldings, frames, stand-alone panels, and so on.

Holding no monopoly on learning or lore, in this book we only communicate our own methods and skills, and hope that whether you are a neophyte, jack-of-all-trades, art lover, artist, craftsperson, house painter, signpainter, or experienced decorative artist, you will find here a guide, a model, a new set of projects, and inspiration.

Yannick Guégan

1

PREPARATIONS FOR PAINTING

INTRODUCTION

All the decorative work in this book is done on surfaces previously painted a uniform tone (white or colored), normally with two coats: we refer to this foundation as the base coat. For this we mostly use high-quality commercial house paints: turpentine- or paint-thinner-soluble alkyds or water-soluble (latex/vinyl) acrylics, sold in cans. The former are called solvent-based; the latter, water-based.

The decoration painted on this surface—designs, ornaments, borders, and imitation (faux) materials—are made with the same kinds of paints but of finer quality, with more covering power. These come in smaller packages, such as tubes or jars, as artists' oil or acrylic colors. Diluted, all of these can be used as glaze, so long as you bear in mind their particular drying times.

In contrast to the fine-art painter, the decorative painter often uses the technique of *removal:* we apply a tinted liquid, paint or glaze, over a different-colored painted base and then partially remove it by one means or another. This method is essential for rendering patinas, stone, and some wood effects. In contrast, other kinds of decoration—for instance, marble and drapery—are rendered with successive applications of paint. Removal is the method of choice when we work on large surfaces such as ceilings, paneling, and walls because it allows us more easily to obtain the very soft and finely nuanced results over a large area. It is more difficult to apply colored glazes over parts of a surface and then to evenly blend and soften the borders.

GLAZES, PAINTS, AND SOLVENTS

PAINT SYSTEMS

Although they are still useful to study, the methods of the masters of previous eras have aged, and the old explanations do not cover all the possibilities available to us today. We have new materials, and with them come new methods.

Painted decoration is accomplished principally with glazes, sometimes with pure or diluted paint. A glaze is a fairly fluid liquid, clear or faintly or strongly colored, which serves as a binding agent. Clear, uncolored glaze visually softens the layers underneath; colored glaze intensifies them. Transparent glaze lets the color below show through, faintly or strongly, and permits the many decorative effects that come from removing areas of wet glaze.

Undiluted paint is used for uniform, opaque decoration, such as flat-painted figures, borders and letters, stenciled ornament, and the like.

Decorative painting is done on interior surfaces (wood, plaster, canvas, glass, or other building materials) or on exteriors (usually cement, but sometimes wood, metal, and other materials).

Interiors

Traditional solvent-based paints, diluted with turpentine or paint thinner: alkyds (or oil paints) for priming and base coats, then oil glazes for the decorative finish, and alkyd varnish for final protection.

Modern water-based paints, diluted with water: acrylic priming, acrylic or vinyl base coats, then dilute acrylic or vinyl for the decorative finish (we often use waterproof liquid acrylic); finish coats may or may not be used with these media. Acrylic paints come in different grades of quality. Our advice is to use *high-quality* acrylic paint for finer renderings, like marquetry, precious objets d'art, or small panels; use *good-quality* acrylic paint for larger surfaces.

The two systems—solvent-based and water-based—are compatible and can be combined, for example:

❖ Dilute liquid acrylic decoration on a flat alkyd base.

❖ Oil glaze on a satin-finish acrylic base coat.

❖ A first glaze of acrylic, followed by a second, solvent-based, glaze.

Exteriors

Acrylic or vinyl exterior (house) paint, or a latex or acrylic resin (these come in a limited range of colors): paints that are compatible with cement, in direct or indirect contact.

Satin or gloss alkyd paints, used mostly on wood and metallic surface, are not compatible with cement in direct contact. As with interiors, oil glazes require alkyd varnish for protection.

Base Coats

Base coats are essential to achieving the desired decorative result. Apply two coats, to thoroughly cover the prepared, primed support. Choose colors (especially for the last coat) depending on the final material or effects desired; in this book the base coats are generally specified. Pick the base coat color closest to what you want from what is available from the manufacturer of the paints you choose. Light tones can be made by tinting white base paints with concentrated colorants (see page 15).

For solvent-based base coats, use light-colored commercial satin-finish alkyd enamel paints (alkyd replaces the old oil paints), or prepare your own (with ground white pigment, linseed oil, turpentine, dryer, and tube color, light tones only).

For water-based base coats, use commercial acrylic (latex) or vinyl paints, preferably satin-finish. Flat-finish paints are used for simple work like imitation stonework and wax patinas.

Many professionals prefer solvent-based alkyd enamel paints for their very sleek, "tight" look. But there are advantages to water-soluble paints: quick drying time, no solvent odor, easy cleanup, and, sometimes, compliance with fire codes.

Glazes and Paints for Decoration

Oil (solvent-based) glaze: combine 2 parts turpentine to 1 part linseed oil, plus 3 percent dryer solution (by volume), and add powdered pigments for the desired tone.

You can also tint glazes with fine tube oil paint, principally for fine work on small surfaces, or for bolder coloration (blue glaze for sky, for example, or white glaze for highlights).

Solvent-based paint: use fine-quality oil paint mixed with a little dryer, or small amounts of alkyd paints diluted according to your needs (remember their quicker drying time).

Water-based glaze: use fine-quality artists' tube acrylics diluted with water; or small packages of decorative or sign-painting acrylic paint, also diluted with water.

Water-based paint: use tube or packaged acrylic paints, as above. Waterproof liquid acrylics (often used for airbrushes) are good for their transparency. Good-quality vinyl/acrylic house paint can also be used.

Base coats

Uniform black (left side) under antique bronze finish

Uniform yellow (left side) under "old penny" finish

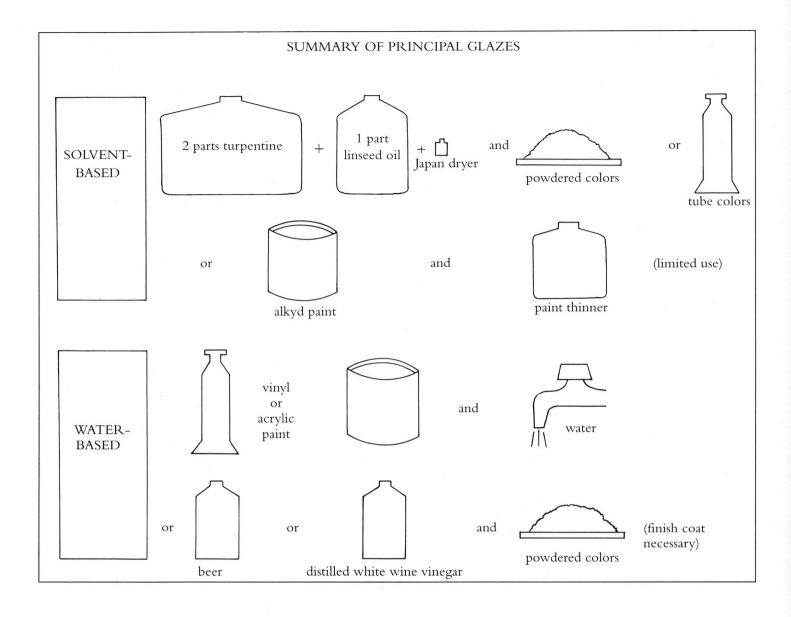

SUMMARY OF PRINCIPAL GLAZES

SOLVENT-BASED: 2 parts turpentine + 1 part linseed oil + Japan dryer and powdered colors or tube colors

or alkyd paint and paint thinner (limited use)

WATER-BASED: vinyl or acrylic paint and water

or beer or distilled white wine vinegar and powdered colors (finish coat necessary)

Solvents

Paint thinner (mineral spirits): use for diluting alkyd paints and varnishes, for cleaning stains and brushes.

Turpentine: use for making traditional oil glaze.

Denatured alcohol (methylated spirits): use for cleaning glass, removing waterproof liquid acrylic glaze, and as a solvent for shellac.

COLORANTS FOR GLAZES

From earliest times, painters have made their colors from rocks, plants, and animals. These powdered substances, called pigments, were applied in water to wet lime surfaces (fresco); later they would be bound in such media as wax, glue (from casein or animal skin), gum, or egg yolks (as in tempera painting, practiced from antiquity to the Middle Ages). Around the twelfth century, the discovery of oil paints (pigments in linseed or nut oil) ended the age of fresco painting. The major drawbacks of oil paint were that it yellowed and, more important, took a long time to dry. With the addition of dryers to reduce this time, oil painting gained currency and developed, bringing significant changes in pictorial technique. Paintings grew more realistic, and stunning trompe l'œil was achieved, with incomparably fine detail. Jan Van Eyck was one of the first great masters to apply these new techniques (see chapter 6). Around the end of the fifteenth century, tempera and oil were often used together.

Oil paint was unchallenged until the appearance, after World War II, of synthetic resins like acrylics, alkyds, and polyurethanes. Designed for the building industry, these new materials dry very rapidly and are very flexible. Acrylics do not yellow. These qualities are very useful (not least in trompe l'œil), offering the subtlety of oils in half the time. Oils are far from obsolete, however; they are very good for bringing out the

PRINCIPAL PIGMENTS FOR GLAZES

raw umber

burnt umber

raw sienna

burnt sienna

smoke

Cassel earth

mineral blue

ultramarine blue

yellow lake

crimson lake

viridian

chrome green

brown ochre

yellow ochre★
(or yellow oxide)

red ochre★
(or red oxide)

fine details of faux finishes, ornament, and elaborate trompe l'œil effects, in transparent glazes or thick opaque strokes.

In the past (and today, for those whose minds are closed to new techniques), a standard rendering of faux marble, for instance, would take at least two days; a more involved rendering, with many coats, much longer. On a dry foundation coated with several layers of the old brew (zinc-oxide paste, linseed oil, turpentine, and dryer) or satin-finish enamel, the painter meticulously imitated the veins and other components of the stone. Retouching each day's work the day after, it took a long time to make a satisfactory imitation. Using dilute liquid acrylic, today you can realize in a day's time an imitation far superior, in its fine play of transparencies, to those of yesteryear. In the space of an hour, you can add seven or eight transparent liquid coats to obtain the many effects and nuances of the marble. We demonstrate this method in chapter 3. However, when necessary we use oil paints, despite the need for several hours' drying time, to add realism and vigor to flat acrylic tones.

The illustration above shows some of the principal pigments we use to color glazes. Yellow and red ochre (marked with

asterisks) are not very transparent pigments, but they are still useful in small amounts in some renderings—faux brick (page 94), for example.

Some other colorants you may need include: zinc white in paste form (used for marouflage; see chapter 7) and powdered bronzes and related products, for metallic effects.

Tint large amounts of glazes required to cover big areas (walls, panels, etc.) by putting powdered colors directly into the glaze; mix well with a brush.

For small-scale work (delicate patinas, decorative panels, lacquerware, and the like), tint glazes by mixing a paste of ground pigment with a little glaze (using a painting knife) or fine tube paints with glaze (using a brush); in either case, mix the paste in with the glaze.

Universal colorants allow you to tint paints, either to alter a ready-made color or to color a white (to a limit of about six to eight percent by volume). You can use tube colors for this purpose, but, given their cost, only for small quantities. Universal colorants cannot be used by themselves as paint for decoration.

PRACTICAL TIPS ON GLAZING

You can apply an oil glaze over a dry acrylic glaze, and vice versa (although the latter technique is difficult and seldom used).

Reglazes are second—or third, or fourth, or fifth—applications of glaze often used for special decorative effect. They yield additional layers of color and depth over all or part of a rendering.

Other liquid applications, made of pigment mixed with beer or vinegar, called distemper, can be directly applied to base coats or over other glazes. These must be sealed with varnish or oil glaze.

In this book, "apply a clear glaze" means use a solvent-based glaze. You can blend and softly blur in this glaze when it is wet. Its main advantage is the slower drying time, allowing unhurried work on large surfaces, or the reworking of an unsatisfying effect after its completion, without fear of leaving visible traces. All oil glazes must be sealed with a clear finish coat (see Protection, page 22).

Before applying water-based glazes to a shiny or somewhat oily base, or over an oil glaze, you must degrease the surface by rubbing with a sponge and a mixture of water and chalk.

Some gouaches and tube watercolors, diluted in water, can be used as fine glazes for delicate work on small surfaces.

A quart of glaze covers 215 to 269 square feet (a liter, 20 to 24 square meters). Flat base coats absorb more glaze than satin-finish foundations.

Wait twenty-four hours for oil glaze to dry between reglazings; the work is fragile and sensitive to the touch for more than twelve hours. Only acrylic glazes or waterproof liquid acrylics and water- or beer-based glazes dry quickly—in about an hour, depending on room temperature.

PREPARATION OF SUPPORTS

Regardless of the surface being decorated or the system employed, professional decorative painters follow a series of operations in invariable order:

1. Preparatory work: the indispensable first step in preparing a surface (examples: removing old paint, washing the surface).

2. Priming: application of primer or filler to fill cracks and other irregularities, sanding, and final priming undercoat.

3. Base coats: the surface color under the decoration proper.

4. Decoration: the realization of the desired design.

5. Finish coats: one or several transparent coats to provide protection.

In the past, artists used various complicated processes to prepare the supports on which the colors were applied. After walls, wood and canvas were (and are today) the most common. To these were applied several layers of gesso or animal-derived glue, and the surface was polished until it was perfectly smooth. For fine lacquerwork, restoration of historic works, or just in the spirit of tradition, we can still follow the old methods, but modern technology allows us simpler procedures. Specialty stores offer prepared canvas and paper supports, and a variety of high-quality media specially made for all sorts of foundations. The range is so extensive that you should always consult your supplier about what materials are right for a particular project.

Follow the basic preparation of supports described below for the projects described in this book to ensure long life for your work. A badly prepared support, with cracks or scaling paint, will cause the decorative painting over it to deteriorate quickly.

Start by cleaning the surface.

CLEANING

Clean old supports as follows:

Old paint and distemper: scrape and wash with hot water.

Old solvent-based paints, flat, satin-finish, or gloss: wash with detergent.

Old water-based paints: wash with water. Use detergent to remove oil and grease.

Blistered or otherwise deteriorated paint: scrape and scrub.

Wax-polish, varnish, polyurethane, and other finishes: scrape and scrub as clean as possible.

Adhesives (wallpaper paste): pull off and scrub, washing away traces of paste.

Clean new supports as follows:

Plaster: smooth and dust off.

Raw cement and cast cement: brush off surface dust.

Raw wood and its derivatives (laminates, fiberboard): dust off.

Degrease tropical woods with a rag and solvent, and seal traces of resin and resinous knots with one or two coats of shellac.

Moldings, cast plaster, terracotta, stone: sand imperfections and irregularities.

Slick supports like PVC plastics, laminates, tiles, mirrors, oven-enameled surfaces, etc.: degrease, wet-sand, and apply a coat of primer to give it tooth (texture) so the decorative finish will adhere.

Ferrous metals: sand visibly rusted areas and coat with a rust-proofing primer.

Nonferrous metals and alloys: degrease and coat with primer to give the surface tooth.

Polyester tracing paper (mylar) needs no special preparation and canvas generally comes ready for use, but if they are to be mounted, the support requires a coat of high-quality solvent-based primer. Then smooth with fine sandpaper or scrape with a painting knife in preparation for marouflage with vinyl adhesive.

PRIMING

Priming readies the surface to receive paint or glaze and makes it smooth by correcting irregularities.

The traditional basic support is primed by applying a first coat of solvent-based primer to the wood or plaster surface. Let it dry; then sand. Coat plaster surfaces with plaster to fill in defects of the surface, wood with a wood filler, to fill in the pores of the wood, and to unify the whole. Then cover with a coat of pure, clear satin-finish shellac.

There are many brands of primer. Check before you select a primer by carefully reading the manufacturer's instructions.

Priming for Solvent-based Media

Fill gross irregularities and imperfections (with plaster of paris, gesso, or a filler such as spackle).

Apply an all-purpose alkyd undercoat (usually white).

Fill minor irregularities and imperfections (with premixed gesso or spackle).

Coat the support with primer (depending on the condition of the support, brush on or spread with a painting knife).

Sand with fine sandpaper, and dust.

Apply base coats (see page 13).

Priming for Water-based Media

Fill gross irregularities and imperfections (with plaster, gesso, or spackle).

Fill minor irregularities and imperfections (with gesso or spackle).

Coat the support with primer (depending on the condition of the support, brush on or spread with a painting knife).

Sand and dust.

Apply a vinyl or acrylic undercoat (optional).

Apply base coats (see page 13).

When you are preparing new or old moldings, or curved or relief pieces such as urns or other castings, it is helpful to use primer that can be brushed on; one or two coats even out nicely when they dry.

Whether you use solvent- or water-based media, you must apply:

❖ a waterproof undercoat for moist or efflorescent bases

❖ appropriate primer for raw, oxidized, or new metal

❖ appropriate primer to give tooth to slick surfaces. You can also prime varnished surfaces instead of removing the varnish.

Old nonabsorbent painted surfaces need not be primed if two new base coats are sufficient to cover the old color. Otherwise, prime to provide an opaque foundation.

PLANNING AND LAYOUT

Depending on the complexity of your design, you may need to make a preliminary study, a sketch, or a complete layout or model (sometimes full scale), partially or fully colored, with the details necessary for its completion. Color layouts allow you to judge whether the colors are harmonious; consult color charts and use paint chips to compare different tones, placing them on your rendering under the appropriate lighting. The final layout or model is what professionals submit to their clients for approval.

Graph paper is useful to work out correct proportions (example: for faux trelliswork or door panels). Tracing paper allows you to transfer designs (especially friezes, repetitive elements, and symmetrical designs) to templates, masks, and stencils or to the supports themselves. Use tracing paper, too, when you need to reverse a design (example: for painting under glass).

Whether or not you make a preliminary drawing, it is important to make an erasable sketch with chalk, charcoal, or a chalkline before the final pencil layout for wall decorations such as friezes and faux paneling, and for other finishes rendered on finished painted surfaces. On some surfaces, however, such as previously painted delicate faux marble or patinas, the final pencil layout cannot be erased. In these cases, use stencils or templates to transfer the design.

MASKING

Often you will need to reserve, or mask, certain areas of a design before applying a coat of paint or to facilitate edging. You can use ordinary masking tape or special straight or curved tapes of various widths; masking films (such as frisket) with peelable backing; and masking fluids (liquid frisket), applied with a brush. Beware of those that leave adhesive marks on the surface (such as some removable aerosol adhesives). For working under glass (as described in chapter 7), you will need special plastic-film masking tape.

SHADOWS AND HIGHLIGHTS

Following convention, the works shown in this book are lighted from the upper left, at a forty-five degree angle. Depending on where your work is to be located, however, you must consider the direction of the real light, natural or artificial, that will illuminate it. A few cases require an imaginary light source from a particular location coming from the center, for example, for a painted cupola on the ceiling.

BRUSHES

Paint applied uniformly for base coats is applied with the following customary painting tools:

- Medium round or flat (bristle) brushes in a range of different sizes
- Paint rollers for covering large surfaces

Use regular synthetic rollers for water-based paints. Use short-napped anti-spatter rollers for solvent-based alkyd paints.

Using rollers gives paintwork a stippled or fleecy look. It is therefore necessary to even out the paint, section by section, with a wide spalter (see illustration #13, page 20). Some subjects, however—stone, for example—call for a stippled base coat, while other work (such as a decorated façade), intended to be viewed from a distance, can be executed with a roller without smoothing.

Decorative glazes and protective varnishes (finish coats) are applied with the same brushes that are used for painting—a range of differently sized round or flat brushes; there are also special oval brushes for varnishing (see #14, page 20).

When you work with water-based media, we recommend that you use synthetic soft-hair brushes; these wear out much more slowly than real hair on coarse foundations.

You should have the following basic decorating brushes, or equivalents:

- an 8-inch (200 mm) patina brush
- spalters—three sizes: about 1½, 2½, and 4 inches (40, 70, 100 mm)
- flat (square) artists' brushes (different sizes)
- brushes for edging (angular fitches or dagger stripers), angled and straight
- *rondins*—two sizes: about ¼ and ⅜ inches (6 and 10 mm) in diameter
- a flogger
- sables (square, medium pointed, small, natural and synthetic hair)
- soft-hair brushes

Spalters, shown in the illustration on page 19, are flat brushes used in decorative painting. *Rondins* are brushes made in France that are similar to small stencil brushes, but softer. They are not readily available in the United States. If you can find soft stencil brushes, these may be used in place of the *rondin*.

SPECIAL BRUSHES

The four brushes shown opposite have special uses in decorative painting:

1. Badger blender. A small, flat, rectangular brush made of real or imitation badger hair.

   Use: blending (or softening) colors in glaze, especially in limited areas, where it works better than the spalter (marbled patinas, shaded stone, wood, mother-of-pearl, etc.)

2. *Chiqueteur.* This round squirrel-haired brush is expensive, and comes in different diameters. Like the *rondins,* it is not

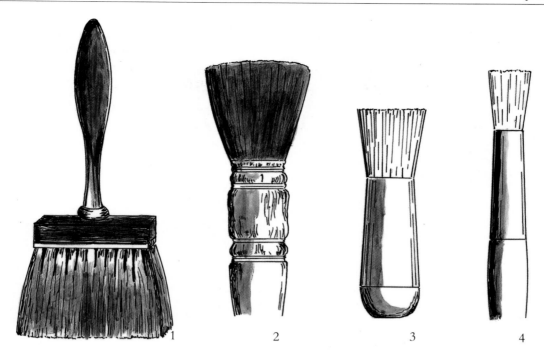

readily available in the United States, but some specialty paint stores do carry it. A nice piece of natural sponge, soaked with paint or glaze, makes an acceptable substitute.

Use: rendering the repetitive speckled effect of granite and jasper.

3 and 4. Hog-bristle stencil brushes. These come in different sizes.

Use: working with stencils and templates.

Nomenclature and Brush Shapes

The range of brushes we use is illustrated on page 20. Brushes vary, of course, from manufacturer to manufacturer, and some experimentation will be necessary to find the right tools for you. The list here is meant as a guide.

1. Round hog bristle brushes in different sizes. The large ones are used for large surfaces, the smaller for filling in.

   Use: applying base coats (of uniform paint), glazes, and varnishes. Reserve these brushes for these applications.

2. Flat hog bristle varnish brushes, in different lengths and widths.

   Use: the same as round brushes, but reserve for small areas.

3. Patina brushes (hog bristle), similar to stippling brushes (#6) but not identical.

   Use: stippling patina glazes; very smooth blends between shades; stippling in wet glaze.

4. Flogger (mixed bristles, horsehair).

   Use: graining some woods by "flogging" through glaze; special effects.

5. Spalters (hog bristle) for applying glaze.

   Use: evening out glazes applied with round brushes, making different effects in glaze (undulations, moirés, streaking, and blending).

6. Stippling brush (hog bristle).

   Use: stippling base paints to obtain a marked grain, stippling glazes over large areas (floor and ceiling patinas).

7. Dusting brush (natural bristles) for cleaning surfaces before applying paint or glaze.

   Use: dusting, stippling bronze glazes and patinas on small areas (for example, wrought iron finishes).

8. Brushes for edging: angular fitches or dagger stripers (bristle or sable, real or synthetic), angled or straight.

   Use: making straight edges with a ruler (decorative stripes, masonry joint, fine shadows, faux molding).

9. Flat brushes (hog bristle, sable, synthetic) in different sizes.

   Use: applying glaze to parts of small areas, shading, marble veining.

10. Sables (natural or synthetic) in different sizes, with pointed or square tips (like lettering brushes).

    Use: edging curves, mortar joints in molding, ornaments, outlining.

11. Soft-hair brushes (squirrel) for applying bronze powder.

12. *Rondins* (squirrel).

    Use: blending and grading edges of light and shadow, and blending fine stippling.

13. Wide spalter for smoothing base coats.

14. Oval varnish brush.

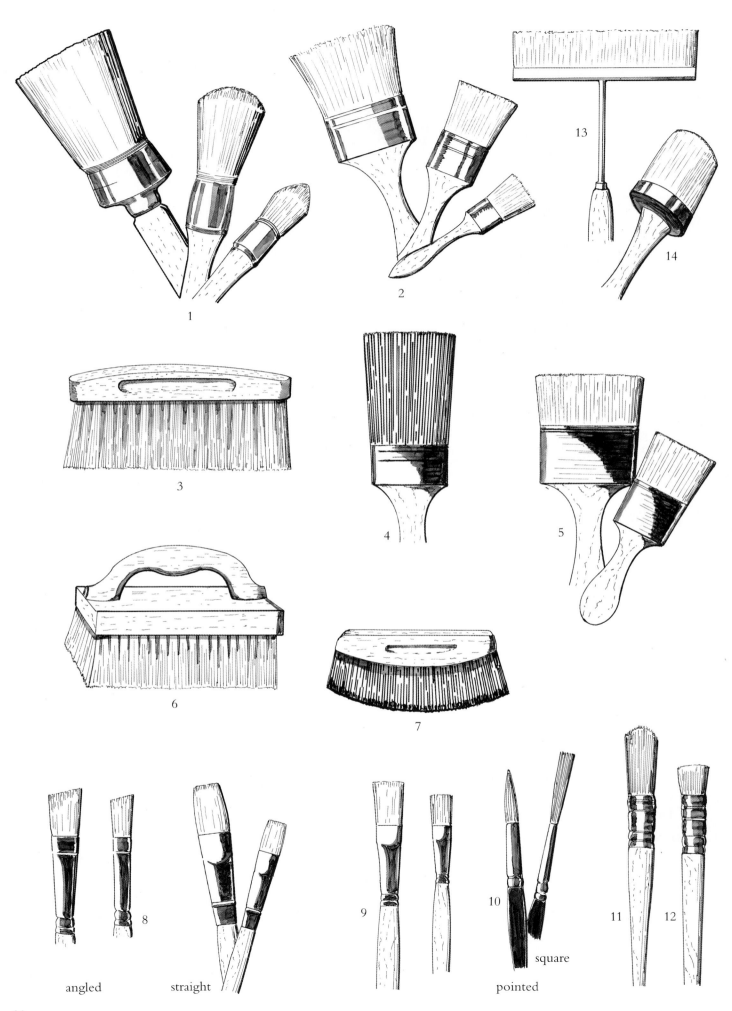

1

2

13

14

3

4

5

6

7

angled   straight   pointed

8   9   10   square   11   12

20

CARING FOR BRUSHES

Brushes for Base Coats

Solvent-based media: submerge brushes and rollers in water nightly. The next day, wring out and rinse in turpentine or paint thinnner before use.

Water-based media: rinse brushes and rollers in water immediately after use, and immerse in water until the next day.

Decorating Brushes

Solvent-based media: rinse bristles in turpentine or paint thinner, wash them with brush-cleaning soap, and store them flat.

Water-based media: wash the bristles with soapy water, rinse in tepid or hot water, and store flat.

Glaze and Varnish Brushes

Solvent-based media: rinse with turpentine or paint thinner and immerse overnight in a solution of two parts linseed oil to one part paint thinner; rinse in turpentine before reuse.

Water-based media: same as for decorating brushes.

OTHER SUPPLIES

In addition to brushes, these items are useful to keep on hand:

Two palettes, one wood and one plastic

A bit of burlap (available from suppliers of upholstery materials)

Metal and plastic containers for paints

Medium and fine sandpaper, and wet/dry sandpaper

Chalk for degreasing oily base coats before applying water-based glazes. Chalk also can be added to solvent-based glazes to give them more consistency and reduce running, without changing their color.

Tapes for masking, ⅜ inch (9 mm), ¾ inch (19 mm), 1 inch (25 mm), and 2 inches (50 mm) wide, for masking edging, borders, masonry joints, and the like. To avoid problems, always remove the tape before the paint, varnish, or whatever is under it dries completely.

One or two medium- or stiff-bristled toothbrushes

A hard lead pencil, chalk, and charcoal for layouts

Gouache- or vinyl-based markers for drawing lines and colored borders (example: cut lines in marquetry, masonry joints)

Sturdy paper or bristol board for stencils and templates

A sharp craft knife for cutting

Tracing paper for laying out ornament or making stencils for pouncing. Tracing paper made of polyester (mylar) is recommended for some projects.

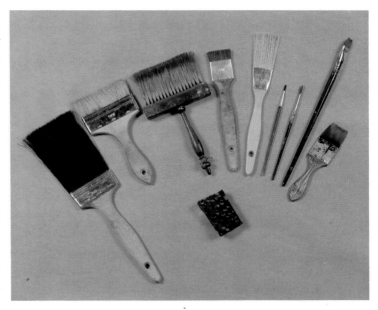

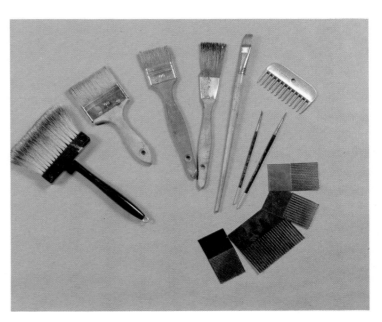

Tools for wood graining: (top) square synthetic sponge and, from left, flogger, spalter, badger blender, spalter, graining brush, artists' brushes, spalter; (bottom) a selection of steel combs for graining, a comb for separating the bristles of the graining brush, and, from left, badger blender, two spalters, graining brush, and fine-pointed artists' brushes

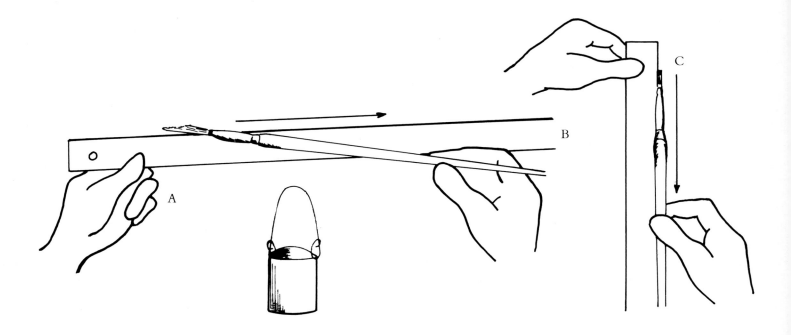

For Patinas

Lint-free white cotton rags for wiping

Two natural (marine) rounded sponges, medium and large

A round metallic scouring sponge

A medium-sized chamois cloth

For Faux Stone

A yardstick (1-meter ruler), a level, and guidesticks for some layouts (see below). A chalkline is also very useful for making long straight lines between two marks; fill it with powder (white chalk, yellow ochre), then snap it along the length of the wall you want to mark.

For Wood Graining

Square synthetic sponges for quick graining and natural (marine) sponges for making burl

A selection of steel combs for graining

An aluminum veining comb to separate the hairs of the graining brush

For Edging (decorative borders, masonry joints, etc.)

A flat yardstick (1-meter ruler) and an 18-inch (.50 m) guidestick of light white wood. Cut guidesticks from very straight commercial molding, preferably with a lip that will not touch the surface to be painted. The brush is guided along the lip. Choose a molding with a cross section that is about 1⅜ inch (35 mm) by ¼ inch (5 mm). Lightly sand the sharp edges, and cover with two coats of gloss varnish or shellac. This finish makes it easy to wipe off stray paint.

A small paint pot: a round tin can with two holes poked for a wire handle. While you are edging, you can hold the pot around your wrist, hang it on the other side of the work, or put it in your pocket.

Practice making borders on paper on a section of wall. Hold the tools as shown in the illustration above; your fingers separate the wall and the guidestick at A; it touches the wall at B; do the same for vertical borders (C).

Depending on your skill, you can render straight lines with ruler and brush, or with the help of masking tape. You can edge curves freehand with a pointed sable, or by painstakingly applying masking film. Some very narrow edging can be accomplished with special felt-tip gouache- or vinyl-based markers that have a conical tip, which allow you to draw waterproof lines on any surface. They come in limited colors.

PROTECTION

Decorative painting executed with solvent-based glazes, water-based glazes such as distemper (beer) and dilute gouaches, or with dilute acrylics and vinyls need one or more finish coats of clear varnish to seal and protect them. The number of coats depends on how much wear the surface will get and how particular you are. Finishes rendered with alkyd paints, oil paints, and acrylic and vinyl paints (normal dilution) do not need to be sealed. Protection is recommended in some cases, however: to provide resistance to bad weather, frequent washing, air pollution, or to produce a special effect, such as a high-gloss finish. The varnishes used for protection include:

Alcohol-based varnishes (shellac, copal varnish). Light-amber-colored, these provide a gloss finish and dry quickly. They have a yellowing effect. Use for small objects and interior surfaces.

Solvent-based alkyd varnishes, flat, eggshell, satin, gloss. These go well with solvent- or water-based glazes, dilute acrylics, etc. You can apply two, three, or four successive coats (let dry between coats), which can be wet- or dry-sanded for a smooth and sleek surface before the application of a final coat. These varnishes dry slowly and yellow, most noticeably over light tones.

Natural white wax, matte when applied with a brush, satin after polishing with rag. Non-yellowing; mix with turpentine, about 3 ounces to a quart (80 grams per liter). Most useful for protection of light-toned designs and patinas on walls.

Water-based acrylic varnishes: flat, satin, gloss. Quick-drying, non-yellowing, these are made for varnishing interior natural woods; they are also good for protecting matte or satin painted decoration. With one or two coats you get a solid result without much yellowing, but check the manufacturer's directions to avoid incompatibilities.

Water-based (latex) varnishes, matte, satin, and gloss. Quick-drying and non-yellowing, these are used for interiors painted with media that are not oily.

Solvent-based polyurethane varnishes. Composed of two substances that must be mixed before use, these give a very brilliant finish. They must be sprayed on with an airbrush in the studio and cannot be applied to oily foundations (oils, alkyds). They are used primarily for decorated furniture. These are specialty varnishes and must be applied carefully following the manufacturer's instructions.

Vinyl varnishes, matte, satin, and gloss. These are made to waterproof fragile paints. They can also be used on any matte paint for decoration. They have a milky look and dry clear. Because of their fluidity, they can also be used as a glaze on flat base coats, for instance, for faux colored stone.

Shellac. Shellac is very useful as an isolating coat or sealant, and it dries very quickly, in just a few minutes. Is is also used to seal over stains and to protect delicate glaze, metallic leaf, and bronzing. Do not use it over oil glaze unless the glaze is extremely well dried.

Crackle varnishes. Clear products made to give a crackle surface, not suitable for protection.

Color harmony based on tones from a wall hanging (left) and monochrome harmony from a scale of graduated tones taken from the base color of the fabric

COLOR CONSIDERATIONS

Before undertaking any painted decoration, you must think about color. Between the conception of your plan and the time that you make your final sketches and models, you must decide on the color scheme. The key to color selection is to work from an existing or planned central element. This theme serves as the basis for overall harmony. The upholstery, wall hangings, floor treatment, furniture—any of these can generate a successful color scheme.

Learn about the principles of color (the chromatic circle, complementary colors, optical contrasts and phenomena); these will help you come up with different solutions for harmony or different harmonies—tone on tones, contrasting tones, neutral tones, monochrome and polychrome schemes. Armed with this knowledge, you will be a distinctive colorist, making patinas complement fabrics, painted marbles set off floor treatments, faux paneling work with the furniture, colored borders underline architectural elements.

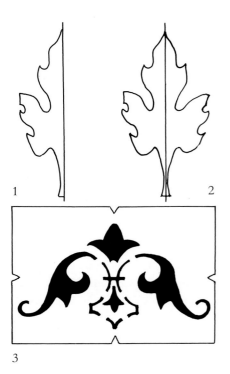

1 2

3

4

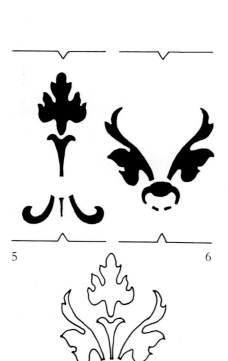

5 6

7

STENCILING

Stencils and templates ensure that a design is transferred exactly to the surface to be decorated and also aid in the layout of large-scale or repetitive designs. Stenciling is a useful technique that complements the decorative methods of the trompe l'œil painter.

We use a simple stencil to transfer designs by the pouncing method (see page 238). Here we describe a more elaborate stencil made by cutting openings in sturdy paper (kraft or drawing paper, bristol board) or slightly flexible plastic.

Rendering the Design

Draw the desired motif to full scale on paper. Cut out the design and transfer it to stenciling paper that has been coated on both sides with one or two coats of shellac or solvent-based glaze. If the design is symmetrical, draw only one half, and transfer it by rotating (flopping) around the axis of symmetry (1, 2).

Making the Stencil

Place the stencil on a smooth hard surface (glass or metal), and cut out the design. Leave uncut attachments in narrow parts, and cut notches to align the stencil on the layout (3).

Using the Stencil

Place the stencil on the surface to be decorated, holding it in place with your hand or with tape. Using a paint-can lid or palette to hold a small amount of not-very-fluid paint, take up a little bit of the paint on the tips of the bristles of a stenciling brush (a round brush with short straight bristles). Go over the stencil with a dabbing motion, wiping the brush off frequently (4).

Note that stenciled designs can be retouched with a brush to add highlights and shadows, strokes of a different color, and other details. You can overlay stencils to add different tones, modeling, or ornament (5, 6, 7).

You can use small foam rollers instead of a stenciling brush, or aerosol paint, which also allows you to shade by applying a different tone in some areas.

Solvent-based paints wash off stencils better than vinyl or acrylics.

Always keep (and keep in good condition) all your old stencils, to use again in future work. Store them in a cardboard folder with dividers of mylar, vellum, or plain tracing paper.

*A selection of tools and materials for decorative painting:
brushes, colors (ground pigments, tube paints, and liquid
acrylic), solvents, gold leaf, and gilders' tools*

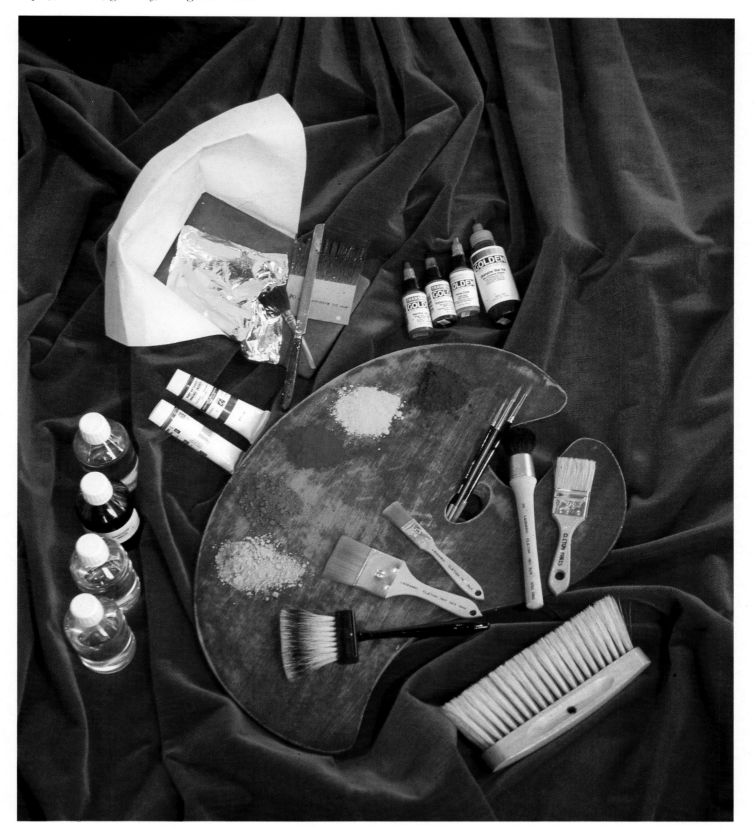

2

BASIC PATINAS AND MATERIALS

INTRODUCTION

We use different elements to decorate our surroundings: furniture, upholstery, floor coverings, lighting, objets d'art, floral art, and so on. But the most important elements are the very surfaces of particular premises, their ceilings, floors, walls, and paneling. The two dimensions of these surfaces constitute the raw material for creating a personalized decorative environment, including colors and textures. It is within this conception of interior design that we employ the trompe l'œil material effects that make up the repertoire of decorative painting. It is not perfectly simple. Rules of good taste must be observed with respect to existing decorative elements.

The most commonly represented materials in trompe l'œil are undoubtedly marble and wood, and these, and more, we shall cover in detail in due course. In this chapter, however, we show how to render a broad range of effects: simple patinas, basic marble and wood grain, stone and brick, bronze, and a handful of other special materials. The most advanced, perfect trompe l'œil is built on mastery of these effects and the elaboration of them.

The patinas and faux materials in this chapter have one thing in common: a generally soft and understated quality. Use them to complement, not upstage, existing furnishings.

PATINAS

In painters' parlance, a patina is a modification, by way of a colored glaze, of existing flat paintwork, often to age it artificially. With the simple application of a dilute, tinted glaze to a base of a different color, you can produce a wide range of decorative effects. We group patinas into four basic categories:

Aging Patinas

The traditional finishes, which soften the harsh tones of fresh paint, are produced by shading parts of the surface. The finishes work well in rooms designed in subdued colors and with antique furniture.

Two techniques are used to obtain an aging patina. The choice of method depends on the type of surface to be treated:

- ❖ Single-glaze aging—for small surfaces, objects, reliefs.
- ❖ Double-glaze aging—for large surfaces, ceilings, walls.

Wax Patinas

These colored finishes are made by rubbing a painted surface with blocks or sticks of tinted wax. When applied to paneling and small pieces of painted furniture, the colored stripes and stippling produced by the wax go well with textiles.

Antique Patinas

Special techniques give a realistic antique look to the surface treated. Among the finishes in this category are stippled patinas, dusty patinas, streaked patinas, worn patinas, and distressed patinas.

Decorative Patinas

Instead of simulating antiquity, decorative patinas are meant to achieve particular effects. We call these patinas colored, ragged, sponged, cloudy, marbled, and pebbled.

When you have mastered these techniques, you can easily use them in combination for myriad decorative combinations. Within an ensemble, though, the effects produced only harmonize to the extent that their tones are in harmony with the surroundings—whence the importance of the colors of base coats and glazes. Practice before going on to the real thing.

Molded ceiling tile, with two colors of single-glaze aging patina.
The reliefs are wiped at the end to produce highlights.
19½ in × 19½ in (50 cm × 50 cm)

1

2

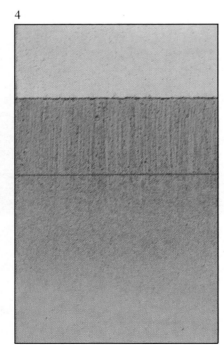

3

4

SINGLE-GLAZE AGING PATINAS

When working with aging patinas, always apply a cool, subdued glaze color over a lighter and more boldly shaded base. Oil glazes are used principally, but water-based acrylic glazes may be used for small areas.

Base coat: as desired

Principal colors: raw sienna (for yellowing); raw umber, Cassel earth, or black (for graying, to get a "dirty" effect), and the dominant color of the base.

Examples, at left, are:

1. Glaze + raw sienna + raw umber

2. Glaze + raw sienna + black + a drop of chrome green

3. Glaze + burnt umber + a drop of raw sienna

4. Glaze + raw umber + a drop of ultramarine blue

Always try out different colored glazes on a sample of the base coat and stipple to blend, so you can see the actual color that will result.

Patinas on Relief

To age three-dimensional surfaces, such as rosettes, cornices, sculpture, ironwork, metalwork, chairs, railings, or painted objects:

Step 1: Apply the colored glaze over the lighter base coat. You may need to even out the glaze with a spalter to keep it from runing or to fill in recessed spots in reliefs that you may have missed.

Step 2: Selectively remove the glaze by wiping vigorously with a dry rag over reliefs and high spots and in the middle of flat areas.

Step 3: Smooth with a spalter so the glazed area and wiped areas blend.

Step 4: Stipple with a patina brush for a fine even grain. Finish by tightly and cleanly wiping the tops of the reliefs and edges.

Step back and judge the effect of the whole.

Note that on small areas of relief, after wiping you can stipple by vertically "poking" or dabbing the glaze with the tips of the bristles of a small spalter. For quick work (on metal rungs, for example), you can stipple with a dusting brush.

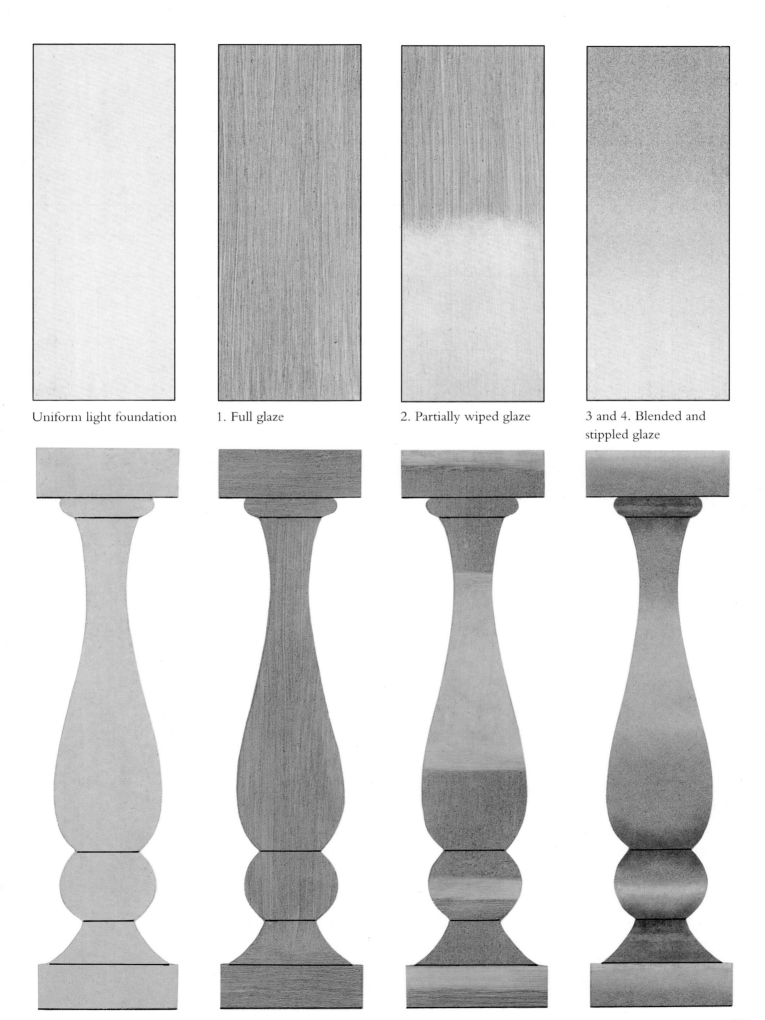

Uniform light foundation

1. Full glaze

2. Partially wiped glaze

3 and 4. Blended and stippled glaze

Patinas on Panels and Wainscoting

Use this method for paneled doors, small panels, dados, windows, and painted furniture. Oil glaze is the preferred medium, to allow time to work, blend, and stipple the whole piece.

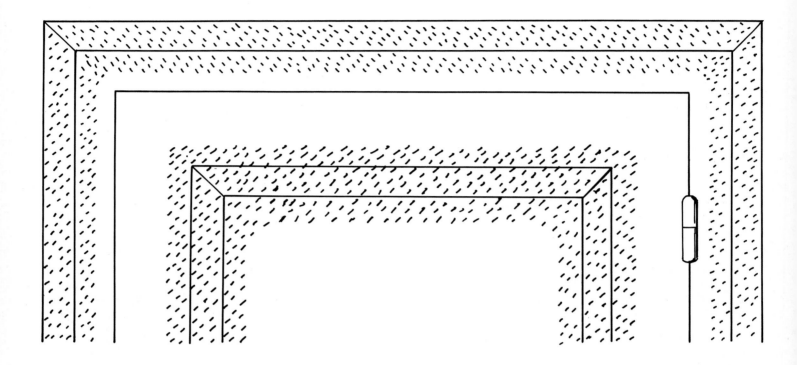

Step 1: Apply the colored glaze to the lighter painted base coat. Even and smooth this coat with a bristle brush or wide spalter, without leaving too much glaze on the moldings or raised surfaces.

Step 2: Remove the glaze evenly from the raised parts of the panels, rounded edges, the middle parts of panels and edges, etc., without wiping too far into the initial base color.

Do not wipe the areas shaded in the drawing above, around the edges of panels and moldings.

Step 3: Blend the borders between wiped and glazed parts with the bristle brush or spalter.

Step 4: Stipple the blended and other, unwiped, glaze.

To wipe flat, uniform surfaces, use a white cotton rag, folded flat. For raised sections, such as molding and other three-dimensional elements, use a narrow, folded strip of cloth, as shown at right. As you wipe, use different sections of the cloth, so that you are always wiping with a clean portion of rag.

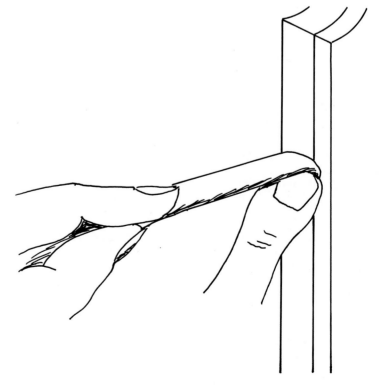

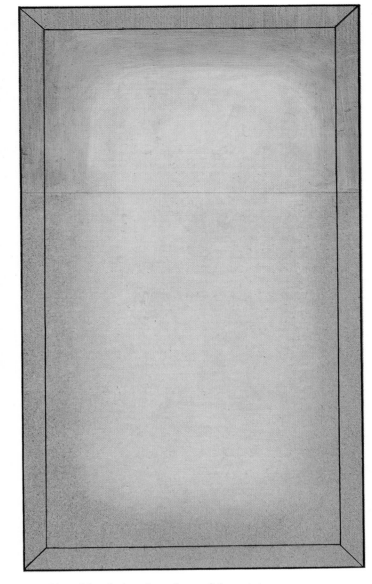

1. Full glaze
2. Partially removed glaze

3. Glaze blended at the edges of the wiping
4. Stippled glaze

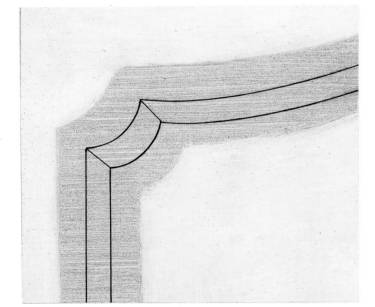
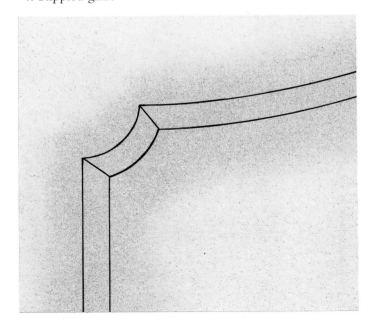

Basic technique for single-glaze aging of a rectangular panel (top) and a panel with curved edges (bottom).

DOUBLE-GLAZE AGING PATINAS

The single-glaze aging process is based on removing glaze in all but the recesses and edges of the treated surface. Double-glaze aging entails the application of a light glaze over the whole surface, without significant removal, and the application of a second, darker glaze in recessed areas. Use separate brushes and containers for each glaze.

Patinas on Medium and Large Surfaces

Use this method for ceilings, walls, panels, furniture, and pillars. You must use oil glaze in order to be able to finish the work before the glaze dries.

Step 1: Apply the first light glaze over the whole piece (wall by wall, door by door, or in manageable sections).

Step 2: Stipple with the patina brush, except in the areas to be glazed a second time for shading.

Step 3: Apply the darker second glaze evenly around the edges of the surface, following the contours of any existing molding.

Step 4: Blend the two glazes, by stippling between them and in the shaded areas. Keep the dark glaze off the lighter areas by using one side of the patina brush for the dark-glaze side of the area where they meet, and the other side of the brush for the light-glaze side. Occasionally wipe the tips of the patina brush bristles with a dry cloth when stippling glaze.

Finish by wiping reliefs and high points clean. (Not shown in the examples opposite.)

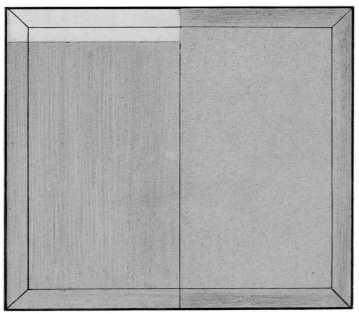

1. Application of light glaze over foundation   2. Stippling

3. Application of dark glaze   4. Stippling dark glaze and the area where the two glazes meet

Patina on paneled door

Placement of dark glaze

Patina on a column

33

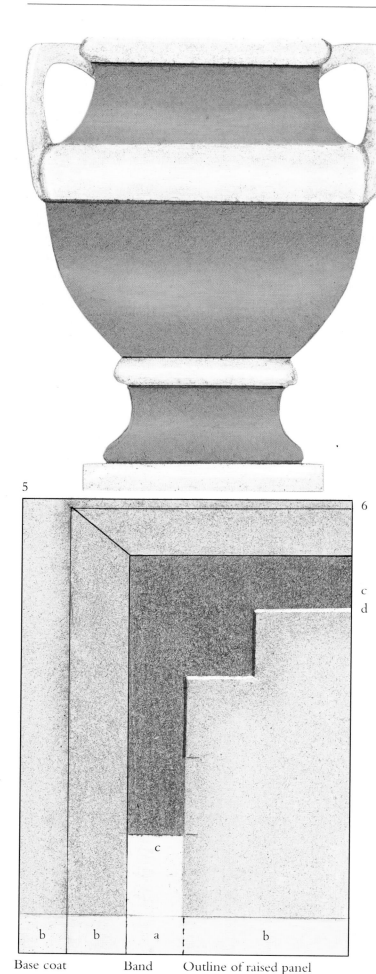

5

6

c

d

b | b | a | b

Base coat   Band   Outline of raised panel

DOUBLE-GLAZE PATINA VARIATIONS

By changing base and glaze colors, you can create different colorations on the same elements and objects, and accentuate chosen parts, as illustrated in the example at left (5) and on the facing page (1–4).

Example 1

The base coats are two different tones of the same color. The glaze is the same all over.

Example 2

The base coat color is the same; the glazes are different.

Example 3

The base coat color is the same, except for the white molding. The glaze is the same. Note that on three-dimensional moldings, wiping the glaze off gives the effect of edging (white or colored, depending on the color underneath).

Example 4

Two different base coat colors, with a different glaze for each.

Example 6

Faux-relief panel.

Step 1: Lightly lay out the outline of the central raised panel on the base coat—the dotted line (a).

Step 2: Apply a uniform light patina over the whole surface, including the moldings (b), leaving unglazed only a narrow band between the molding and the center panel (c). Mask this area with tape.

Step 3: After the first coat dries, apply a slightly darker glaze to the narrow band (c) around the panel; stipple without going over the edges.

Step 4: Finish by edging in light and shadow to produce the relief, and make a clean distinction between the two glazes (d). Blending the outside edges suggests a thick panel with rounded edges; you can also make the edges of the panel appear curved.

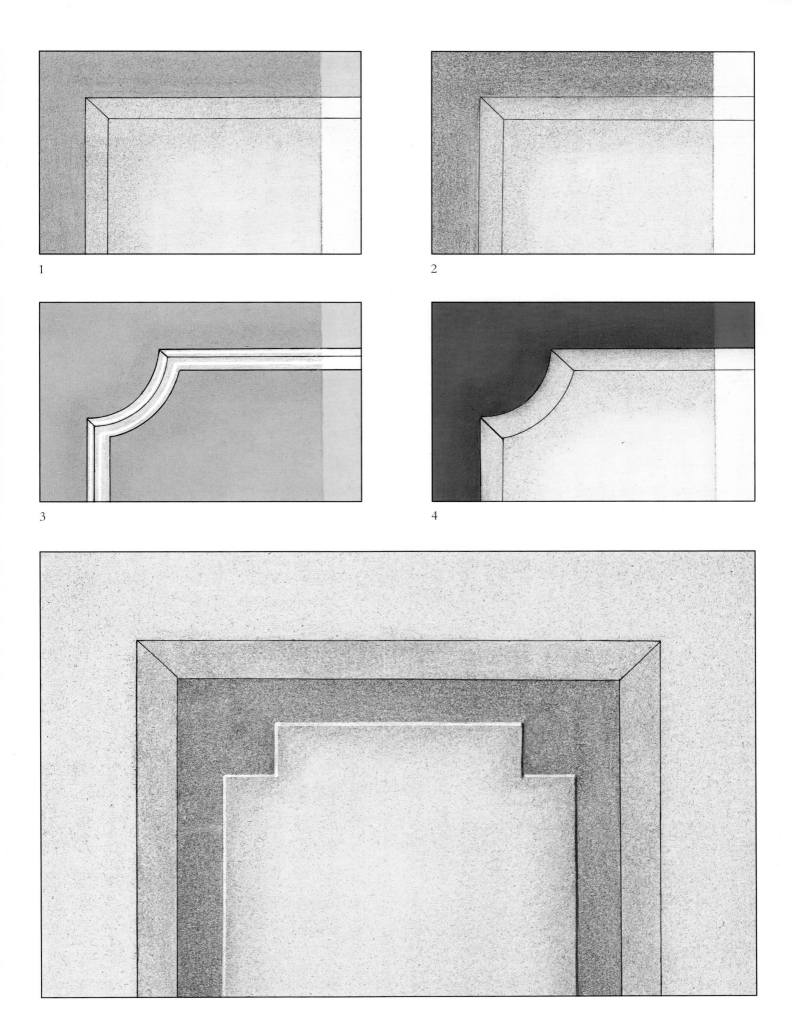

Faux relief panel

Commercially manufactured and home-made wax crayons

Smooth base coat   One pass of the wax   Several passes in different colors

Base coat   Colored wax   Metallized wax

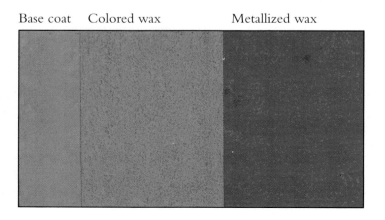

WAX PATINAS

Wax patinas are made by rubbing a painted surface with pieces of colored wax, as though coloring with crayons. The final effect depends on the base coat treatment. If the foundation is smoothly painted with a brush, you get a streaked look. If the foundation is painted with a roller or stippling brush, you get a stippled look.

For the base coat use matte vinyl or acrylic (or even ordinary matte alkyd applied with a roller).

Making Wax Disks

You can buy sticks of colored wax, but the range of colors is limited.

To make your own wax, use white wax and powdered pigments. Cut off the bottom of a small tin can, to make a cylindrical mold. Coat the mold with a little grease, such as automotive grease, and place it on a smooth surface (glass or metal); affix it to the base with glazier's putty.

Break a slab of white wax into small pieces, put them into a metal pot, and heat on the stove. Watch it carefully. When the wax is melted, pour it into the mold, simultaneously adding the pigment bit by bit and mixing well with a small rod. (It is useful to have help here.)

When the wax has cooled, an hour or two later, remove the disk from the mold.

Streaked Patina

Drag a wax disk along the surface. If there is a grain, apply with the grain, not against it.

Stippled Patina

Lightly drag the colored wax (held flat) over a stippled foundation.

If you want to add another effect over a wax patina—for example, extra glaze for supplementary coloring or decoration, or to produce the effect of a raised panel, first isolate the wax patina with a coat of appropriate sealant.

Wood panel with molding, with streaked wax patina, faux raised panel, and stenciled ornament.
43 in × 27½ in (110 cm × 70 cm)

ANTIQUE PATINAS

Antiquing gives surfaces a grayish (or dirty) and worn antique look. The following methods can be used singly or in combination. Use them for furniture, wainscoting, paneled walls, and antique pieces.

Stippling and Dusting

Apply a darkish glaze (zinc white + raw umber + black), heavier in recessed areas and around moldings.

Stipple for a fine grain.

You can blow or sprinkle a little gray pigment on the glaze before it dries completely.

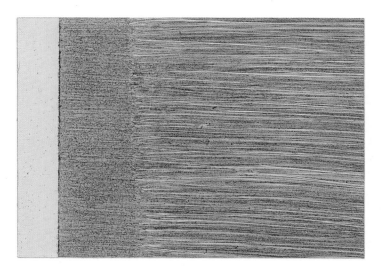

Streaking

Using a paint brush, vigorously apply a glaze (as above) on a smoothed base coat.

Streak the glaze with a spalter or a piece of burlap.

When the glaze has dried, streak raised portions with sandpaper or a rag moistened with solvent to remove the glaze.

Scraping

Over the base coat, apply two or three coats of different-colored paints, letting each dry before applying the next. Casein paints, available from art supply stores, work best.

Then scrape these glazes with steel wool or a metal scouring pad, more or less forcefully, depending on the effect you want. Finally, polish with a wool rag or lambswool.

When tinting these glazes, follow the same rules as for aging patinas. You can obtain interesting effects by spattering the finish—for example, with dark brown spots.

It is difficult to apply the exaggerated antiquing patinas over large surfaces, walls, and panels; traditional aging patinas suffice for these projects. The following examples, however, work for frames, moldings, sculpted woodwork, and the like. The effect produced by each method is shown on the facing page.

Example 1

Base coat: a light or middle tone, toned down with raw umber (white + yellow oxide + raw umber + a drop of red)

Apply a fluid coat of darker paint (here, strong green); wipe the reliefs vigorously with burlap or a rough rag.

Using a flat artist's brush, apply a dark glaze to the recesses of moldings, or other crevices; then, depending on the size of the work, stipple with a spalter or *rondin*. You can finish by edging with a more opaque glaze, in a more understated color.

2

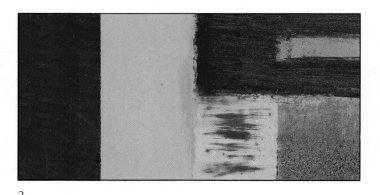

1

Example 2

Base coat: Mars red (or red oxide with a drop of chrome orange). In water gilding, this is the color of the foundation under the gold leaf.

Apply an opaque coat (bluish here).

Apply an aging patina over the whole surface.

Then, with sandpaper, bring out the red base on high points and relief. You can also do this by wiping away parts of the succeeding coat.

Finish with touches of gold-colored bronze on the relief (see page 80).

Example 3

3

The reverse of Example 1, this has a washed look produced by using a very light-colored paint over a darker base.

Base coat: a strong color (here, yellow oxide + raw umber + a bit of white)

Cover the whole with a very light color; then wipe reliefs and the middle of flat surfaces.

Apply an aging glaze to recesses, and stipple.

For a crackled effect, apply commercial crackling varnish to any of the above.

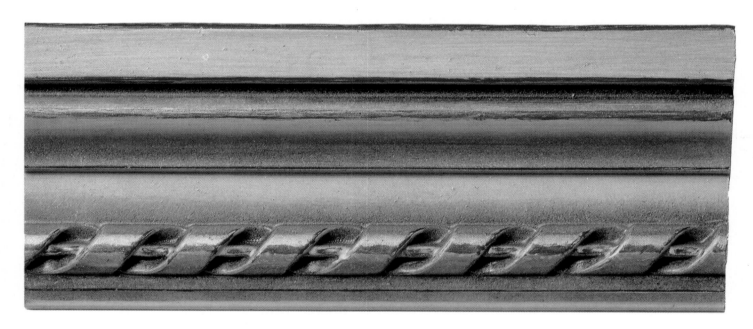

1

2

3
4

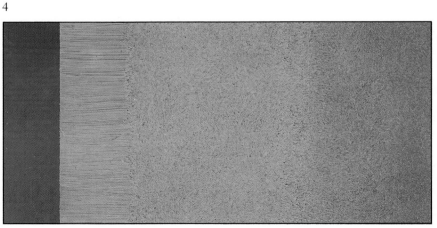

42

COLORED PATINAS

To produce these patinas, a colored glaze is applied to a differently colored base coat, for a decorative play of transparencies, often with lively and bold hues.

Basic Method

Apply a glaze over the whole as usual. For patinas that require much stippling, use slow-drying oil glaze. Glazes made from dilute acrylics, which dry more quickly, are useful only for smaller areas. Stipple with a patina brush for a uniform grain over any brush marks.

Depending on the harmonies you seek, some base coats might be (as shown at left and on the facing page):

1. White

2. Light colors—for deeper coloration, you can apply the glaze more thickly over the edges or other parts of the panel, and stipple those areas more lightly.

3. Bright colors

4. Dark colors—in this case the decorative effect is often obtained with a light glaze against a dark base. The application of light glazes over very colorful bases is also the basis for different effects like the scraped antique patina and liming (a bleached or whitened effect).

5. Bands—applying two or three colored glazes in horizontal bands allows smooth color shifts with stippling and blending of wet glaze where the bands meet.

2

3

4

5

1   Tone on tone

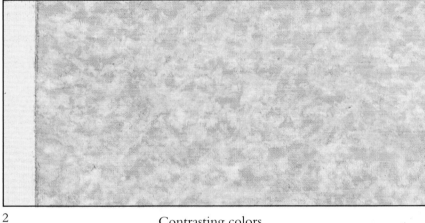
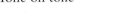

2   Contrasting colors

3
4

SPONGED PATINAS

Sponged patinas are produced by evenly dabbing the glaze with a sponge, or "walking" the sponge through the glaze along particular paths. Depending on the movement and force, you get different effects. Dabbing yields a soft and subtle effect if the color of the glaze is close to the color of the base. Vinyl and acrylic paints are the best choices for sponging.

Dabbing (1, 2)

Apply glaze over the whole surface.

Dab the surface evenly with a moist natural sponge. The markings will be more distinct in water-based glaze than in oil glaze. Use the same repeated motion, with the same side of the sponge.

Depending on the area to be covered, you may have to move quickly, before the glaze starts to dry.

Variations

A stronger pattern (3) is obtained by using a thicker glaze (with more colorant).

A medium pattern (4) is obtain by using a flat artificial sponge.

Sponged patina sample on tracing paper
29½ in × 15½ in
(75 cm × 40 cm)

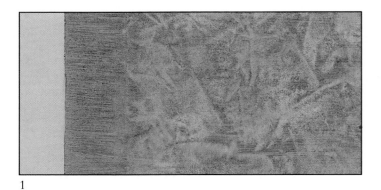

1

2

3

4

RAG-ROLLED PATINAS

Rag-rolled patinas are produced by walking or rolling a crumpled rag over fresh glaze, removing glaze so the base color shows through. The effects obtained depend on the type and weave of the cloth and the pressure of the hand behind it.

Basic Method (1)

Apply a colored glaze (generally close to the base color) to the whole surface.

Place a rag, rolled into a rough cylinder, at the top of the surface, and roll it through the glaze, toward the bottom, with your fingertips. Use the same rag for the entire area to be covered. You can use a moistened rag with water-based glazes. Using moist chamois on glazes also gives interesting effects.

Finger position for rag-rolling

Rag-rolling (2)

Use more pressure to produce a stronger effect.

Rag-rolling (3)

Rag with a soft balled-up cloth, dabbing to produce a very fine grain.

Rag-rolling (4)

Use thick crumpled material such as suede in place of a rag to get marked folds and reflections, for a buckskin effect.

*Examples of leather-colored (yellow or chestnut)
rag-rolling from a book of samples shown to clients.
Rag-rolling gives the look of tanned or chamois skins.
Base colors are rather lively and bold; the glazes are
strongly colored with raw and burnt sienna.*

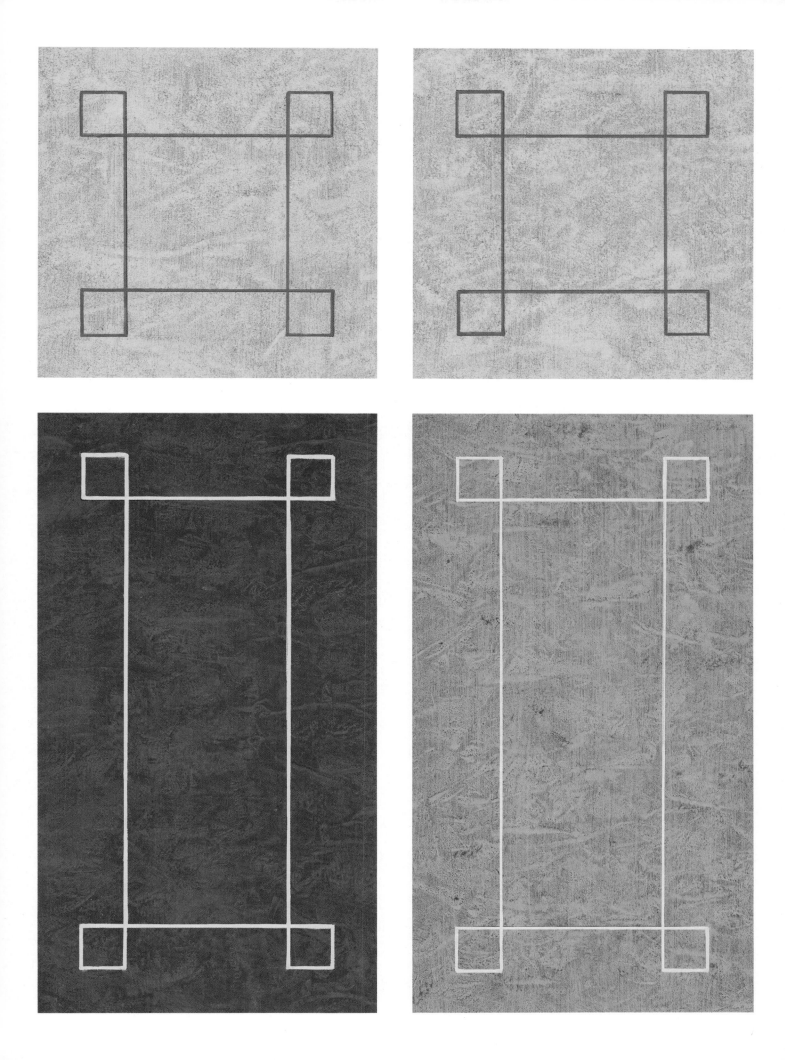

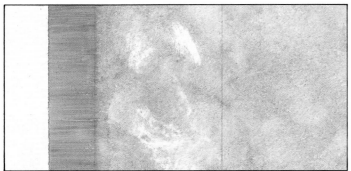

CLOUDY PATINAS

As the name implies, these patinas look like cloud formations, with lighter and darker masses. The pleasing smoothness comes from the final stippling. If you work in tones of blue, you will get a good imitation of a sky with a neutral character. While you stipple, you can use the rag to modify the results. Now and then step back to judge the effect of the whole.

Sky

Apply a blue glaze over a white base coat.

Using a dry rag, wipe scattered, rounded cloud shapes.

Stipple the whole with a patina brush.

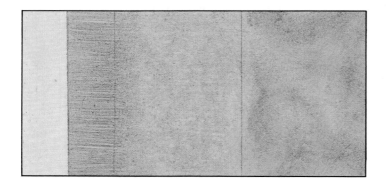

Simple Clouds

Apply a colored glaze (generally close in tone to the base coat) over the whole surface.

Remove glaze by wiping with a rag in a repetitive fashion.

Stipple the whole with the patina brush.

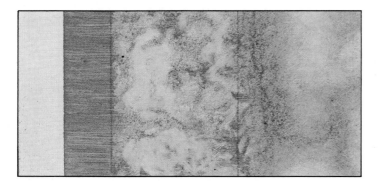

Double-Glaze Clouds

Apply a slightly colored glaze (close to the base color) over the whole surface and stipple.

Apply a more strongly colored glaze in places, and stipple these reglazed areas.

Clear-Glaze Clouds

Apply a glaze that is lighter in tone than the base coat (generally it will contain white).

Remove glaze by wiping with the rag in a repetitive fashion.

Stipple the whole with the patina brush.

Cloudy patina on ceiling with dome effect (top)
A range of differently colored cloudy patinas (bottom)

49

MARBLED PATINAS

These decorative patinas, with simple and soft veining, suggest marble. Their texture should be understated, however, to distinguish between them and the careful imitation of particular marbles, as described in chapter 3. Marbling can be executed with oil glazes and paints, or with acrylics alone.

Simple Veining

Apply a lightly tinted glaze (close to the base color) over the whole surface. Stipple the whole.

Form some veins with the edge of a flat brush. Smooth them with a small spalter, and soften by stippling.

Simple Marbling

Apply a clear or lightly tinted glaze to the whole surface.

Form a network of veins, irregular and spread out.

Blend this veining with a small spalter.

Apply a second glaze, lightly colored but darker than the first glaze, in open areas.

Soften the whole by stippling.

Multitoned Marbling

Proceed as for simple marbling, then apply a white glaze in spots, and stipple.

You can also apply some separate touches of a third shade.

Brecciated and Pebbled Marble

More elaborate patterns and markings. The pebbly network is not stippled.

Marbled patina wall finishes

Panels, edges, and plinths with patina made by sponging or rag-rolling the first glaze, stippling, and veining with white glaze, smoothed and stippled. The columns on either side are multitoned marbling.

Like the example above, the panels, edges, and plinths were color-glazed, stippled to produce a fine grain, and then veined. The columns are multitoned.

Color darker than the base coat   Lighter than the base coat

Jasper patina   Multicolored jasper

Granite patina, light and dark   Medium granite

Ragged granite patina

JASPER AND GRANITE PATINAS

Jasper and granite patinas are produced by dabbing a base coat with a sponge wet with paint (or glaze) of various colors. These are the only patina methods we use based on adding rather than taking away paint. Many effects are possible, including overlays of colored spots, coarse-grained jasper, and coarse- and fine-grained granite. Acrylic and vinyl paints are very useful for rendering jasper patinas.

Simple Jasper

Make a fluid paint tinted to go with the base coat. Put a little in a flat lid or other shallow container and lightly soak one side of a natural sponge in the paint. Dab the surface with the sponge, and repeat, moving regular distances between dabs.

Replenish the paint on the sponge from time to time as needed.

Multicolored Jasper

Render simple jasper, as described above. Then apply other colors, letting each dry before the next application.

Coarse-grained Granite

The example is monochrome; the pebbling is produced by using two or three tones of the base coat color.

Fine-grained Granite

Use thinner paint and more compact sponges. Alternatively, use a thick rag rolled into a round wad to produce a similar result.

Parchment-colored jasper-patina wall panel within chamois granite patina (top)
Monochrome dado, with off-white jasper patina, two-tone granite patina, and interlace border (bottom)

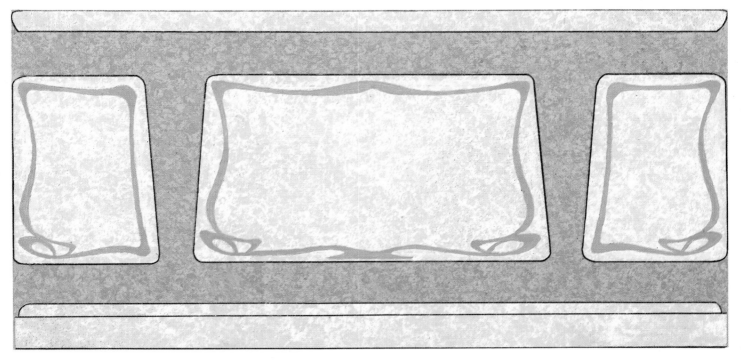

FAUX STONE

Imitation stone is used in many different ways in decorative painting. The choice of stone will depend on the intended use.

❖ Freestone is traditionally used for foyers, stairwells, halls, stately living rooms, ceiling vaults, large fireplaces.

❖ Ashlar and rubble masonry, with elements of various shapes and colors, are used for rustic-style rooms, interiors of country homes, low dividing walls, moldings.

❖ Stonework construction elements are used for frescos, panoramas, scenic design, and architectural structures.

Freestone is a common stonework that is based on the assembly of pieces of cut fine-grained stone, according to a set geometric pattern, in construction. Start by making a pencil layout of the arrangement on a base coat of a flat color, and then paint the mortar joints over it with straight, narrow lines. Rendering freestone is mainly edging work with ruler and brush. For a more realistic decorative look, you can shade each stone before rendering the joints.

For ashlar and rubble masonry, again you start by making a layout of the stonework on a homogeneous base, using pencil, charcoal, or chalk. The individual stones are then colored in different ways. This allows you to imitate a range of rocks, from those with precise characteristics like millstone to ruder rubblework with its varied shapes and colors. When you have finished rendering the stones, render the mortar joints called for by the layout, rectilinear or irregular according to your chosen arrangement.

Both freestone and ashlar and rubble masonry are also useful for trompe l'œil wall decoration: columns, arches, and other architectural elements.

Niche wall section in shaded freestone with white mortar joints; statuette with ivory patina

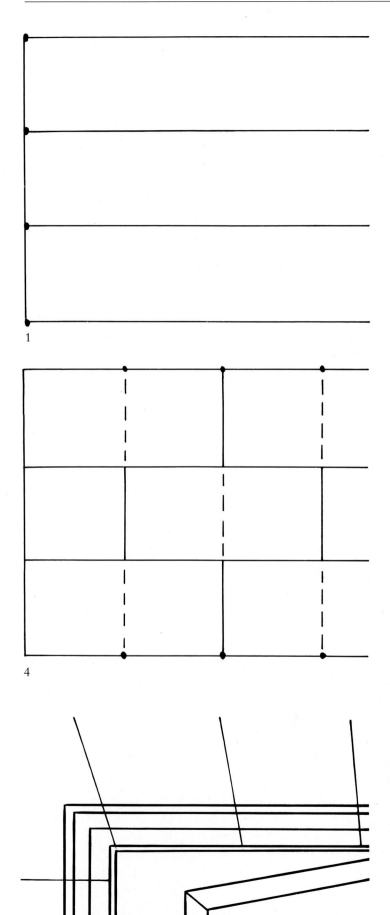

1

4

5

FREESTONE

Base coat: stone color. Apply two coats of matte (flat) or satin paint, stippling with roller or stippling brush.

Stone colors vary from cream to grayish-cream to medium beige to pinkish beige. Some examples are shown opposite. If you tint white paint, use small quantities of concentrated colorant. Do not use gloss paint; when stippled, it will not give the desired relief effect.

Layout

First determine the height of the rows of stone (called courses) by dividing the height of the wall, from floor to ceiling, for courses about 13 inches (33 cm) high. The stones should be approximately twice as long as they are high, ideally 26 × 13 inches (66 × 33 cm). Depending on the size of the room, wall, or partition to be painted, however, they may range from about 8 inches to 15 inches (22 to 40 cm) high.

Example: for a wall 102 inches (2.60 m) high

102 inches divided by 9 stones = 11.3 inches (2.60 divided by 9 = 28.8 cm)

102 inches divided by 8 stones = 12.75 inches (2.60 divided by 8 = 32.5 cm)

For ease of calculation, make the stones 12¾ inches tall × 25½ inches long (32.5 × 65 cm)

1. With a pencil, tick off the height of each course from the floor to the ceiling (not counting attached baseboards and cornices).
2. Draw a horizontal in the middle.
3. Tick off the other horizontals above and below; then draw these using a ruler or chalkline.
4. Mark the first half-stone at the top course, and then draw the rest of the vertical joints.
5. Around openings such as doors and windows, first draw keystones (see examples, pages 64-66).

Note that you can incorporate door frames in the stone arrangement by continuing the stones onto the frame, as shown in illustration 5, left.

Render mortar joints with matte paint, usually white and somewhat fluid (one part matte alkyd paint to one part zinc or titanium white, with a little oil, a little turpentine, and dryer).

For corners, follow the system used in real stonework: whole cornerstones alternate with half-stones. This method makes the vertical joints perfectly symmetrical.

Stone colors

You can substitute black for raw umber

White + yellow ochre + a little raw umber + a drop of medium chromium yellow

White + raw umber + a little red ochre

White + yellow ochre + a little raw umber + a drop of burnt umber

White + yellow ochre + a little red ochre + a drop of raw umber

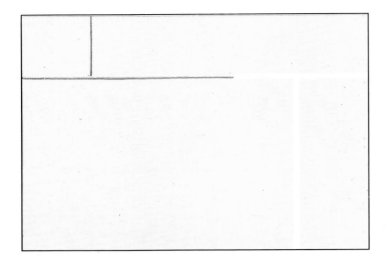

UNIFORM AND TONED FREESTONE

Uniform Freestone

The base coat determines the final color of uniform (flat-color) stone; the mortar-joint edging gives the stonework its realistic look. White joints sometimes need a second coat, mainly when the pencil layout underneath is too heavy.

Glaze applied

Toned Freestone

Freestone is toned by applying a lightly tinted glaze to each stone, coloring within the lines of the layout. To alternate lighter and stronger-colored stones, use three or four differently tinted glazes made with raw umber and raw sienna (burnt umber on beige base coats). For example:

* an almost colorless slightly yellow glaze
* a grayish raw umber glaze
* one or two other intermediate glazes

Apply the glaze thinly to the stone, and finish in one of two ways:

1. Streak the glaze horizontally, more or less forcefully, with a wide spalter. Working with oils, a sponge, or folded burlap gives a similarly striped look.
2. Evenly stipple the glaze with a patina brush. The grain may look more or less marked, depending on how far away you are.

Whichever method you use, wipe up any glaze that drips onto adjacent stones.

Finish by edging joints.

Glaze applied

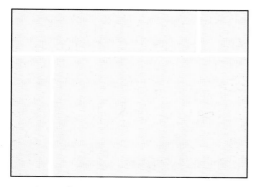

Uniform freestone

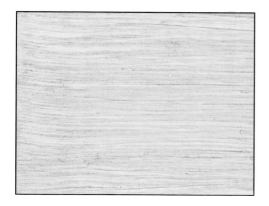

Streaked glaze

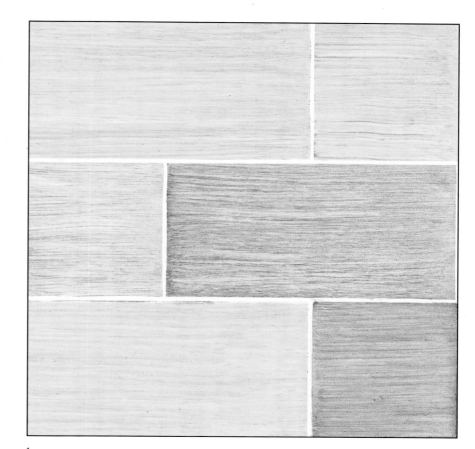

1

2

Stippled glaze

SHADED FREESTONE

Shaded and Veined Freestone

Prepare a clear glaze and two other lightly tinted glazes, as for the preceding toned stonework.

Cover one or several stones at a time with clear glaze.

Apply colored glaze as desired.

Smooth and blend around the colored areas with a spalter or wipe with a rag.

Stipple or streak as desired.

Working along the width of some stones (or a little obliquely), add some wide shaded streaks, and blend; add some yellowish, whitish, or grayish veins.

Spatter with a little brown and white.

Edge the joints.

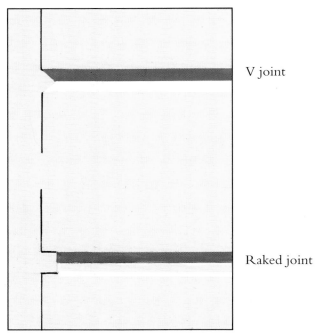

V joint

Raked joint

MORTAR JOINTS

Joints can be white, ochre, light gray, or medium gray. They can also be made with tinted glaze for a more realistic effect.

In addition to the simple plain-edged joint, made with a flat color, you can also make joints that appear carved or hollowed, with light and shadow. By convention, the placement of the shadows represents light coming obliquely from above, at an angle of 45 degrees, from the left or right, depending on the placement of the wall and existing lighting.

Shaded and veined freestone

V joints   *Raked joints*

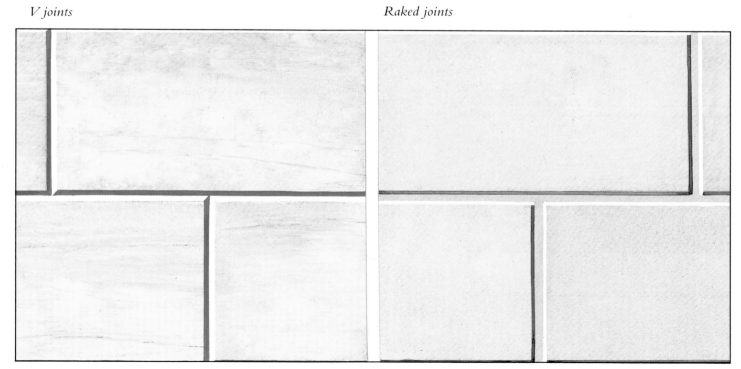

1   2

FREESTONE IN RELIEF

Raised Panels

There are several different methods to add relief to freestone. Single or double raised panels (illustrations 1 and 2) are rendered with light and shadow; the narrow white edging of the panels requires some mastery. Artists' gouache-based markers can be useful here and for shadows, if the available colors are suitable.

Other Reliefs

Chamfers around the perimeters of the stones (3, opposite) and diamond points (4, 5) are rendered in four colors, one for each facet. There are two methods for accomplishing this.

Using flat paint (3 and 4)
Paint the whole surface with a medium-light base coat (A); draw the edges, and paint the three other facets following this layout. Use masking tape to keep the edges precise. For a good monochrome, make enough of the dark tone (D) so it can serve as the sole colorant, mixed with white, for tones A, B, and C. The facets on the left are in the plain base tone.

Using four glazes (5)
Paint the whole surface with a stone-colored base coat.

Lay out the edges.

Glaze, stipple, and blend each facet. Remember to let each section dry before proceeding to the next.

Keep the edges precise by using masking tape.

1
Stone with
single raised
panel

2
Stone with
double
raised panel

general tone
A
medium light

light tone B

medium dark
tone C

dark tone D

4

5
stone-color
base coat

1. Stone with single relief

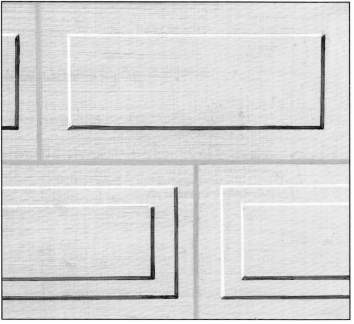

2. Stone with double relief

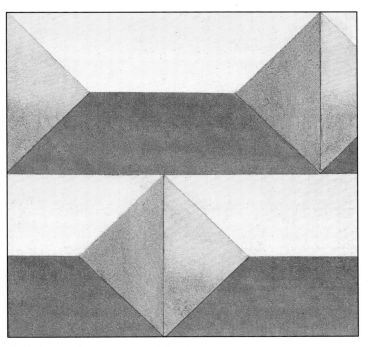

3. Chamfered stone

4. Diamond-point stone (flat paint)

5. Diamond-point stone (glaze)

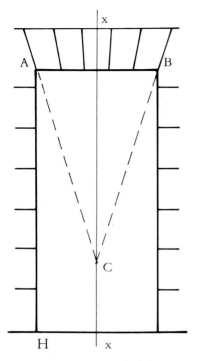

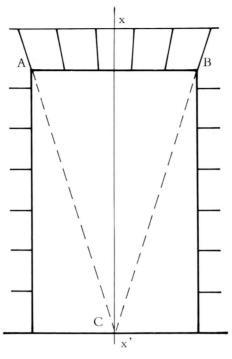

1. Recommended for narrow openings

2. Recommended for wider openings

FREESTONE LINTELS

Flat arches, the horizontal lintels over openings in walls (doors, windows, bay windows), are made of oblique stones called voussoirs, always in an odd number, with a central keystone.

Layout

Divide the horizontal AB into five or seven parts (or more, for wider openings).

Find point C on the xx' axis, and from this point draw the diagonal edges of the stones, following the divisions made in AB.

To find point C

Professionals use different methods; here are simplified versions of two:

1. Add the width AB to the height AH. Divide the sum by two, and drop that far down from the intersection of AB and xx', toward x'.

2. Establish the xx' axis, and place point C at the center of the base of the opening.

Layout of other flat arches

Crossette

Staggered crossette

Harp

Uniform freestone on wall with closed bay, with flat crossette arch and faux-relief keystone

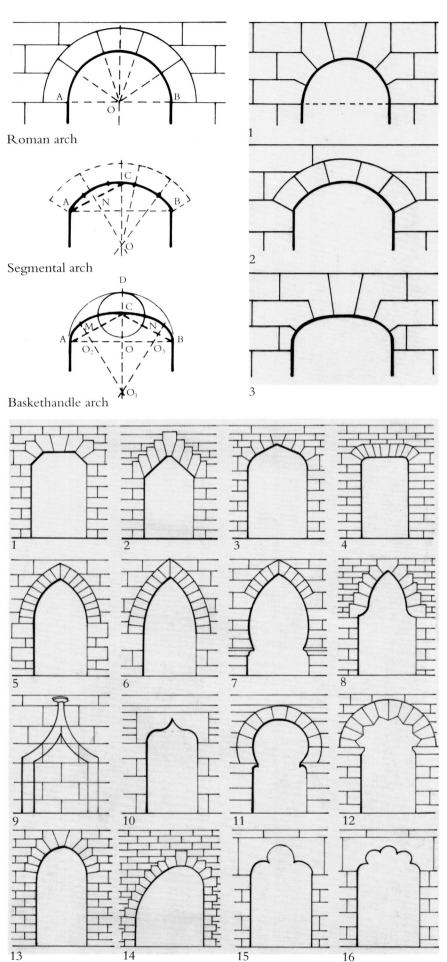

Roman arch

Segmental arch

Baskethandle arch

FREESTONE ARCHES

Arches are another way to build around openings in walls (doors, windows, bay windows). Arches consist of springers, voussoirs, and keystones, and come in different styles: Roman, Gothic, etc.

Roman Arch

This arch is a perfect semicircle.

To make one, draw the horizontal AB to the desired width. Then draw a semicircle from the midpoint O. Divide into a number of stones, and tick them off. Then connect O to each division. The tops of the stones are a second half-circle.

The arch is made of crossette voussoirs.

Segmental Arch

Segmental arches are a fraction of a circle, and the variable central point O is always below the horizontal AB.

First determine points A, B, and C. Connect A and C; from midpoint N of AC draw a perpendicular; this intersects the vertical axis at O, the center of the arc to draw.

Baskethandle Arch

First determine points A, B, and C.

Trace the semicircle determined by ray OA.

Connect AC and BC. Place point D at the intersection of the semicircle and the vertical axis. Make a circle centered at C with the ray CD, to determine points M and N. Draw the medians of AM and BN; these give the centers of the three curves at O1, O2, and O3.

The arch is made of crossette voussoirs.

Other Arches

1. Truncated
2. Corbelled
3. Tudor
4. Depressed baskethandle
5. Gothic
6. Lancet
7. Lanceolate
8. Doucine
9. Inflected
10. Ogee
11. Saracenic
12. Zigzag
13. Elliptical
14. Recumbent
15. Round trefoil
16. Round cinquefoil

Shaded freestone (with mortar joints), on wall with faux window and Gothic arch

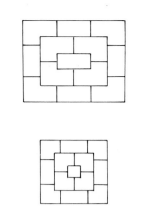
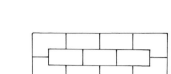
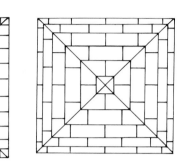

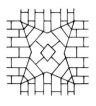

STONEWORK ARCHITECTURAL ELEMENTS

Vaults

Stone vaults have differently arranged stones, depending on whether they are flat, curved, or composite. Several arrangements are shown at left.

Balusters

Balusters are the short pillars that, together with a rail on top, make up a balustrade.

Trompe l'œil stone balustrades can be an interesting element to incorporate within wall frescos. A variety of baluster designs are shown opposite.

Rendering balusters

When the base wall decoration is finished or laid out, draw the balustrade. Start by making (erasable) horizontal lines for the base and rail, and then mark out the vertical axes of the balusters. You may make a stencil for the whole baluster, or make a half-template and flip it over along the vertical axis to achieve perfect symmetry.

Arrangement of stone block around an oval œil-de-bœuf, with coursed ashlar (see page 70) around it.

Œil-de-boeuf

An œil-de-bœuf is a round or oval opening, often in the upper part of a facade (or wall or gable), allowing a decorative arrangement of surrounding masonry.

Various baluster shapes (top)
Real stone balustrade at the edge of a terrace (bottom)

1

ASHLAR AND RUBBLE MASONRY

The use of small regular or irregular stones in walls offers many different arrangements.

Coursed Ashlar Masonry (1, 2)

On a stone-colored base coat of your choice, draw regular horizontal lines, and then irregularly spaced vertical joints to form stones. With a flat bristle brush, make some strokes a little darker than the base, mostly in the lower parts of the stones; soften these strokes with a sponge or brush.

Repeat with a light tone, mostly in the upper parts of the stones.

Paint the mortar joints with cement gray, lightly rounding the corners.

3

5

Random Ashlar (3, 4)

On a stone-colored base coat of your choice, draw a rectilinear arrangement of stones, following one of the layouts opposite.

For the rustic look, follow the directions for example 1 above.

For a freestone surface, shade or spatter, following the directions for freestone (pages 56–60).

Paint the mortar joints with cement gray.

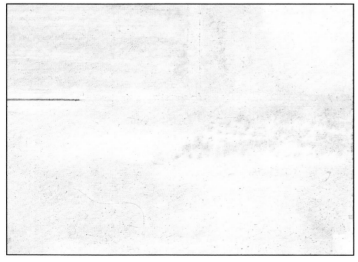

Rubble Masonry (5, 6)

On a light stone-color base coat, draw horizontal courses, and draw the shapes of the irregular stones laid out in each row.

Shade, lightly texture, and dab with a sponge. Add some white strokes to represent pointing and cleaning.

Paint fairly wide mortar joints around the stones, in a tone close to the light base color. This suggests the use of lime in reworking old joints.

1

2

3

4

5

6

Rubble Masonry, Opus Incertum Style

Opus incertum is an irregular arrangement of stone dating back to ancient Roman walls.

On the base coat, draw differently shaped stones, placed so as to avoid large voids.

Texture as for coursed or random ashlar (page 70).

Finish by painting angular, irregular mortar joints. For a high-quality rendering, it is important to add shadows to these joints—they add the three-dimensional quality that makes the stonework look real. Paint the joints with flat color, as for normal rubblestone. Then add a dark strip of paint or glaze along the bottom and one side of the stones, according to the desired lighting. Blend this strip by stippling with a spalter or *rondin,* or by smoothing with a straight edging brush and ruler for rectilinear shadows.

"Polygonal" Rubble Masonry

Draw five- or six-sided stones on the base coat, in a pleasing composition (opposite, center).

Then use the method described for ashlar masonry (page 70).

Millstone

Millstone is irregularly shaped and riddled with holes. The colors are yellow oxide and "burnt bread."

Base color: white and yellow ochre

Draw the shape of the rocks with a pencil.

Color each stone with a different amount of burnt and raw sienna colored glaze.

Wipe bare spots in the glaze with a rag, and stipple with a sponge wet with water or turpentine (depending on whether you are working with water- or solvent-based colors).

With a whitish glaze tinted yellow ochre, make some light blotches with a piece of sponge.

To produce the holes, mottle with the end of a sponge and very dark glaze (burnt umber and raw umber).

Paint the mortar joints with opaque cement-colored paint.

Rubble masonry in random arrangement (top)
Rubble masonry in polygonal arrangement (center)
Millstone in regular arrangement (bottom)

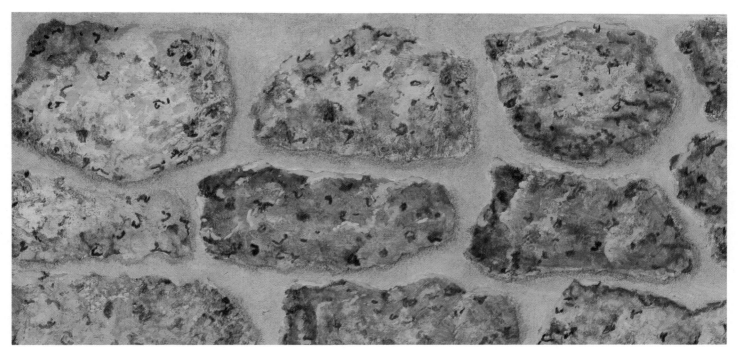

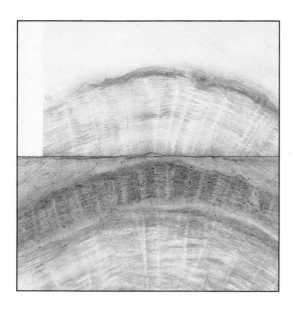

OTHER STONES

The stone effects shown here require preliminary layout, like freestone. They can also be arranged in tile-like rectangular pavers.

Ribbon-patterned Stone

Some stones have colored veins that twirl into ribbons.

Base coat: stone yellow, beige, light gray, or white

Cover each stone with clear glaze.

Form sinuous veinings, close to the base color, in each stone. Immediately make undulations with the spalter.

Finish with some stronger colored lines following the same curves.

Comblanchien

Comblanchien is a beige construction stone, used as accompaniment with more strongly colored elements.

Base coat: white or light beige

Apply over the whole surface a slightly opaque beige glaze (white + yellow ochre + red ochre + black).

Mottle parts of the wet glaze with a natural sponge, first with light beige, and then with dark beige.

Using a pointed sable, with raw sienna and burnt sienna, draw two or three restrained veins.

Add some light blotches that might be fossils, and some dark gray touches around the mottling.

Travertine

Travertine is a limestone deposit with undulating markings made by underground spring water. (For more detailed travertine, see page 160.)

Base coat: a light tone (white + yellow oxide + a drop of raw umber)

Apply a slightly opaque beige-yellow glaze over the whole surface.

Make two or three slightly colored wide bands by dragging, using a small round bristle brush, with a glaze of raw umber and a drop of burnt sienna and a glaze of raw sienna and a drop of black, and blend the whole with a spalter.

Draw sinuous narrow lines with a pointed sable.

Add light spots to imitate the characteristic travertine voids filled with beige-colored putty, and edge them with a little brown ochre.

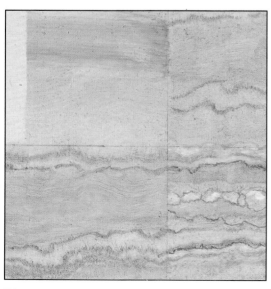

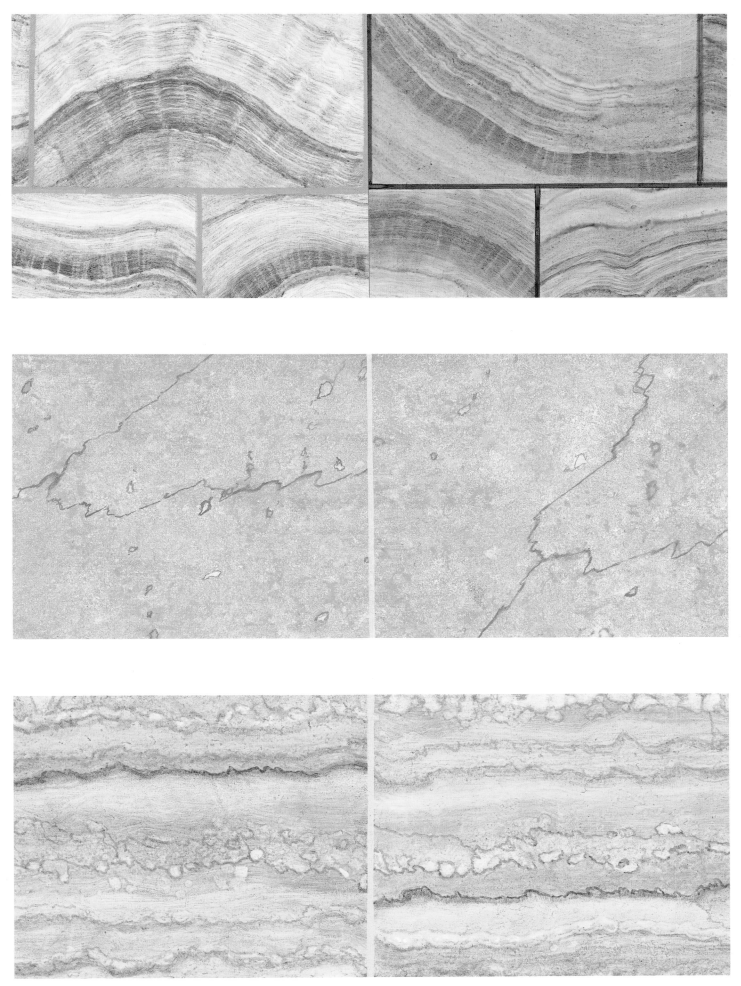

FAUX BRONZE

Real bronze, an alloy of copper and tin, is used as an interior decorative element in many ways: bronze sculptures, furnishings, light fixtures, and so on. In decorative painting, we can imitate bronze (or gold and silver) and give surfaces a metallic look with various materials. Among these are:

- Packaged paints (e.g., liquid gilding)
- Bronzing powders and varnishes (separate items) or non-toxic colored mica powders
- Aerosol sprays
- Metallic gouaches, inks, acrylic colors, and waxes.

These products are stable in a dry environment, but are sensitive to water, humidity, and bad weather. Varnishing prolongs their life, though at some expense to their initial sparkle.

HOMOGENEOUS BRONZES

The direct brush application of bronzes to painted surfaces should be reserved for work on small surfaces: gilt edging, small ornaments, etc.

On larger surfaces, the final sheen may be reduced by the visibility of brushstrokes. You must then use the traditional method of application with gilding size (see pages 241–243) or, for more everyday projects, aerosol bronze might do.

PATINAED BRONZE

Patina glazes on homogeneous bronze produce a more authentic and less artificial effect.

BRONZE POWDERS

This method consists of highlighting parts of a surface with bronze powders for decorative metallic effects.

SIMULATED BRONZE

This technique consists of imitating bronzes solely with appropriately colored paints and oil glazes. The greatest advantage of the technique is the stability of the work over time, as there is no fear of alteration of metallic pigments as with the other methods.

VARIATIONS

In addition to the effects listed above, other special effects can be obtained with bronze powder.

Bronze powders
Main shades (which can be mixed together), from left to right,
top to bottom: pale gold, yellow gold, lemon gold, dark gold,
"old penny," aluminum, silver, copper

HOMOGENEOUS BRONZES

Here we apply a uniform metallic treatment, in a chosen shade, to a surface.

Homogeneous Bronze Directly Applied

Brushing on bronze powder mixed with bronzing varnish works best for decorative edging and braids, interlacing, small ornaments, stenciled designs, edging on reliefs, and small objects. Because the brushstrokes remain visible, this method does not work well for larger surfaces.

Paint the prepared mix directly onto the finished surface; no special base coat is required. Some skill is necessary for edging with a ruler, as it is difficult to wipe off bronzing.

Homogeneous Bronze on Gilding Size

This professional method yields excellent results, but is also more delicate work. Use it for large surfaces, moldings, casements, objects, sculptures, and small pieces of furniture.

Apply two base coats of gloss or satin-finish enamel, in a color close to the color of the bronze.

Apply a coat of twelve-hour gilding size, evenly and without missing spots.

The next day, over this adhesive coating apply a coat of bronze powder in a mixture of equal parts water and denatured alcohol. For a small piece, you can apply the bronze powder directly onto the gilding size with a soft brush; collect excess powder on a piece of smooth paper under the object being bronzed.

After a few hours, finish up by rubbing with cotton and a soft brush. This removes any excess powder and polishes the surface.

A coat of varnish slows the decay of sensitive metallic pigments. For plain surfaces or quicker projects, you can use aerosol bronzes; follow the manufacturer's directions on the can for base preparation (usually matte white).

*Examples of bronzing (powder and varnish) applied freehand
directly by brush in ornament and decorative border*

Carved molding in pale gold; bronze powder on gilding size

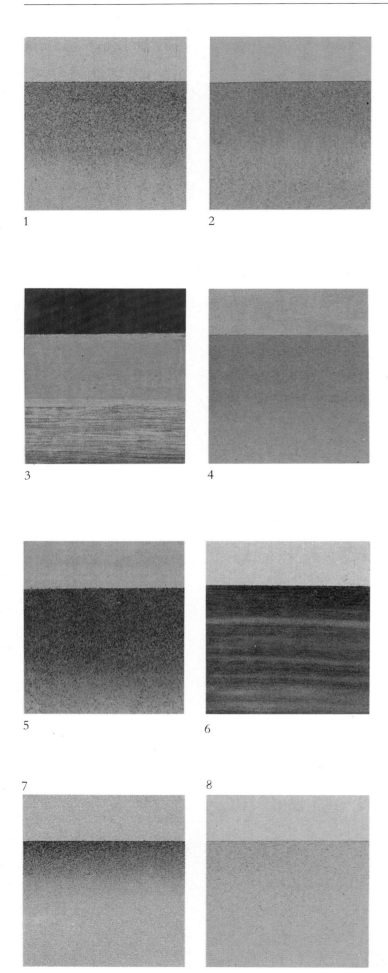

1

2

3

4

5

6

7

8

BRONZE PATINAS

Imitation bronzes are aged with patina glazes. In preparation, to avoid altering the metallic surface, first seal it with an isolating coat of varnish.

Basic Method

Make a bronze base, and apply a coat of shellac or alkyd varnish diluted with a little turpentine.

Apply the aging patina with tinted glaze.

Finish with a last coat of gloss, satin, or matte varnish.

The possible colorings are unlimited, depending on the shades of bronzes and the patina applied. Some examples are shown at left, as follows:

1. Yellow bronze aged with raw umber glaze.
2. Yellow bronze shaded with a burnt-sienna and burnt-umber glaze.
3. Yellow bronze (in the style of water gilding), worn to show the coats below. The bronze is applied over the whole red base coat, and then partially removed, after it dries, with turpentine or fine sandpaper.
4. Verdigris antique bronze with yellow-green glaze.
5. Dark antique bronze, with dark green glaze (black, raw umber, chrome green).
6. "Gun-barrel" bronze with dark glaze (Prussian blue and black), streaked with a rag, over an aluminum base. Another way to achieve the same effect is to rub a white bronze metallic glaze over a base painted dark steel blue.
7. White aluminum bronze with a light glaze of ivory black.
8. Silver bronze with light yellow glaze (drops of raw sienna and medium chrome).

Aged Yellow Bronze

Three quarters of the frame (opposite, clockwise from lower left) illustrate the successive steps:

Priming (common to all examples)

Base coat (yellow) and gilding size

Gold bronze, polished and varnished, to seal

Aging patina

Yellow Bronze Water-gilding Style

The lower-right quarter of the frame (opposite):

Base coat (red) and gilding size

Gold bronze, wiped off the relief

Varnish and optional painted green patina

Final varnish coat

Shaded yellow bronze and dark antique bronze

81

1

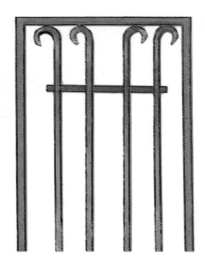

2

3

BRONZE POWDERS

This technique is the opposite of bronzing with a patina. Instead of applying bronze over all and covering parts with glaze, here you apply glaze over all, and apply bronze to only selected spots. (Metallic waxes, sold in small bottles and applied with a finger or rag, give quick and satisfactory results.)

As with aging patinas, the method is based on the use and proper placement of three colors:

❖ A dark tone for the lower part of panels, spindles, railings, recesses, and the like

❖ A medium tone for intermediate parts

❖ A light tone for reliefs, high points, extremities of volutes, etc.

Yellow or Gold Bronze (1)

Base coat: satin-finish yellow paint (yellow ochre, lemon yellow, and raw sienna, depending on the shade of the bronze)

Apply a clear glaze over the whole piece.

Apply the tinted glaze (raw sienna, raw umber, burnt umber) for the dark tone.

Stipple this glaze, running it into the intermediate areas (in the clear-glazed base).

Apply the light glaze with gold bronze, and stipple.

Red or Florentine Bronze (2)

Base coat: satin-finish reddish-brown paint (Van Dyck brown or burnt umber)

Apply a clear glaze over the whole surface.

Apply an oil glaze with a very little bit of red bronze on intermediate parts.

Stipple this glaze, running over into the dark parts.

Apply the light glaze with red bronze, and stipple.

Wrought Iron (3)

Base coat: black satin-finish paint

As for red bronze, but use white "aluminum" bronze powder. Black glaze applied as a patina on aluminum gives a similar result.

Yellow bronze vase, red bronze vase, bronze antique highlights in metallic wax, and violet bronze highlights in metallic wax

1

2

3

4

SIMULATED BRONZE

These techniques resemble bronze powders, requiring the application of three stippled and blended colorings. The important difference is the substitution of tube oil colors for metallic powders; these oil colors are mixed into glaze, rendering as closely as possible bronze metallic reflection. As the effects are limited, this technique is used principally for the following applications.

"Old Penny" (1)

Base coat: satin-finish tobacco-colored paint (yellow ochre, a bit of raw umber, and perhaps drops of black and red ochre, depending on the metal to be simulated)

Cover the surface with clear glaze.

Apply a tinted glaze (raw umber + a drop of burnt umber) for the dark tone.

Stipple this glaze, running over into the intermediate parts.

Apply the light tone with yellow ochre tinted glaze (use drops of raw umber and white).

Antique Bronzes

Different colorations are possible, with the same three-tone method.

Conventional Bronze (2)

Base coat: strong green satin-finish paint (chrome green deep, raw umber)

A dark tone—glaze tinted chrome green deep and raw umber

A medium tone—clear-glazed base

A light tone—glaze tinted yellow ochre with a drop of sienna

Shade with burnt sienna and burnt umber.

Green "Egyptian" Bronze (3)

Black glaze on copper green base. An alternative is verdigris glaze on black base.

Art nouveau green bronze (4)

Base coat: light green satin-finish base (white + medium green + a little yellow ochre)

A dark tone—medium green, raw umber, and raw sienna

A medium tone—the same tint, but thinner

A clear light base tone

The simulated bronze effects are shown here on real reliefs, but they can also be used in trompe l'œil ornament with flat tints for relief (light tone, middle base tone, dark tone), as in the design at lower right, opposite, which is rendered in antique bronze on a flat, painted surface.

"Old penny" bronze vase, antique bronze on green vase, antique bronze on black vase, and antique bronze motif painted on flat surface

SPECIAL EFFECTS

The following examples demonstrate different ways of using bronze: bronzes applied over all (on gilding size or with aerosol), decorated with colored glaze, or painted homogeneous bases decorated with bronze glazes. A finish coat of varnish is necessary for these methods. Note: Isolate the glaze containing bronze with varnish before overlaying glazes.

Oxidation with Vinegar (1)

Base coat: gold bronze (using gilding size)

Let dry, then wet the bronze with distilled white wine vinegar, either by placing paper toweling wet with vinegar on the bronze or, if the surface is vertical, by blotting with a sponge wet with vinegar.

Oxidation with Colored Glazes (2)

Base coat: gold bronze (by any method), sealed with an isolating coat of varnish

Using a sponge, with green-yellow glaze, make a cloudy patina, and mottle with light verdigris. You can also spatter drops of turpentine to make splotches here and there or add other color effects.

Cloudy Lacquer (3)

Base coat: a strong color

Apply a glaze containing a moderate amount of bronze.

Wipe, stipple, and sponge with the edge of a free-form natural sponge barely moistened with turpentine or other solvent.

Stippled Granite (4)

Base coat: bronze (in your choice of shade), sealed with a coat of varnish

Using a *chiqueteur* or the equivalent, pebble once or several times with colored glazes.

"Modern" Effects (5)

Base coat: a strong color

Apply a clear glaze over the whole.

Form repetitive effect of your liking (hatching using a spalter, crumpled rag or other tool, with bronze).

Using a *chiqueteur* or the equivalent, mottle and add supplementary color glazes (blue in the example opposite).

Oxidation with vinegar, imitation oxidation with glaze, cloudy lacquer, stippled metallic effects, and modern metallic effects

OTHER MATERIALS

These pages present some complementary materials chosen for their similarity (in method and level of difficulty) to the foregoing techniques. These renderings are simple, but can lead the way to more refined work.

LEATHER

Base coat: medium chrome + yellow ochre + cadmium orange + a little white for yellow leather; yellow ochre + chrome orange + a little red + a little burnt umber for chestnut-colored leather

Apply a tinted glaze that is close to the base tone; wipe with a dry rag, and stipple to produce the fine grain.

Use a folded rag to apply more strongly colored glaze to produce the more pronounced markings.

PARCHMENT

Base coat: white + yellow ochre + drops of light chrome and raw umber

Apply over the whole a more or less yellowish glaze (raw sienna and raw umber, depending on the desired look—the light or darker, aged look depends on the coloration of the glazes). Proceed as for a sponged or cloudy patina.

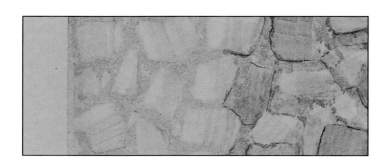

Stipple the whole surface and let dry.

Add some touches of whitish glaze, and some markings with a more strongly colored glaze.

CORK

Base coat: white + yellow ochre + a little red ochre, depending on the desired look

Apply over the whole a colored glaze (raw sienna and a little burnt sienna).

For the particles that make up the cork, wipe the wet glaze; let dry and, using a small spalter, recolor some of the bared spots in the glaze. Then make some additional particles.

For sheet cork, which comes from close to the bark, use a spalter and rag to make undulations in lighter parts.

Add some brown spots (raw and burnt umber) and pinkish reflections with glaze (a drop of red ochre + white).

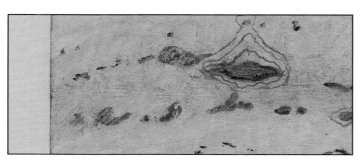

Yellow and chestnut-colored leather, light and aged parchment, and two kinds of cork

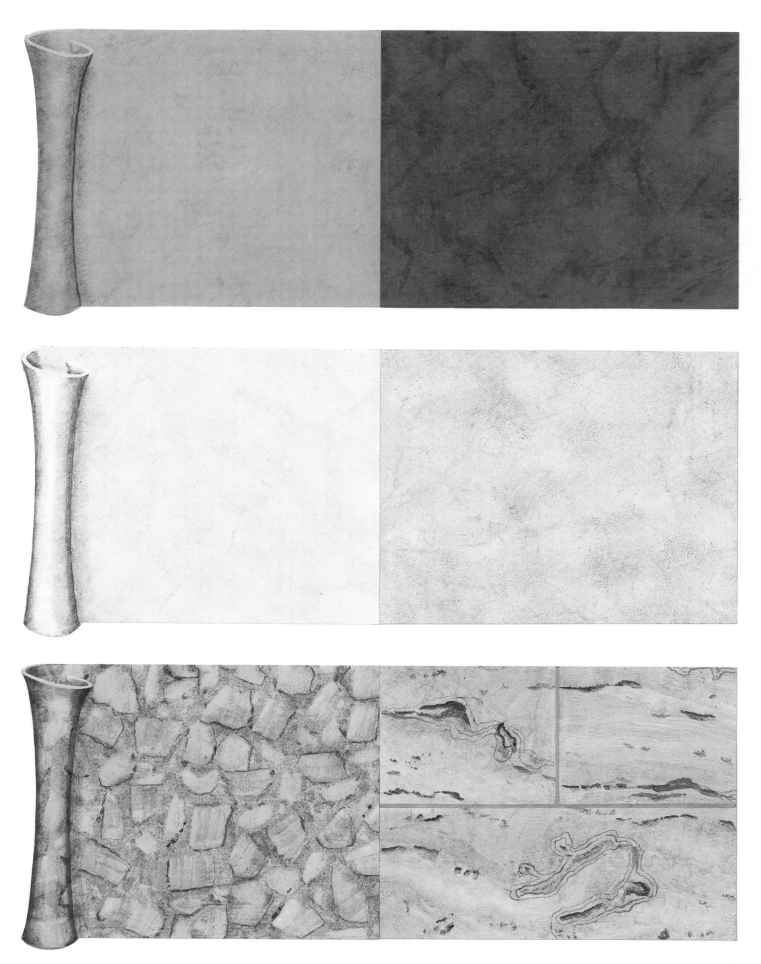

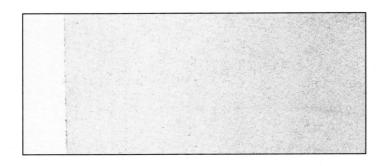

These materials are used on small surfaces, inlays, edging, objects, veneer effects, etc.

IVORY

A very light-colored bony material that goes well with any other material.

Base coat: white + a little yellow ochre + a drop of vermilion

Apply a lightly tinted glaze (raw sienna + a drop of raw umber).

Follow method for single-glaze aging, wiping reliefs and stippling recesses.

On three-dimensional objects, a final coat of white wax polished with a cloth helps to capture the natural luster of ivory.

TORTOISESHELL

Tortoiseshell comes in red and yellow (blonde).

Base coat for yellow: slightly orange bold yellow

Apply a moderately opaque glaze (raw sienna with a little burnt sienna).

Using a wet natural sponge, wipe oval spots and blend the resulting markings.

Reglaze, lightly stipple, and add dark spots with burnt umber.

Base coat for red: orange-toned vivid red

Apply an opaque glaze in burnt sienna with a little black.

Wipe to produce a cloudy effect or long, oval spots.

Blend the markings.

Reglaze parts with a mixture of burnt sienna and crimson lake, lightly stipple, and add some almost black spots.

MOTHER-OF-PEARL

Mother-of-pearl lines the inside of some shells, and has a nice iridescent look.

Base coat: white + a very little bit of yellow ochre + a drop of medium chrome yellow

Apply a thin clear glaze over the base coat. Make some well-spaced streaks, barely tinted pink (with crimson lake), and others tinted very pale green to produce the luminous effect.

Blend the whole with a soft brush or badger blender, pulling the brush in different directions.

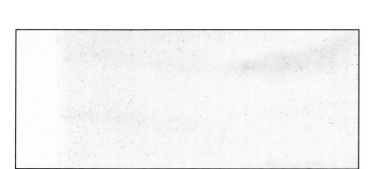

Faux materials on relief panels

*Light and aged ivory border, red
tortoiseshell center in reverse-diamond-
pattern marquetry*

*Ivory-patina outer and inner border,
mother-of-pearl molded frame, yellow
tortoiseshell center in four-way
marquetry*

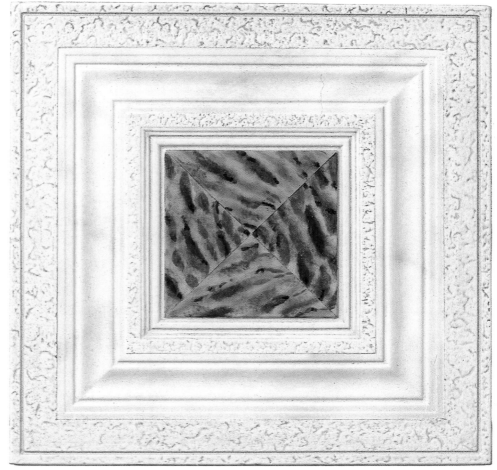

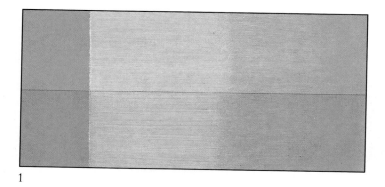

1

TERRACOTTA

Oven-baked clay has a soft look and pleasing colors. This material—used in sculpted and molded objects, wall plaques, and the like—is easy to imitate.

Base coat: white + yellow ochre + a little cadmium orange or orange-yellow, depending on the desired color

Using a very dilute matte white paint, proceed as for a single-glaze aging patina, wiping the surface vigorously so as not to leave any white except in the recesses. Smooth with a spalter and lightly stipple.

White matte acrylic or vinyl paint is recommended for this work.

GRANITE

The pebbled look of granite is achieved by the successive applications of colored pebbling. Apply each coat with a piece of very open-textured natural sponge wet with thin paint or colored glaze. Keep the paint on a flat surface or in a paint-can lid, for easy refilling of the sponge.

For additional granite effects, see chapter 3.

Dark Gray (2)

Base coat: white + black + a drop of ultramarine blue

Sponge once with medium gray.

Let dry. Sponge again with darker coal gray (black + a drop of white).

Sponge finally with light gray.

Finish with a coat of varnish.

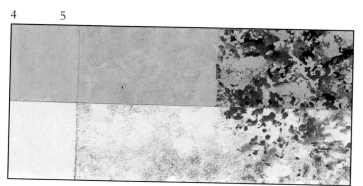

2

Light Gray (3)

Base coat: same as above

Sponge once with off-white (white + a drop of yellow ochre). Let dry. Sponge once or twice with medium and coal grays. Do not put too much glaze on the surface.

Finish with a coat of varnish.

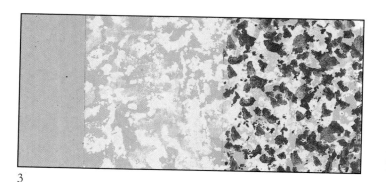

3

4 5

Pink (4)

Base coat: same as above

Sponge with a light tone (white + yellow ochre + cadmium orange). Let dry. Sponge with a caramel tone and add some dark brown pebbling.

Finish with a protective coat of varnish.

Example 5 shows granite characteristic of Tarn, in the south of France.

Imitation-terracotta pot

Granite samples

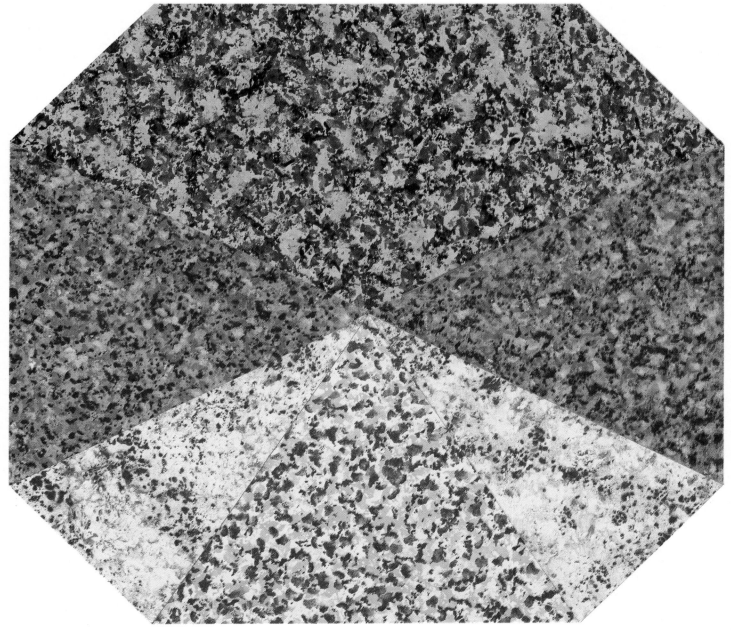

BRICK

Good faux brickwork requires an accurate layout and precise edging. You must also consider the different looks that are possible through color variation, traces of firing, and bond.

Layout

There are many sizes of brick, which vary from country to country. Standard sizes, however, range up from 4 × 2⅔ × 8 inches (7 × 22 × 11 cm) inches; facing bricks may be thinner, and some oversize bricks may be up to 8 inches (20 cm) long.

These measurements include the thickness of the mortar joint, so the actual manufactured bricks are smaller; similarly, in trompe l'œil, the final proportions of the brick are reduced by the width of the edging.

Basic Method

Apply a uniform base coat, in the desired matte-finish color. Lay out the arrangement of bricks in light pencil.

Partially or wholly shade the bricks with tinted glaze to simulate flashing. (Stay inside the lines!)

Some common bonds (uniform red brick)

| Running bond | Flemish bond (English corner) | Flemish bond (Dutch corner) |

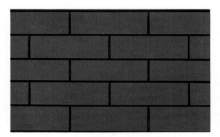 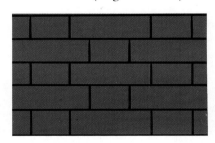 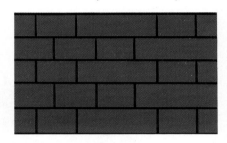

Paint the edging to simulate mortar joints. The mortar may be off-white, medium gray, or cement-colored. To make the joints more realistic, you can include cast shadows.

Geometric designs and arrangements can be obtained by coloring or shading bricks in a predetermined pattern.

Flashed Red Brick

Base coat: red ochre + drops of white and yellow ochre

Apply a tinted glaze (burnt sienna and burnt umber) over each brick. Wipe, varying the shading according to the design.

Stipple to soften the wiped strokes. The edging will mask any places you have gone over the borders between bricks.

Finish with matte or satin varnish.

Antique Yellow Brick

Base coat: yellow ochre + white + a drop of raw umber

Apply a light glaze (raw sienna and raw umber), varying shading as above. Reglaze in places with a slightly darker glaze, and stipple.

Spatter with brown.

Finish with matte or satin varnish.

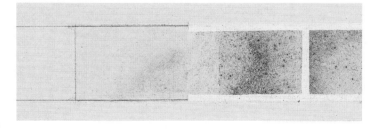

Ironspot Brick

Base coat: yellow ochre + white + orange-yellow + a drop of red ochre

Apply a reddish glaze (burnt sienna and burnt umber) and stipple the shadows. Reglaze with raw sienna and orange-yellow, adding brown and mauve-toned marks. Spatter with brown.

Finish with matte or satin varnish.

Flashed red brick

Red brick with header

Uniform orange brick

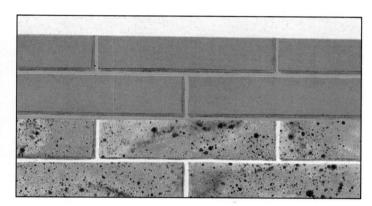

Thin modern brick (top)
Thin gray mottled brick (bottom)

New uniform yellow brick

Yellow ironspot brick, aged by mottling

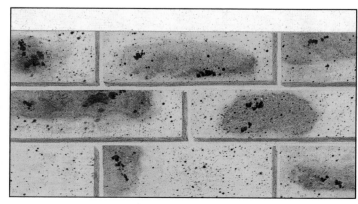

Light ironspot brick

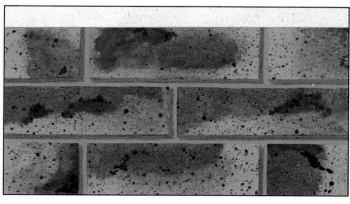

Dark ironspot brick

Base-coat colors

Light oak 1

Dark oak

Medium oak 2

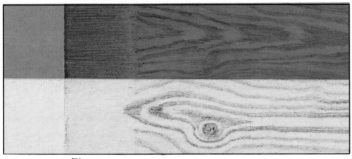

Fir

Fir 3

Rosewood

Dark walnut 4

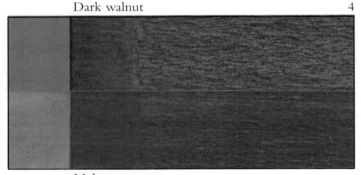

Mahogany

Limed oak 5

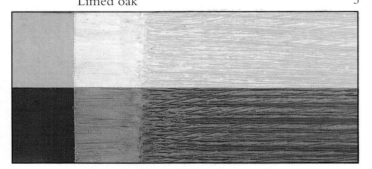

Contemporary colored and limed

WOOD

These simplified imitations of wood are based on the application of a colored glaze to a lighter painted base, whence their similarity to classical patinas. For more detailed rendering of wood, see chapter 4.

The grain effects are produced by overlaying glazes. In all cases, varnishing (matte or eggshell) is necessary for liming effects. The base colors for the woods are shown at the left of each sample.

Combed Oak (1)

Apply a colored glaze and comb parallel lines with the steel combs designed for imitating oak.

Wipe the glaze off the comb after each pass.

Plume or Vee Grain (2)

Apply a thin, barely tinted glaze over the surface. Using a sable or artist's brush, draw the grain with colored glaze.

Apply the same glaze over the whole of the rest of the surface.

Wipe with a rag, following the contours of the grain.

Straight Grain (3)

Apply a glaze tinted according to the color of the chosen wood, and wipe lengthwise with folded burlap, making the "rises" by halting the movement of the rag.

Wood Grain (4)

Apply a colored glaze and "flog" with a flogger, pushing the brush away from yourself, not pulling it toward you.

Limed Wood (5)

This imitation of naturally whitened wood with a coating of filler is obtained by applying a whitish glaze on a painted base. Wipe forcefully with a rag, and comb with a steel comb.

You can also grain as desired.

The limed look, very much prized in today's decoration (for woodwork and painted furnishings), is close to the white antique patina shown on page 40.

Faux parquet, with different base-coat colors, produces different decorative results (top) Faux marquetry on paper support, cut and glued in position (bottom)

3

MARBLE

INTRODUCTION

Marble is an indispensable element of trompe l'œil art. Nature is generous with marble, offering thousands of varieties. But it is not necessary to be familiar with every one to create superb interiors. A few dozen will suffice.

Perpetual geological movement transforms the planet day after day. Rocks are buffeted ceaselessly by various cataclysms, incursions of water, erosion from the wind, and abrupt changes in temperature. Over millions of years, the material is modified, creating a host of marbles: *veined marbles, breccias* (marbles composed of large chunks embedded in a limestone bed), *brocatelles* (marbles with smaller fragments), *granites* and *porphyries* (with still finer fragments), and finally, some almost uniform marbles.

The boundaries between these types of marble are not perfectly sharp: a veined marble may have large chunks, and breccias, with fragments of various sizes, may be veined.

For purposes of imitation, you need to study the markings

and colors that characterize each kind of marble. An inaccurate rendering of a large breccia, with fragments placed in an unbalanced and disharmonious way, can ruin an interior design. So you must get the forms and colors right.

Our objective is to lead you to discover, appreciate—even love—and imitate as best you can these natural treasures called marbles. Your imitations will only improve with regular practice.

Marble with pronounced veining and brecciation and strong coloration is decoration unto itself. On the other hand, when the marble is to be part of an elaborate frieze with other architectural and ornamental elements, choose a more restrained variety, so as not to overload the eyes.

To really fool the eye of the viewer, you need to master not just the markings and colors of marble but also perspective and the history of style. Visit museums and historic buildings to admire the masterworks, and copy them up close.

THE MARBLES

A good faux marble is more than a few veins painted on a colored base. To imitate marble well requires some research, and you should take the time to examine closely, if possible, the marbles to be copied, to observe the subtle veining that runs through the finely nuanced opposing base color and other characteristics of the particular marble. You can use samples of real marble or fine painted marble as your models. When you have become proficient, you can even invent your own varieties.

Here are a few of the best-known and most imitated marbles. These are, of course, marbles that are (or were) accessible in Europe, marbles primarily from France, Italy, and Spain. American suppliers will have some of them, but also a rich selection of American native marbles as well as marbles imported from all over the world. Since the names of marbles are generally established by the producer, we give the French name and an English equivalent, where available or useful.

VEINED MARBLES

Vert de Mer (Mediterranean Green)

Spread across the Mediterranean basin, the beautiful Mediterranean Green, with its white-green spider-web veining on a blackish background, is both one of the most sober and widely used marbles. It is used in almost all antique and modern styles. Its colors and markings harmonize readily with virtually any decor.

Levanto (Red Levanto)

"Cousin" of Mediterranean Green, Italian Red Levanto is distinguished by its dark red background spotted with tiny emerald pebbles. Its use is identical to that of Mediterranean Green, in large or small surfaces. It works particularly well with Empire-style decor, where reds and greens are prized.

Jaune de Sienne (Yellow Sienna)

The striking Yellow Sienna, from Italy, is just as sought after as Mediterranean Green. Both are composed of two main colors, but Yellow Sienna reverses the contrast, with a light background and dark veining. Its strong yellow color goes perfectly with Louis XIV- and Empire-style interiors, bringing them incomparable warmth and radiance.

Campan Mélangé (Mixed Campan)

Campan Mélangé is one of the richly veined marbles, widely used in Versailles and elsewhere. This pleasing marble from the Pyrenees is very different from the above three, but it is just as celebrated, by virtue of its unique markings: a chain of dark green rings on a base of dark red and medium-green parallel bands, shot in places with white splinters.

Campan Rose (Pink Campan)
Vert-Vert (Green Campan)

Close relatives of Campan Mélangé, Campan Rose and Vert-Vert were relatively neglected in past centuries because of their paler coloring. They have come into favor today, because their pale tones fit in better with the lighter contemporary interior. They have similar veining; their distinguishing feature is their base coloration: pink for the Campan Rose, light green for Vert-Vert.

Griotte (Morello Cherry)

Griotte, from the Cévennes region of France, shares with its compatriot Campan similar veining and rings, but is distinguished by its red color. It is so rich in effect that you will not want to use too much of it: a little bit goes a long way. It looks nice with gilt ornamentation.

Three blackish veined marbles:

Portor (Portoro)

Elegant Portoro, also called Black and Gold, hails from the same places as, and yet is very different from, Mediterranean Green. Its gold veins, coiled or in parallel bands, contrast with its finely shaded black base. As with Griotte, limit imitations to small areas.

Saint-Laurent

Black Saint-Laurent (also called Pyrenees Black and Gold), with its fine splintery fissures in rusty white against a brownish black foundation, is a superb embellishment for large surfaces.

Imperador

The markings of Spanish Imperador are close to those of Red Levanto, but its coloring is different: monochrome brown-rust-ochre yellow.

Some grayish veined marbles:

Saint-Anne

Dark Saint-Anne is a cloudy veined marble, with scattered light ribbony swirls and fine veins set against a slate-gray base. Its somber, even sad, tone limits its use, but it is often the marble of choice for fireplaces, plinths, or frames.

Blanc Veiné (Veined White)

Italian Veined White (also called Bianco) is light and sober, with a gray-black foundation lightly striped by very fine grayish-green veins.

Bleu Turquin (Turquoise)

Also from Italy, Bleu Turquin is similar to White Veined marble but possesses a more insistent coloration. It has a blue-gray base set off by darker veins.

Napoléon Gris (Gray Napoleon)
Napoléon Rosé (Rose Napoleon)

The Gray and Rose Napoleons, from Pas-de-Calais, are flecked veined marbles, whose all-purpose coloring suits dignified projects that are contemporary in style.

Jaune Fleuri (Yellow Fleuri)

Yellow Fleuri, from the Jura mountains, is characterized by a network of very fine reddish veins on a pale yellow foundation.

These last four marbles are soft, understated marbles that, in general, best serve as accompaniment to marbles with more striking patterns.

CLOUDY MARBLES

The cloudy marbles all have cloud patterning on a reddish foundation. Depending on the variety of marble, the base color can range from red-orange to brown-wine, the clouds from white to dark gray, and from large to very small. The most notable are:

Languedoc

From the south of France, the striking Languedoc (also called French Rose) is certainly the best known marble. You can see brilliant examples in the Grand Trianon at Versailles and other equally luxurious structures. It has a red-orange foundation strewn with white clouds.

Cerfontaine
Rouge Royal
Rance

Less commanding than Languedoc, these three marbles from Belgium and the north of France resemble one another; all are grayish. They fit into any sumptuous interior.

LARGE BRECCIAS

The large breccias are very beautiful, sometimes hard, marbles, generally composed of large angular chunks embedded in dark limestone strewn with a multitude of small- and medium-sized fragments of contrasting color. Gracing numerous palaces and luxurious homes, these magnificent marbles are for interiors with "character." Take care to consider how they are used in relation to their decorative or visual weight.

The most famous breccias are:

Brèche Violette (Violet Breccia)

Violet Breccia, from Ariège, in the Pyrenees, is composed of a mixture of often enormous mauve- and wine-colored fragments contrasting with whitish to yellow fragments, held together by a mauve-toned to greenish-brown bed.

Fleur de Pecher (Peach Flower)

The blue-violet Italian Fleur de Pecher is softer in form and color than its cousin Violet Breccia.

Sarrancolin

Sarrancolin, also from the Pyrenees, is the most varied of the breccias. Sometimes it resembles Violet Breccia, with large, medium, and small chunks mixed in with tiny ones in a rusty-brown bed; sometimes it is just the opposite, with a linear design made up of nearly parallel reddish stripes against a background ranging from grayish to greenish. Fissures caused by geological movement give a very nice decorative effect. Sometimes it resembles the veined marbles in monochrome blue-green or rusty yellow. And sometimes it combines all these characteristics at once.

Grand Antique

The robust Grand Antique, from the Pyrenees, comes only in black and white. Its brecciation is scattered and always angular, even down to the smallest fragment.

Brèche Grise (Gray Breccia)

Close in tone to White Veined, Italian Gray Breccia is composed of soft gray formations of large, somewhat angular masses ringed in darker gray.

LITTLE BRECCIAS

Like the grand breccias, the little breccias are composed of a conglomeration of chunks in a contrasting limestone bed; the stones of the little breccias, however, are very small, sometimes minuscule, and scattered about. Less likely to clash with other elements or overpower a design, they are the marbles of choice for small panels, columns, pedestals.

Brèche Verte Antique (Antique Green Breccia)

Antique Green Breccia (also called Verde Antico), from the Mediterranean basin, is made up of many small, angular fragments ranging in color from deep black to soft green, mixed with pure white stones, against a nice vivid green background.

Brèche Caroline (Caroline Breccia)

The warm Caroline Breccia is the same type of breccia as Antique Green, but with a monochrome yellow-coral bed strewn with brown, black, and white splinters.

BROCATELLES

The brocatelles are little breccias made up of still smaller, more angular, more regularly arranged fragments embedded in a dark ground.

Violet Brocatelle
Yellow Brocatelle

The yellow-mauve Violet Brocatelle, the more beautiful marble of the two, was used so frequently in past centuries (notably in the eighteenth century, during the Regency–Louis XV period) that it has become rare these days. Spanish Yellow Brocatelle, lacking the mauve nuances, has replaced it today.

FLECKED STONES

Flecked stones are common stones with very fine-textured grains, like granites and travertines. Although the porphyries are flecked, they fall in the category of semiprecious stones.

Also used in past centuries, flecked stones are popular today as a pleasant and neutral design element.

GRANITES

There are many varieties of granite: gray, blue, pink, yellow, and so on.

TRAVERTINES

Anything but uniform, the travertines display, in addition to flecking, sinuous stripes and geode formations. Yellow travertine comes from Italy, orange from Iran.

SEMIPRECIOUS STONES

The semiprecious stones include onyx, malachite, lapis lazuli, and porphyry, among others. Because of their value, imitate these stones sparingly. Use them as elements for the richest decoration on vases, bowls, sculpture, columns, small panels, and jewelry.

Gold Onyx and Green Onyx

Algerian gold onyx and Mexican green onyx are the most renowned, for their undulating bands on a base of remarkable transparency.

Malachite

The superb deep green malachite, with its parallel wavy bands, resembles a miniature onyx. You can admire large works made of malachite in museums such as the Malachite Salons in the Winter Palace at St. Petersburg or at the Trianon at Versailles.

Lapis Lazuli

Lapis lazuli is similar to Languedoc marble, but is deep blue flecked with gold.

Porphyries

The porphyries resemble the granites, but the fineness and polish of their flecking mark them for grander projects, such as you might see in the Museum of Decorative Arts in Paris, or in other palaces. The best known porphyries are the pink, red, brown, and blackish.

*Panel in Mediterranean Green
and Imperador
35 in × 47 ½ in
(.9 m × 1.20 m)*

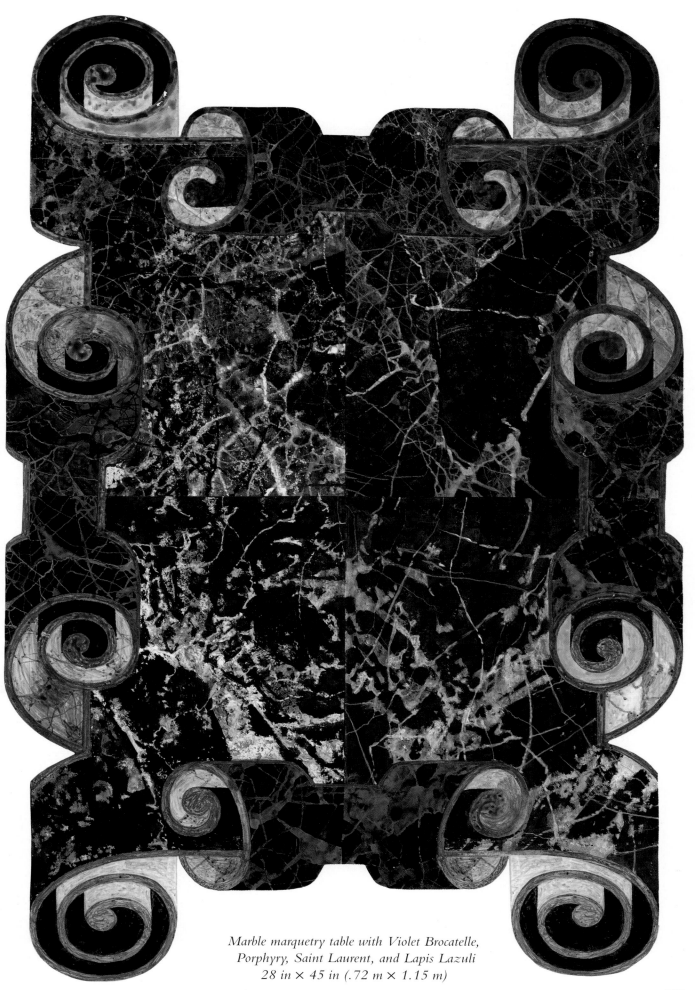

Marble marquetry table with Violet Brocatelle,
Porphyry, Saint Laurent, and Lapis Lazuli
28 in × 45 in (.72 m × 1.15 m)

BASIC METHOD

Refer to chapter 1 for the preparation of the support, brushes, and materials.

As demonstrated here with a Gray Breccia, we render marble entirely with acrylics (except where otherwise specified), to obtain a specific effect. With dilute acrylics, on a base coat of clear satin enamel, you make the stone "beds" of marble; then, with a wet spalter you go over these areas to make the first outlines of veins and the embedded fragments. Finally, you smooth with a sponge and a badger blender. This work dries very quickly, and you can proceed almost immediately to reglazings.

You can use tube acrylics, diluted, or work directly with undiluted waterproof liquid acrylic. (The acrylic must be waterproof, or you risk diluting the work below.) Dilute the acrylic with water to the desired transparency.

Oil glazes (see page 13 for composition) are useful when you want a soft, blended look, or the decoration calls for a material "aged" by time (as in an old building) or by weather (as in exterior work). Remember to take into account that you must let each glazing dry for twenty-four hours.

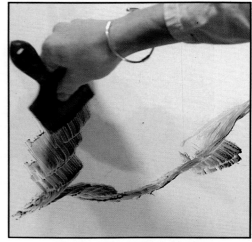

Using a spalter, apply very dilute color.

On the wet color, stipple with a damp sponge to make bare spots.

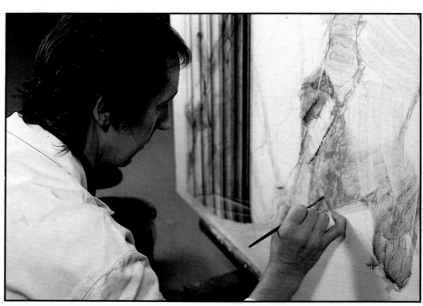

With a synthetic brush, apply light coloration to form the bed of the gray breccia.

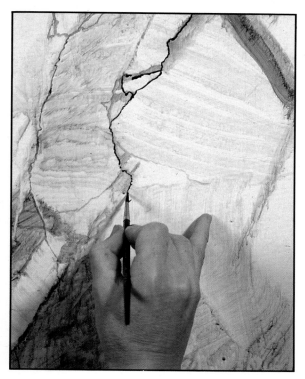

Draw lines, in a color that will stand out, in the bed you have made.

Stipple the lines, so that the edges of the stroke are not definite.

A view of the whole.

Soften with the badger blender to blend the color. By always smoothing in one direction, you will get little fissure-like fringes in the breccia.

Varnishing. With water-based acrylics you get overlaid color without diluting the foundation or having to wait to varnish between layers. The transparency is immediate.

MEDITERRANEAN GREEN

Base coat: white

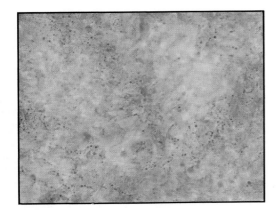

Glaze the surface with very dilute raw umber.
Then stipple vigorously with a wet sponge.

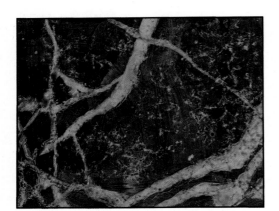

Repeat using very dilute phthalo green.

Using a glaze of two parts black to one part phthalo green, form large, irregular chunks.

Stipple this layer with a damp sponge. Using a stiff, square brush, render the veins around the stones by removing color. Stipple this work.

Repeat these steps until the whole surface is filled.

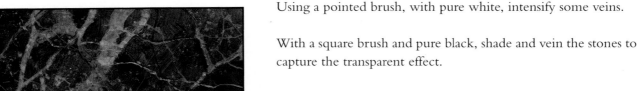

Using a pointed brush, with pure white, intensify some veins.

With a square brush and pure black, shade and vein the stones to capture the transparent effect.

Finally, stipple once more with very dilute raw umber.

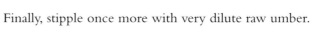

Panel with Greek frieze
30 in × 45 in (.76 m × 1.15 m)

VEINED WHITE

Base coat: white

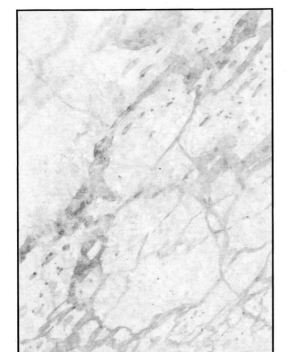

Using a pointed brush, with very dilute gray (ultramarine blue + black + a drop of naphtha red), draw in the veining.

Stipple immediately with a damp sponge.

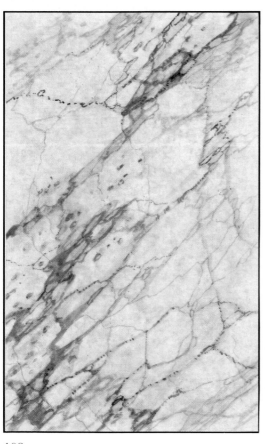

Retouch the main veins with a mixture of black and ultramarine blue. Take care not to make the lines too continuous.

Over this work, using a sponge, dab more or less self-contained spots to form the beds. Stipple and smooth immediately. Glaze the whole surface with a very dilute glaze, using a drop of naphtha red to give depth to the marble.

Streak faintly with raw umber, and stipple again.

Veined White is an understated marble, delicate and restrained.

Panel
30 in × 45 in (.76 × 1.15 m)

LAPIS LAZULI

Base coat: cobalt blue + white

For the first stippling use a sponge, with a mixture of crimson lake and a drop of chrome yellow.

Using a square brush, with a mixture of ultramarine blue and crimson lake, make ribbon-shaped beds.

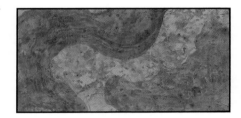

Stipple again with ultramarine blue.

Retouch parts of the ribbon shapes in white with a pointed brush. Glaze the whole with very dilute raw umber.

Finally, on a coat of wet gloss varnish, scatter small specks of gold leaf.

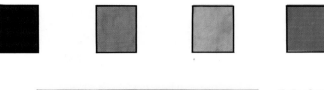

BROWN PORPHYRY

Base coat: Van Dyck brown

Using a natural sponge, stipple with bluish-gray (white + cobalt blue + black).

Stipple with a mixture of yellow ochre and chrome yellow.

Finally, stipple with old rose (crimson lake + ultramarine blue + burnt umber + white).

VIOLET BROCATELLE

Base coat: white

Using a square brush, apply strokes of very dilute yellow ochre; then use a damp sponge to stipple vigorously.

Repeat the same steps with cadmium yellow.

Repeat once more with very dilute violet.

To render an elegant Violet Brocatelle, tone about two-thirds of the surface yellow and tone a third mauve.

In the areas that will be violet, apply some dark touches (ultramarine blue + black + naphthol red + red ochre). Ring these with dark violet-black veins. Ring the yellow areas with gray-mauve veins. The irregular "trembling" lines of these rings should form a light pattern of fragments.

With pure white, detail some tiny fragments on the mauve chunks and add some subtle faults in the yellow.

Finally, lightly stipple the dark areas with very dilute pink (cadmium red + white).

SAINT-LAURENT

Base coat: black

Cover the dark base with a very dilute yellow (white + yellow ochre + a drop of golden yellow); then use a damp sponge for a light and scattered stippling.

Soften with the badger blender.

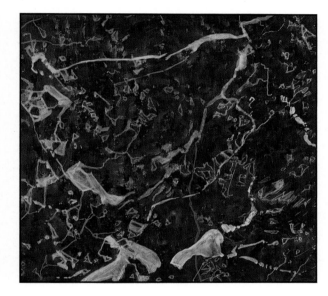

Using a pointed brush, with the same colors, draw long, fine fault lines, heavier lines, and veins that cross each other in all directions over the whole surface.

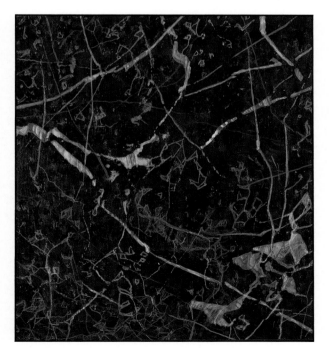

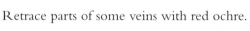

Cover the whole surface with very dilute burnt sienna, then stipple with the damp sponge.

Retrace parts of some veins with red ochre.

Repeat with very dilute white.

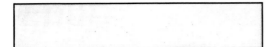

LANGUEDOC

Base coat: white

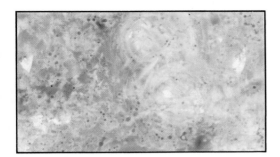

With very dilute gray (black + ultramarine blue), brush cloud shapes over the whole surface.

Stipple with a damp sponge.

Cover about two-thirds of the surface with red (red ochre + yellow ochre + burnt umber + a drop of black).

Over the red and gray, using a large brush with a very dilute mixture of ultramarine blue and black, add more shapes.

Wipe in some light and irregular bare spots with the sponge to shade these forms.

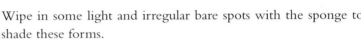

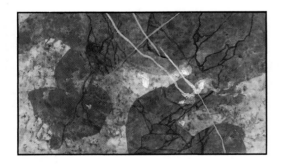

Retouch and vein in pure white, then stipple with a damp sponge. Draw a network of fine veins (burnt umber + ultramarine blue + red ochre), mostly in the red parts, to render the brecciation.

Stipple the whole vigorously, using a damp sponge with a very dilute mixture of yellow ochre and raw umber.

Complete the imitation with a very delicate web of veins in some of the clouds, with a mixture of red ochre and yellow ochre.

Panel with airbrushed molding
37 in × 60 in (.95 m × 1.52 m)

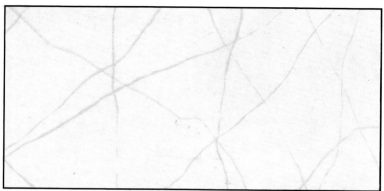

GRAY BRECCIA

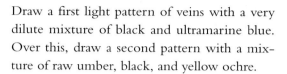

Base coat: white

Draw a first light pattern of veins with a very dilute mixture of black and ultramarine blue. Over this, draw a second pattern with a mixture of raw umber, black, and yellow ochre.

With a mixture of ultramarine, black, and a drop of raw umber, form the chunks. Using a damp sponge, stipple before this work dries. Then smooth lightly with a badger blender.

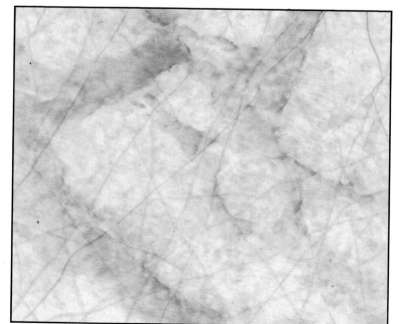

Cover the whole surface, leaving some parts lighter than others, with a very dilute mixture of yellow ochre and raw umber. Before this dries, stipple with a damp sponge. Using a pointed brush, with a mixture of black and ultramarine, retouch the network. After this dries, using a sponge, with white, form crystals over the whole surface.

Finally, use the square and pointed brushes, with a very dilute mixture of black, green, and raw umber, to retouch the largest parts of the bed and some veins.

Panel
27½ in × 43 in (.70 m × 1.10 m)

GRAND ANTIQUE

Base coat: white

Make very angular dark chunks with black acrylic.

Using a pointed brush, with white acrylic, draw fine veins and tiny fragments in the black stone.

Vein the white areas with gray-blue (ultramarine blue + black) and Van Dyck brown.

Oil Glaze

Cover the whole surface with an oil glaze tinted with a drop each of Van Dyck brown and burnt sienna.

With a crumpled rag, remove areas on the wet glaze.

Finally, retouch and intensify some of the white fissures with oil color.

Panel
30 in × 45 in (.76 m × 1.15 m)

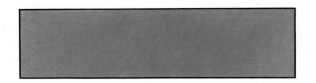

RANCE

Base coat: gray (white + black + a drop of ultramarine blue + a drop of yellow ochre)

Using a square brush, form reddish (red ochre + yellow ochre) shapes, with jagged and sinuous gray parts showing through.

Stipple lightly with a damp sponge.

Inside the reddish shapes, dab some more or less extended lighter spots (white + yellow ochre + a drop of red ochre + a drop of burnt umber).

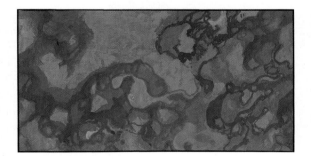

Set off some of the dark parts with very dilute brown (red ochre + burnt umber).

With the same color, make some ribbonlike veins in the reddish areas.

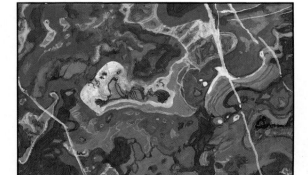

Retouch the gray areas first with pure white, then with dark gray (white + black + ultramarine blue), and finally with black.

Draw some fine fault lines in pure white.

Add some fine rust-colored veins (white + yellow ochre + burnt sienna) in the peach-toned areas.

Intensify all but the whitest areas with a coat of raw umber. Using a toothbrush, spatter first with burnt umber and, finally, with white.

Panel with granite border
17 in × 23 ½ in (.43 m × .60 m)

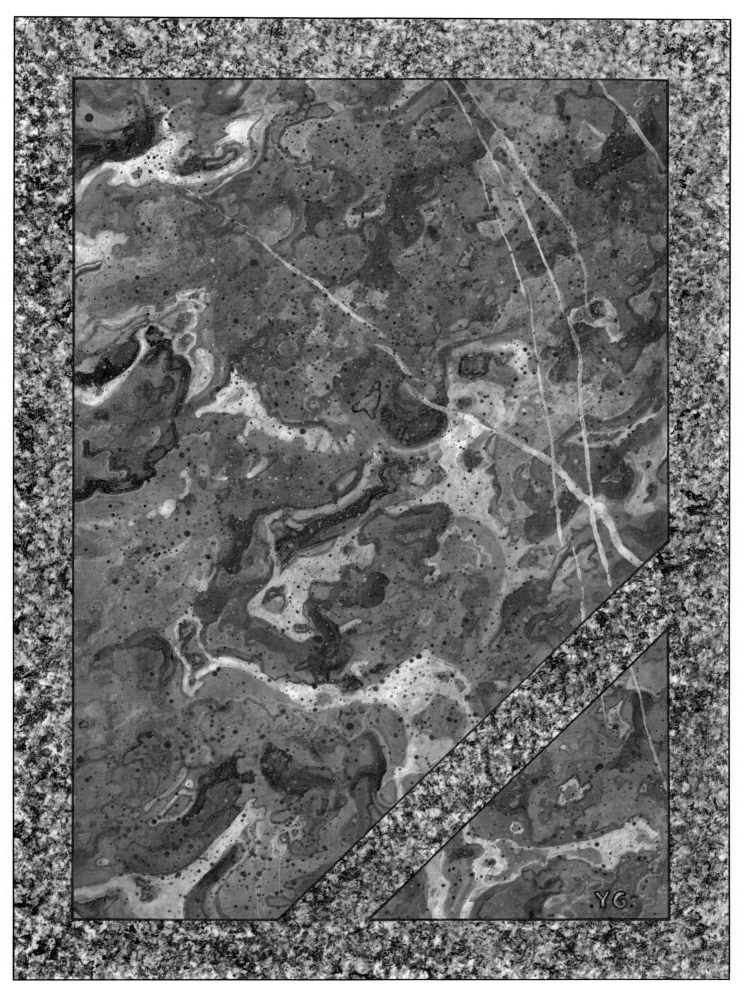

*Model for a
Louis XV–style
marble surface,
with Grand
Antique, Gray
Breccia, Rance,
and Campan*

*59 in × 94 in
(1.50 m ×
2.40 m)*

Panel,
Campan
Mélangé
with Yellow
Fleuri and
Veined
White

30 in
× 45 in
(.76 m ×
1.15 m)

CAMPAN MÉLANGÉ

Base coat: grayish-green (black + chrome green deep + white)

Using a square brush, form beds of varying width, in dark tones from red ochre to Van Dyck brown; then stipple with a damp sponge.

Go over the reddish parts with a very dilute mixture of naphthol red and ultramarine blue; then stipple again to obtain nuances of color.

Add dark green spots (Hooker green + ultramarine blue + black) on the green parts.

In the same color, with the pointed brush, form pebbling over the whole surface, in the same direction as the beds. On the dark green parts, draw some lighter green veins.

Stipple the whole with a very dilute cream color (yellow ochre + white), and emphasize some fragments.

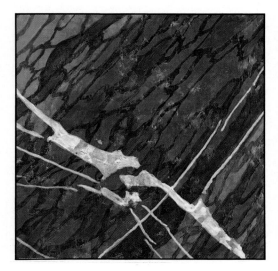

With very dark red (red ochre + raw umber + a drop of black), retouch fragments in the reddish beds.

Glaze the whole with very dilute raw umber.

With two coats of pure white, form fissures, mostly against the direction of the beds. Stipple them with extremely fine spots in a very dilute gray (black + ultramarine blue) for transparency.

YELLOW FLEURI

Base coat: light yellow (white + yellow ochre + a drop of golden yellow)

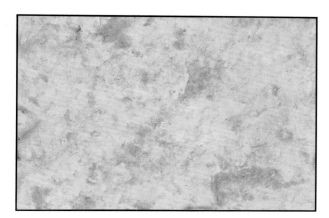

Cover with very dilute raw umber, applying more in some places, then stipple with a damp sponge, leaving comma-shaped marks of dark color going in all directions.

Repeat with yellow ochre.

Using a pointed brush, form some fault lines and some "commas" with very dilute white. Stipple with a damp sponge.

Over the whole work draw a network of very delicate intersecting veins, with a mixture of raw umber and yellow ochre.

Again using the pointed brush, with very dilute naphthol red, form another network of delicate and trembling veins, going in all directions, intersecting. Lightly stipple with a damp sponge; then, with the same red, retouch some veins to intensify the network.

Retouch some veins with very dilute yellow ochre for nuance.

Make tiny points on the major veins with a mixture of naphthol red and ultramarine blue.

Finish by stippling the whole surface with very dilute white.

IMPERADOR

Base coat: honey (white + yellow ochre + cadmium yellow + red ochre + golden yellow)

Using a square brush, with a very dilute mixture of burnt umber, black, and a drop of red ochre, make small- and medium-sized chunks.

Intensify some fragments with very dilute black; then stipple the whole surface with the same tone.

Stipple again with very dilute burnt sienna.

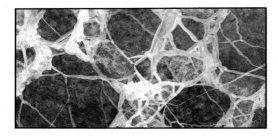

Using a pointed brush, with white with a drop of yellow ochre, on the light ground form small fragments separated by white beds of varying size. Ring some stones with the same color.

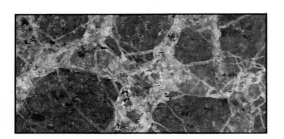

Stipple vigorously with raw sienna, and repeat lightly three more times with white, with red ochre, and finally with burnt umber.

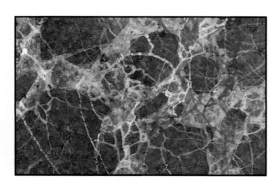

Finally, retouch some veins with pure white and others with burnt sienna.

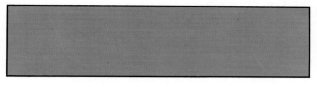

CAMPAN VERT-VERT

Base coat: gray-green (white + chrome green deep + black + a drop of yellow ochre)

Cover with very dilute raw umber, then stipple with a damp sponge.

Repeat with white.

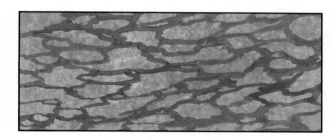

Using a pointed brush, draw a network of lines with medium green (Hooker green + black + a drop of white).

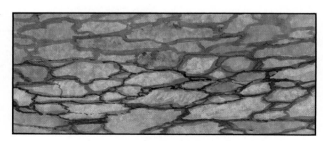

Shade some stones with very dilute raw umber, others with very dilute pinkish white (cadmium red + white).

Retouch one or two lines of the network with dark green (Hooker green + black).

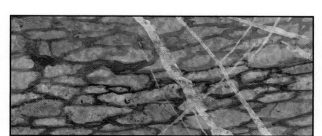

Against the direction of the beds, form white fissures with the pointed brush. Glaze the whole surface with very dilute raw umber, and stipple with a damp sponge. With a light mixture of ultramarine blue and black, make some grayish streaks on the white fissures. To finish, very lightly stipple some parts with very dilute ultramarine blue.

128

Marble marquetry
with Imperador
lozenges surrounded
by Campan Mélangé
and Vert-Vert, with
granite border
30 in × 45 in
(.76 m × 1.15m)

Caroline Breccia and
Rose Napoleon
pedestal, with bronze
vase and trelliswork,
in perspective view
39 in × 79 in
(1 m × 2 m)

129

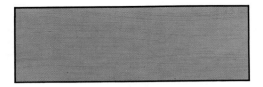

CAROLINE BRECCIA

Base coat: putty (white + raw sienna + cadmium yellow + red ochre + black)

Using a sponge, stipple with raw sienna.

Stipple again with a mixture of burnt sienna and raw umber, and again with black.

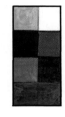

Using a square brush, make small fragments with beige (yellow ochre + white), light chestnut (red ochre + raw sienna), and dark chestnut (black + burnt umber), and even smaller ones with pink (red ochre + raw sienna) and dark blue (black + ultramarine blue).

With a fine-bristled brush, paint a multitude of tiny splinters (yellow ochre, white, red ochre, and burnt umber); then lightly vein some fragments by stippling them with light and dark shades. Finally, stipple the whole with raw sienna.

ROSE NAPOLEON

Base coat: tan (white + raw sienna + red ochre)

Using a sponge, stipple with raw sienna.

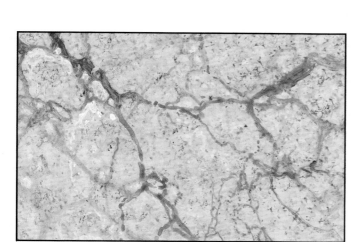

With a pointed brush, form a network of veins in two tones: raw sienna and a mixture of burnt umber and burnt sienna.

These two sets of veins, within beds, make medium and fine brecciation.

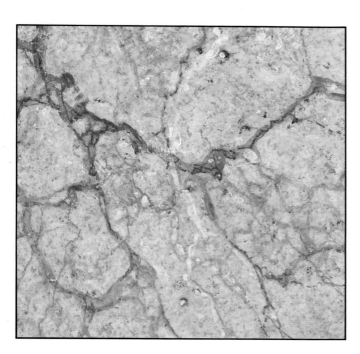

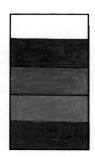

With the pointed brush, paint strokes of pure white in the main network, and form light white fissures; then retouch some dark veins with burnt umber and others with red ochre. Then lightly stipple the whole with raw sienna; repeat with very dilute purple.

SARRANCOLIN

Base coat: white

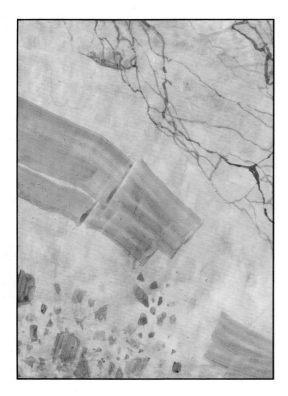

Sarrancolin is greatly varied in its markings and coloration.

Cover the whole surface with a very dilute mixture of raw umber and a drop of brilliant yellow; then use a sponge to stipple. Add some grayish blue here and there, then a dilute ultramarine, then stipple with the sponge. Next use a very dilute blue (cobalt blue + a drop of black) and shade by wiping glaze with a crumpled rag. With the same color, lightly vein this part.

In another section, streak the surface with the square brush and very dilute red ochre. With the same tone, draw some fragments and an accompanying network of fine veins.

In another section, form some fragments with a very dilute mixture of naphthol red, black, and ultramarine blue.

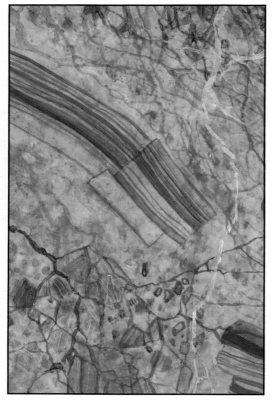

With a very dilute mixture of ultramarine blue and black, glaze and stipple with the sponge to nuance. Then form some fine veins of the same color. Detail the streaks in medium red (naphthol red + black); next, in the sections with small fragments, add strong veins in the same color.

Glaze the whole surface with a very dilute mixture of raw umber and a drop of yellow ochre, then stipple with a wet sponge, and soften with the badger blender. Form some rust-colored (burnt sienna + yellow ochre) veins, and then some white fissures, and small white veins. In rust (naphthol red + red ochre + black), intensify the streaks so the stone looks like a strip of bacon.

Glaze with very dilute raw sienna, and stipple with the sponge.

Panel
33 in × 47½ in (.84 m × 1.20 m)

RED LEVANTO

Base coat: red (red ochre + vermilion + black)

Using a square brush, form large and small fragments, first with vermilion, then with a mixture of black and Hooker green.

Stipple the whole, first with a very dilute mixture of cobalt blue and black, then with pure cobalt blue.

With the square and pointed brushes, form a wine-colored (white + vermilion + cobalt blue) web of veins; then stipple with a damp sponge.

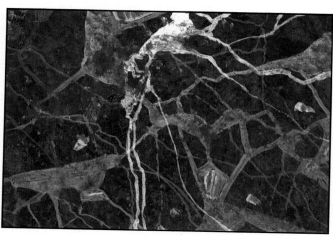

Draw some green (Hooker green + white + yellow ochre) veins in this web; with the same color, draw some fragments like emeralds, then retouch them with a few strokes (white for light parts, Hooker green for dark parts). Place a white fissure (or fissures) close to the principal network. Finally overall, stipple with pure ultramarine blue, and spatter with vermilion and the wine color.

Panel
30 in × 47½ in
(.76 m × 1.20 m)

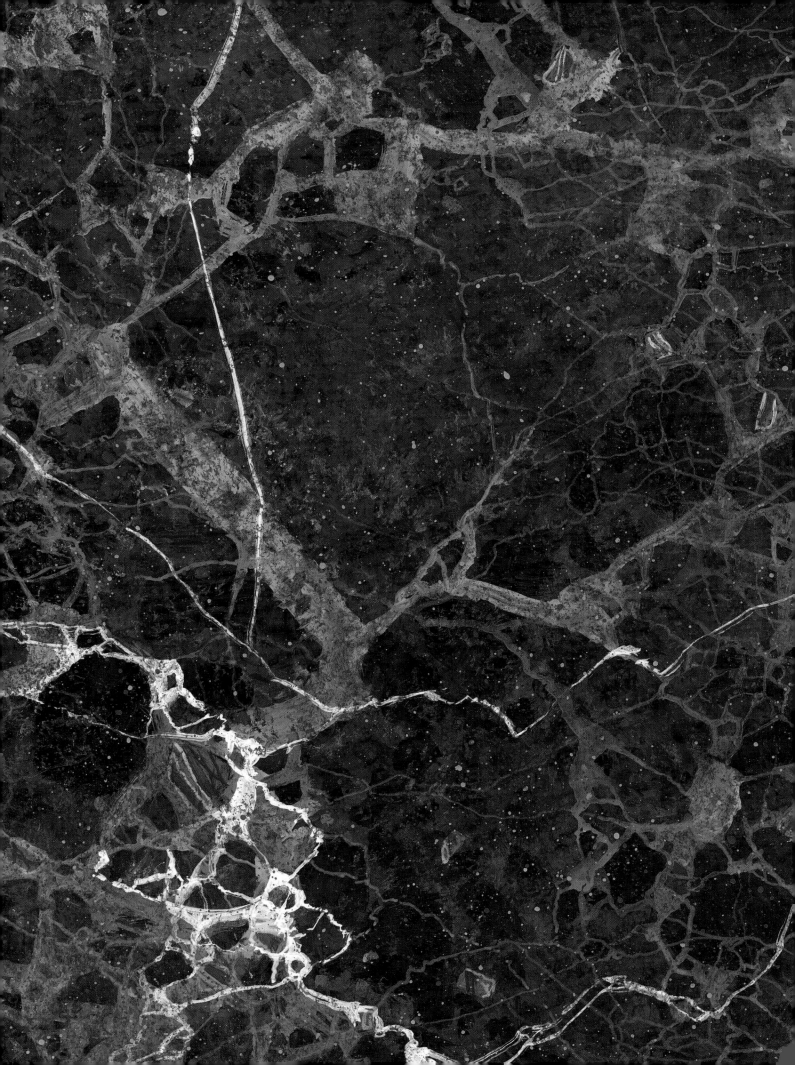

RED GRANITE

Base coat: red (yellow ochre + red ochre + vermilion)

Gray and yellow granite are rendered in the same way as red granite, but with different colors:

Gray granite: cobalt blue + black + white; three stipplings—cobalt blue, then white, then black.

Yellow granite: white + raw sienna; three stipplings—a mixture of raw sienna and burnt umber, then white, then black.

Cover the whole surface with burnt umber; then stipple with a damp sponge.

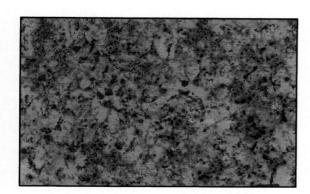

Repeat with very dilute ultramarine blue; take care to cluster the marks.

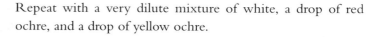

Repeat with a very dilute mixture of white, a drop of red ochre, and a drop of yellow ochre.

With a very dilute mixture of burnt umber, naphthol red, and purple, stipple with a damp sponge, baring parts of the previous paintwork.

Using an artist's brush, with a mixture of white and cadmium yellow, make some slightly squarish light spots. When these are dry, go over them with very dilute burnt umber; this will give an effect of sparkling mica. With a pointed brush and very dilute black, connect the dark spots so as to render the pattern of stones. Finally, stipple with very dilute burnt umber.

*Panel of gray,
yellow, and red granite
10 in × 14½ in (.25 m × .37 m)*

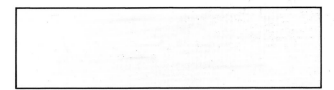

GREEN ONYX

Base coat: white

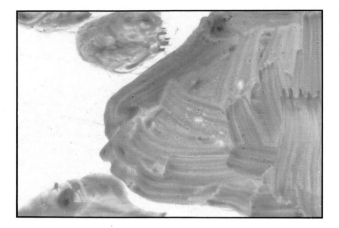

Lightly cover the parts that will end up green with a mixture of Hooker green and cobalt blue; these areas should have very sinuous and ribbony shapes.

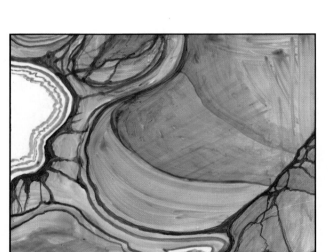

Streak these green forms with the same color.

Using a pointed brush, with burnt sienna, form circular markings in the white areas, sweeping around the green forms, and leaving a central node open.

Retouch this light rust color with burnt umber to produce the fissures that issue from the core.

Again with burnt umber, proceeding outward from the borders, add some veins in the green areas.

Add rings to the core with very dilute burnt umber.

Streak with a stronger green (cobalt blue + Hooker green + a drop of burnt sienna) on the green parts, sometimes crossing over into the rust, to get the effect of transparency.

Retrace the new fissures with pure white to detail, then add some white veins.

Cover the whole with a very dilute white to blend.

With burnt umber, retouch parts of this work to intensify some fissures. Finish the central node by adding a multitude of small veins in every direction.

To increase the transparency, go over the whole with a gloss varnish.

Panel
23½ in × 39 in (.60 m × 1 m)

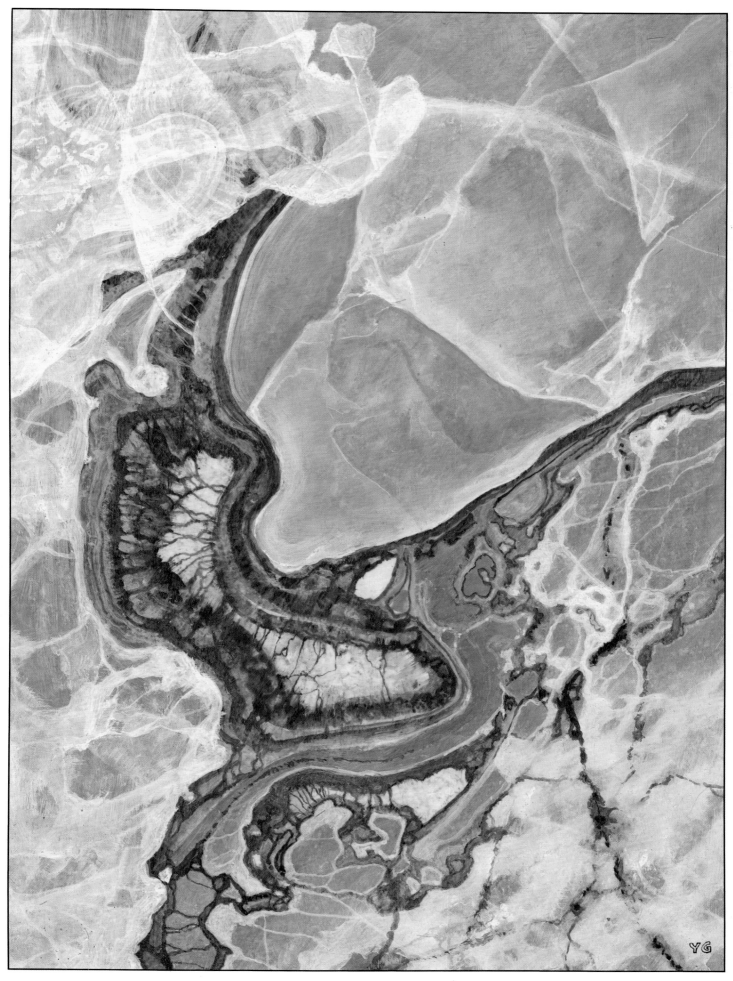

139

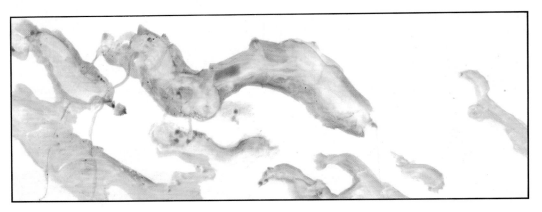

CERFONTAINE

Base coat: white

Using a square brush with very dilute gray (ultramarine blue + black + naphthol red), form long cloud shapes, more or less interconnected.

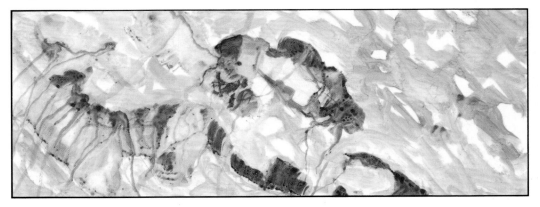

As with Languedoc marble, two thirds of the surface will be reddish; apply this tone (red ochre + yellow ochre), leaving pure white voids. Add a mixture of red ochre and yellow ochre to simulate the transparent effects of the marble. Then stipple with a damp sponge, and reinforce parts of the clouds with a mixture of naphthol red, ultramarine blue, and black.

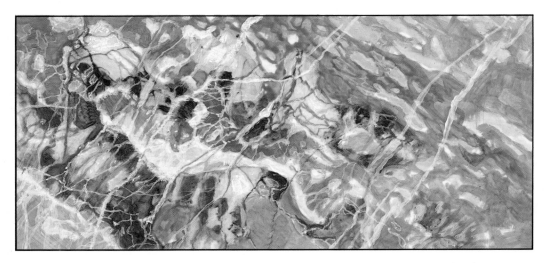

Retouch some of the red areas with a very dilute mixture of burnt umber and red ochre. Form some veins and fissures with pure white, and whiten parts of some gray clouds with very dilute white. Stipple the whole with very dilute red ochre. Stipple a last time with very dilute raw umber.

Panel of Cerfontaine
with frame of Belgian Black
30 in × 43 in
(.76 m × 1.10 m)

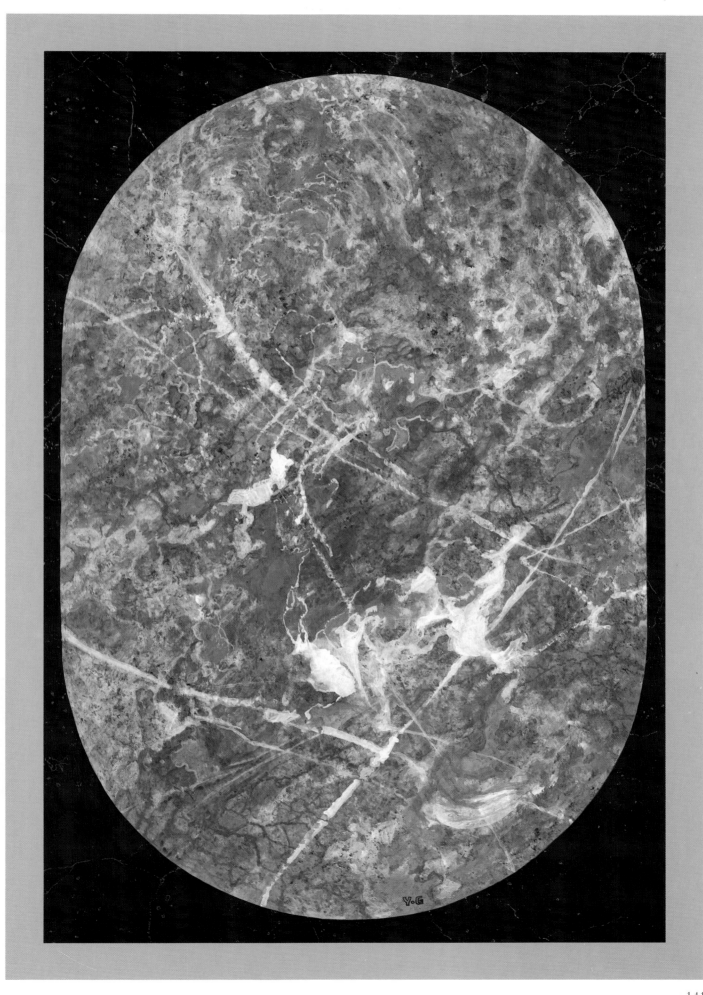

PORTORO

Render Portoro, like Grand Antique marble, with waterproof liquid acrylic.

Base coat: black satin enamel

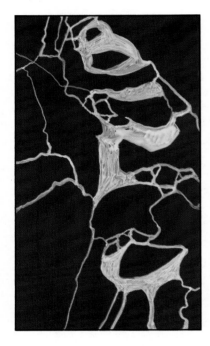

Using a pointed brush, with light yellow (white + vivid yellow) ink, form an irregular chain of "smoke rings." The unique markings of Portoro are sinuous and very airy, and occur in roughly parallel bands.

With the same light yellow, go over the first layer of rings a second time; then, adding white, draw in light veining. These fine veins fit into the yellow chain of rings, and link the parallel bands.

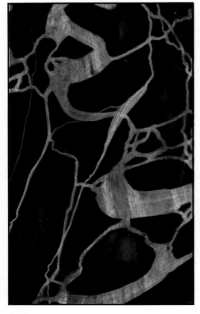

Streak the yellow rings with a very dilute gold (burnt sienna + a drop of burnt umber). Nuance the black base behind the chain with a very dilute grayish mixture of white, black, burnt umber, and a drop of crimson lake.

Oil Glaze

Glaze the whole surface with an oil glaze tinted with burnt umber and a drop of Van Dyck brown. With a rag, wipe parts of the "chain" to get the effect of transparency.

Panel
32 in × 47½ in
(.82 m × 1.20 m)

ANTIQUE GREEN BRECCIA

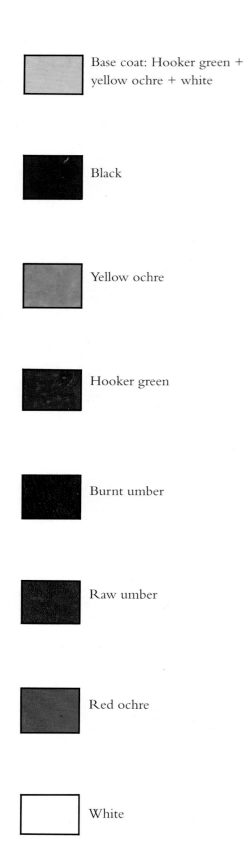

Base coat: Hooker green + yellow ochre + white

Black

Yellow ochre

Hooker green

Burnt umber

Raw umber

Red ochre

White

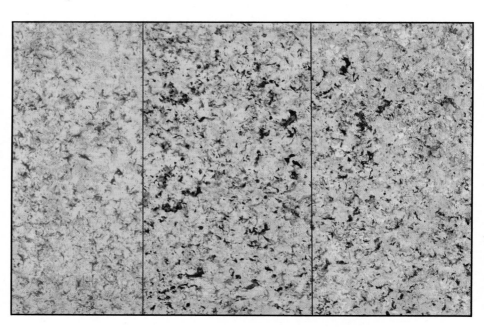

Glaze with a very dilute mixture of Hooker green and yellow ochre; then stipple with a damp sponge.

Repeat with a darker mixture of yellow ochre, Hooker green, and burnt umber; repeat with black, and repeat with a lighter mixture, yellow ochre and white. All three glazes should be very dilute.

Using a flat brush, form light-colored fragments with a mixture of yellow ochre and white; brown fragments with a mixture of chrome green, raw umber, and burnt umber; dark green fragments with a mixture of green, black, and red ochre; and light green fragments with a mixture of Hooker green, yellow ochre, red ochre, and white.

Inside the larger chunks, draw variously colored fissures (black, white, red ochre, Hooker green, yellow ochre) with a pointed brush. Finally, make some small fragments with white.

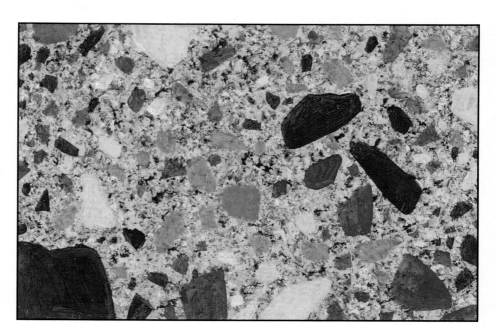

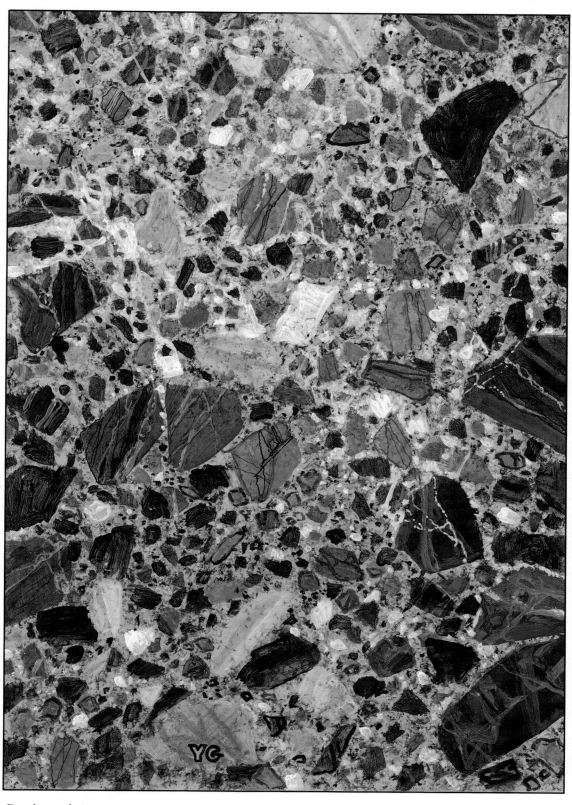

Panel actual size

Panel of Fleur de Pecher and Yellow Sienna,
with Empire-style drapery (see study, page 324)
67 in × 90½ in (1.70 m × 2.30 m)

Panel of Fleur de Pecher
29½ in × 39 in (.75 m × .99 m)

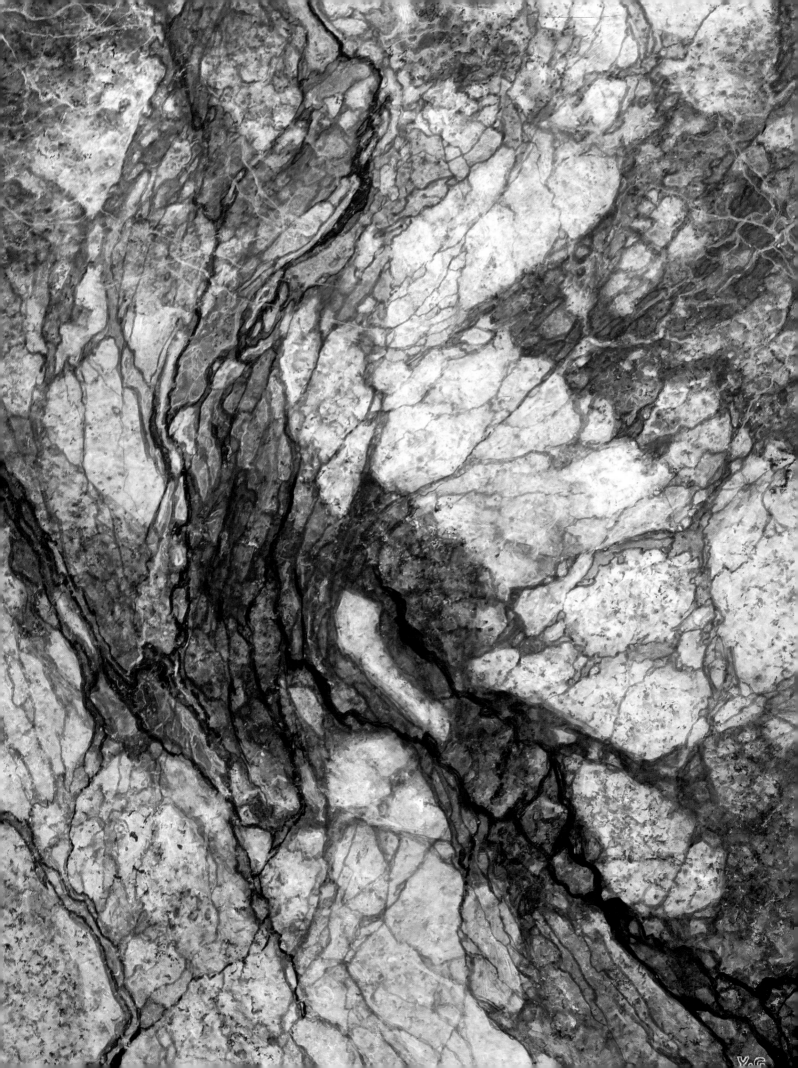

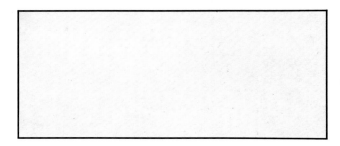

FLEUR DE PECHER

Base coat: white

Stipple with a mixture of white and yellow ochre.

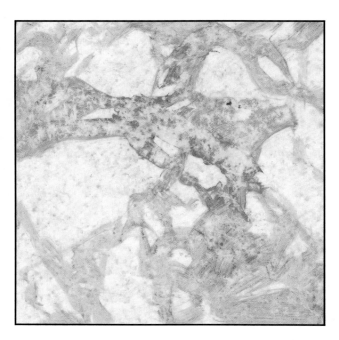

Using a square brush with very dilute ultramarine blue, form brecciation; then stipple with a damp sponge.

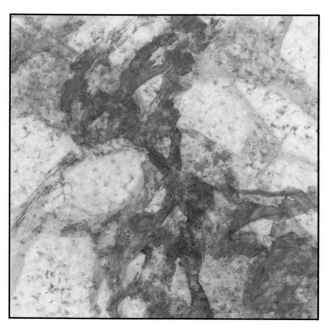

Stipple the whole once again with cobalt blue; then reinforce the breccia with a mixture of ultramarine blue and crimson lake. Stipple again with a very dilute mixture of crimson lake and a drop of raw sienna.

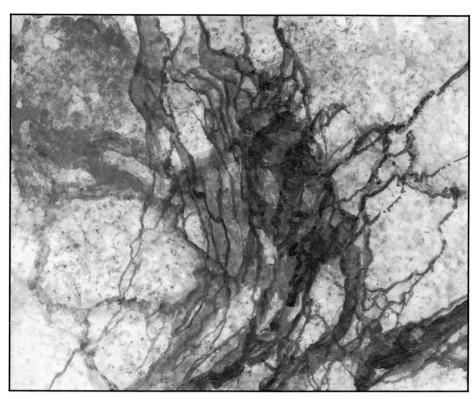

Using a pointed brush, form in the main bed a network of fine dark veins, with a mixture of black and chrome green. Draw one or two stronger veins with ultramarine blue and cobalt blue and intensify a few other veins with chrome green. Then stipple the whole with a cream color (yellow ochre + white).

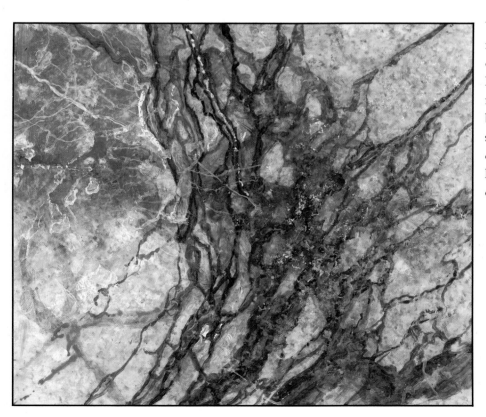

With the pointed brush, form many light white veins; with ochre nuances, intensify some light-colored fragments; reinforce a green vein more broadly with black. Finally, stipple three times with very dilute solutions of crimson lake, ultramarine blue, and cream color.

GRIOTTE

Base coat: medium red (red ochre + vermilion + a drop of yellow ochre)

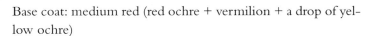

Cover the whole surface with dilute yellow ochre, and stipple with a damp sponge.

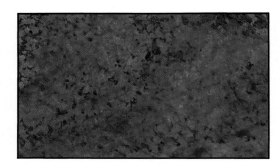

Cover again, this time with burnt umber, then stipple, leaving some dark parts. Soften with the badger blender.

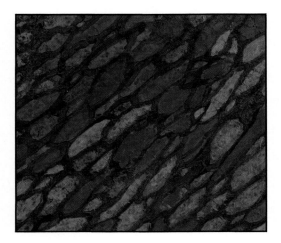

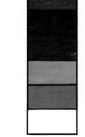

Using a pointed brush, form a network of dark oval-shaped stones, with a mixture of black, ultramarine blue, and burnt umber. Detail some fragments with a lighter tone (white + yellow ochre + cadmium red), and lightly stipple.

Add darker tones (burnt umber + cadmium red) to some other fragments and lightly stipple.

Cover the whole surface with a very dilute darker mixture of ultramarine blue and black, and stipple.

Add a few thin fissures (or cloudy areas) with pure white.

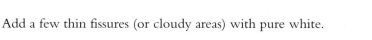

YELLOW SIENNA

Base coat: white

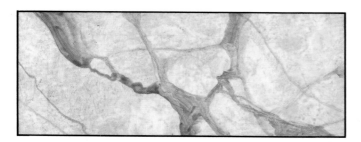

Cover the whole surface with a very dilute mixture of yellow ochre and golden yellow; then stipple vigorously with a damp sponge. You can make the white areas at this stage by wiping away more of the yellow.

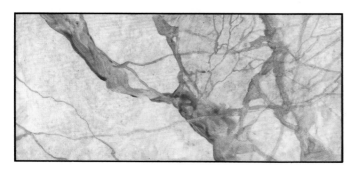

Using a square brush, with a light brown tint (raw sienna + burnt sienna + golden yellow), form the first light network of markings, establishing the general character of the marble.

With a mixture of burnt sienna and cadmium orange, darken some fragments in the general direction of the bed.

Stipple lightly with a damp sponge.

Using a pointed brush, with the same tone, detail the small veining on these fragments.

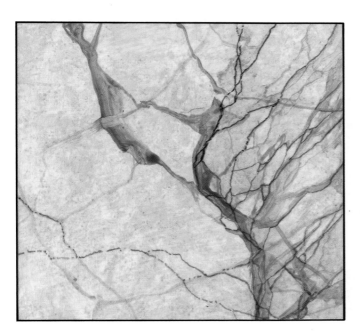

Form a delicate network of somewhat transparent veins on the existing bed, with a mixture of Hooker green and black.

Oil Glaze

As with Portoro and Grand Antique, cover the whole surface with an oil glaze, in this case tinted with burnt sienna. Using a crumpled rag, vigorously wipe some fragments.

Finally, draw very dark veining (black with a drop of chrome green light), mainly on the principal bed.

Panel of Yellow Sienna and Griotte
33 in × 47½ in (.84 m × 1.20 m)

Panel of Yellow Sienna with Mediterranean Green border
23½ in × 39 in (.60 m × 1 m)

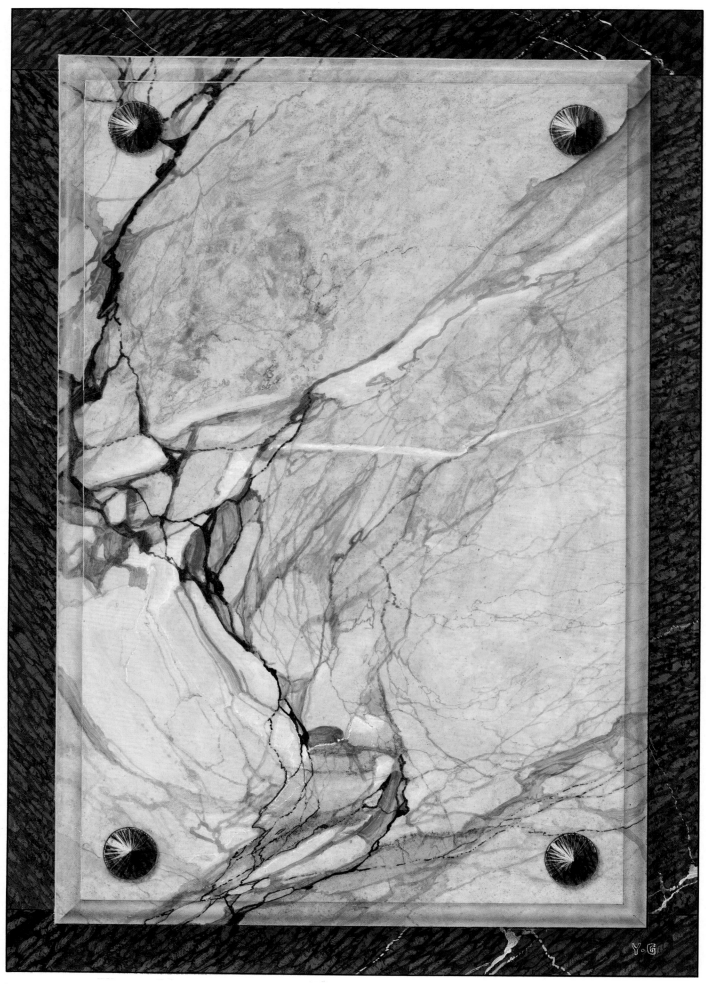

152

VIOLET BRECCIA

Base coat: white

Using a square brush with the colors given below, form large and small fragments, rounded or in distended ovals. Mix smaller with larger ones, like a cascade of stones. This robust marble has strong markings, contrasting beige, gray-blue, wine, rust, deep purple against a more or less pure white foundation. Your palette thus will be varied: burnt umber, black, cobalt blue, ultramarine blue, yellow ochre, raw sienna, naphthol red, raw umber, brilliant yellow, and white.

After forming these stones, take your pick of very dilute color and stipple with a damp sponge to break the regularity of the forms just applied.

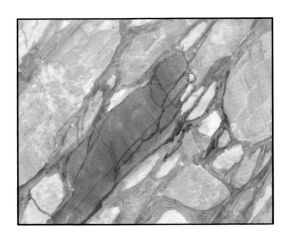

Once you have laid down the principal colors, use the pointed brush to form the main bed. The veins of this bed will surround and, in some places, penetrate the stones you have already formed. The bed should vary in width and color (from slate gray to wine to putty yellow).

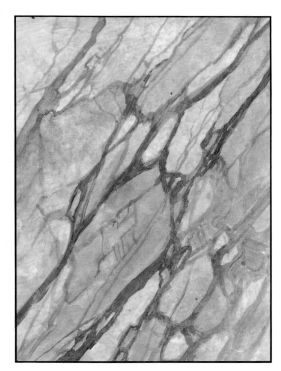

With the same, but less dilute, colors, detail some of the veins. Cover the whole surface with very dilute raw sienna, then stipple with a damp sponge.

Repeat with raw umber, and then again with pure white.

Finally, cover with an oil glaze tinted with pure white, and smooth over the stones; then remove glaze by wiping gently with a crumpled rag.

Panel of Violet Breccia with malachite;
the tops of the flowers are gold leaf on gilding size
33 in × 47½ in (.84 m × 1.20 m)

155

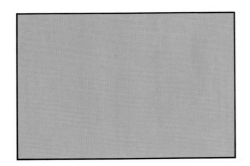

MALACHITE

Base coat: sea green (white + Hooker green + cobalt blue)

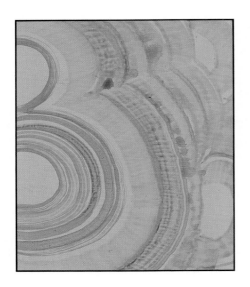

Using a square brush, with very dilute green (Hooker green + cobalt blue), sketch the markings. Start with a central node and surround it with rings—some in stronger tones with more cobalt blue, others with more Hooker green. As you finish a node, mask it with tape while you graft other nodes onto it.

Retrace this work with fine, irregular circular lines, using first Hooker green and then black.

Oil Glaze

Glaze the whole surface with a tinted oil glaze (viridian + a drop of burnt umber.

While the glaze is still wet, retouch some rings with pure white.

Wipe gently with a dry rag across the periphery of the circles to produce a shimmering effect. Smooth with a spalter or the badger blender.

Because it takes a long time to achieve a good imitation, limit malachite to small surfaces.

Louis XIV–style pillar of Antique Green, with gold pedestal and porphyry vase, on Gray Breccia background with Rance border
39 in × 73 in (1 m × 1.85 m)

SAINT-ANNE

Base coat: medium gray (black + white + a drop of yellow ochre)

Using a pointed brush, with pure black, make dark strokes going in all directions.

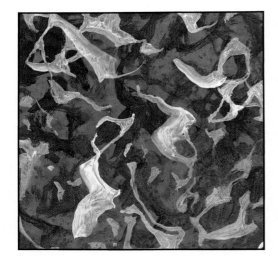

Cover with a very dilute mixture of black and yellow ochre, and stipple the whole with a damp sponge.

With a pointed brush, add white strokes of various strengths and lengths. Some of these may occasionally connect with one another.

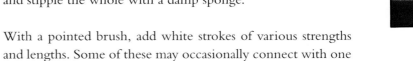

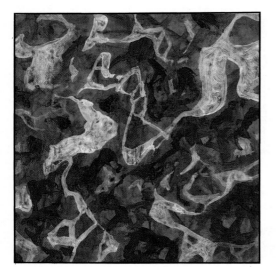

Reinforce some of the gray parts with black.

Cover with very dilute raw umber, and stipple with a damp sponge.

Repeat with yellow ochre.

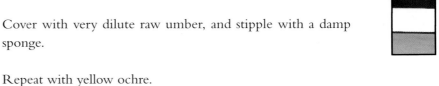

Panel
28 in × 39 in (.73 m × 1 m)

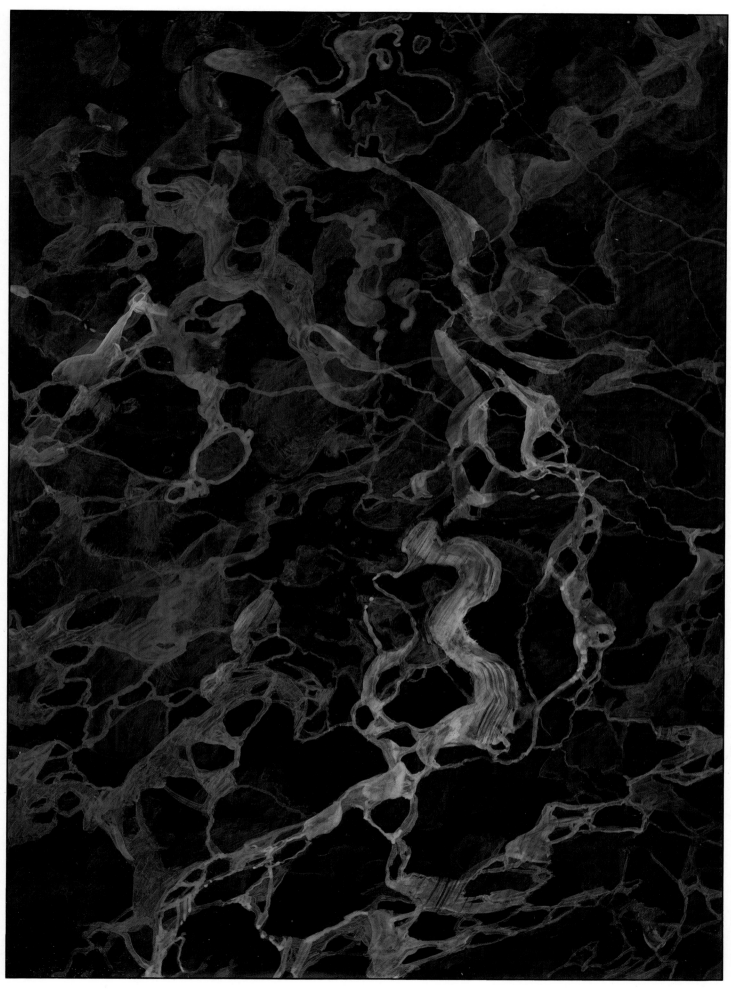

IRANIAN TRAVERTINE

Base coat: sulfur yellow (white + medium cadmium yellow)

Cover the whole surface with very dilute white, then stipple finely.

Repeat with cadmium orange.

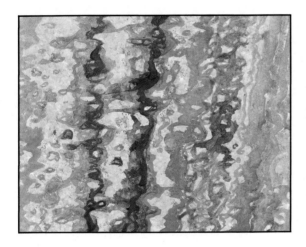

Using a pointed brush, form delicate, parallel beds, first with a dark tone (naphthol red + burnt umber), then with an orange tone (cadmium orange), and finally with a reddish tone (naphthol red + raw umber).

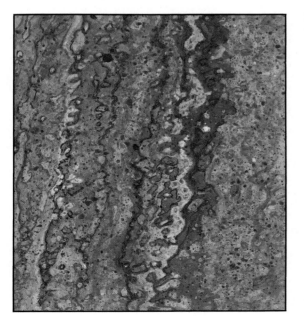

Cover the whole surface with very dilute raw sienna, then stipple with a damp sponge.

With the pointed brush, retrace the marking with burnt sienna, and then with white.

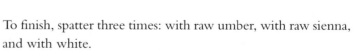

To finish, spatter three times: with raw umber, with raw sienna, and with white.

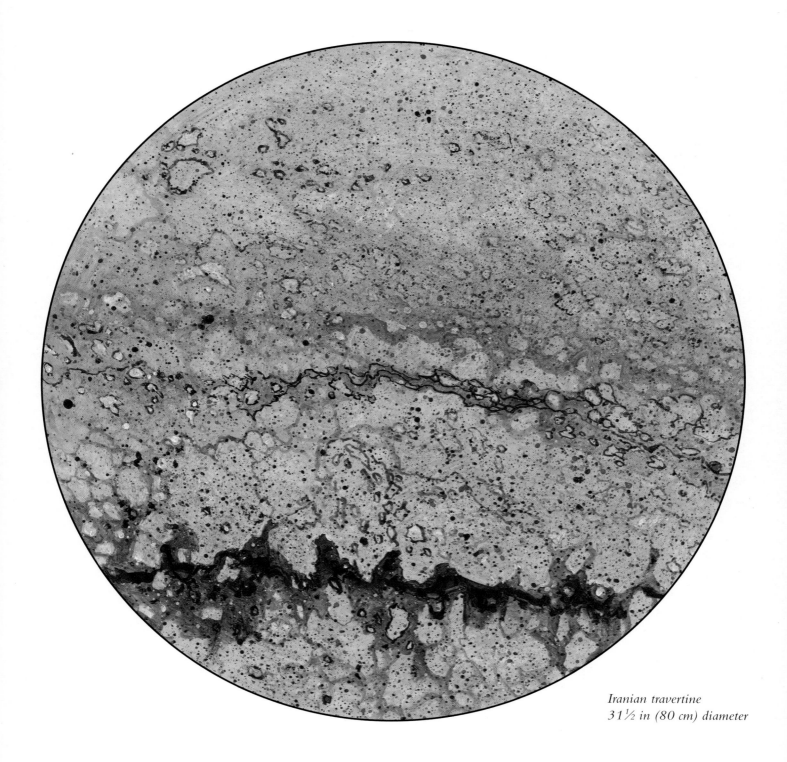

Iranian travertine
31½ in (80 cm) diameter

4

WOOD

INTRODUCTION

Since antiquity, as we have noted, trompe-l'œil art has been admired and appreciated. For ages, these realistic paintings have imitated relief (rendered in light and shadow) and every sort of material to evoke a fantasy world, as can be seen in the work of so many of the great artists of ancient Pompeii, the Renaissance, and the sixteenth, seventeenth, and eighteenth centuries. In these compositions, faux wood was only a minor element, not the main object of the decoration and thus not very finely worked.

Then, around 1500, easel painting appeared. Here (as opposed to fresco, mosaic, or ceiling paintings), the imitation of wood became more important and more detailed, because the paintings were made to be seen and studied more closely. But still, these imitations were not at a high level because they were intended as accompaniment to a much more elaborately and carefully rendered foreground—often still lifes and trophies of the hunt—executed on wood panels, furniture, interiors, cupboards, alcoves, in painterly disorder. Again, the great artists of the time carried on the tradition.

In the nineteenth century the imitation of wood was highly valued, and today, with the renewed interest in trompe l'œil, artists of international renown are practicing the craft. But the quality of the work varies wildly. With the improvement of products and techniques, a new "utilitarian" employment of the art has appeared. It has two distinct tendencies: one that is artistic and decorative, and another that churns out inartistic "fake" faux wood by the mile. Although they have solidity and stability to recommend them, the great number of inferior imitations have spoiled the general taste for faux wood.

With the contemporary renaissance of artistic and decorative (as against mass-produced and assembly-line) trompe l'œil, we are no longer confined to flat doors and tabletops; we can make whole decors in faux marquetry, in accord with existing furnishing, in perfect harmony with the contemporary interior.

Before actually painting an imitation of wood, become as familiar as you can with the object that you are going to render. There is a world of difference between an oak whorl and an elm burl, between sycamore and rosewood. You must master these differences and subtleties, for in trompe l'œil you aim for the best possible reproduction of the real thing. You must first, then, study the reality, for copies of copies inevitably result in degradation.

First of all, the tree is a living being—your companion. Its species, its breadth, its color, its indelible scars: these give each tree its character, and you must match the wood to the project. For example,

❖ the majestic oak serves well for projects that require both size and solidity (timber-frame buildings, ships, stairs, massive furniture)

❖ the less imposing fruit-bearing trees (pear, lemon) are destined for more delicate furniture

❖ mahogany's color and figure enhance the simplest furnishings

❖ the fragile birch, somber gray rings on silvery white, the plane tree, with its tattered gray-green bark

❖ the plane tree, with its tattered gray-green bark. . .

What a pleasure it is to observe and contemplate the thousands of varieties of common and rare species! Learn to look, and to preserve. If we must cut down these living beings for our worldly needs, let it be for the better of our humanity, and of our world. Trompe l'œil offers a unique opportunity to enjoy rare woods for both enjoyment and conservation.

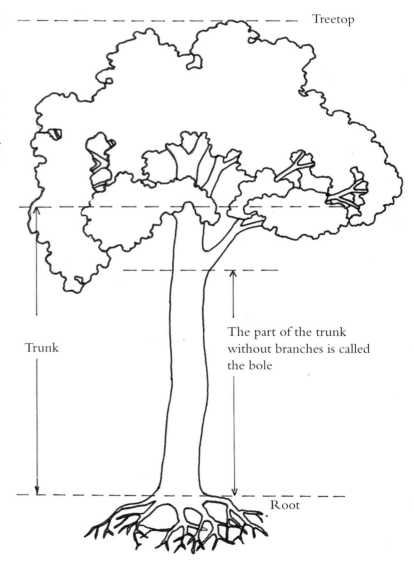

All the branches and foliage of the treetop form the crown

Treetop

The part of the trunk without branches is called the bole

Trunk

Root

FIGURE

All wood has a particular grain, or pattern of markings, called *figure* by woodworkers, that derives from the way it is cut. The proper use of figure shows it off to best advantage. Trees come in many sizes, and there are many ways to cut them. Tree-cutting professionals must be familiar with numerous esoteric complexities of the craft. Painters and decorative painters, fortunately, need only concern themselves with what is important to the painted rendering of figure. Instead of explaining the way wood is cut with the carpenter's technical rigor, we will use a simpler terminology, but one that is still clear and sufficient enough for our uses.

GROWTH AND GRAIN

Around the heart (pith) of the tree, growth rings annually mark its lifeline. Depending on the type of tree, the trunk grows so much taller and so much broader over time. Different ways of cutting through fibers, vascular tissues, and growth rings yield different figures.

❖ Cutting vertically along a tangent (flat-sawing or plain-sawing) brings out the whorls and vees of the heartwood grain, growth rings seen in longitudinal cross-section. We adopt the woodworker's term, plume, to describe this figure.

❖ Cutting the same trunk vertically along radii (quarter-sawing), into wedge-shaped segments, yields rays (again using the woodworker's term), resulting from the bias cut across the growth rings.

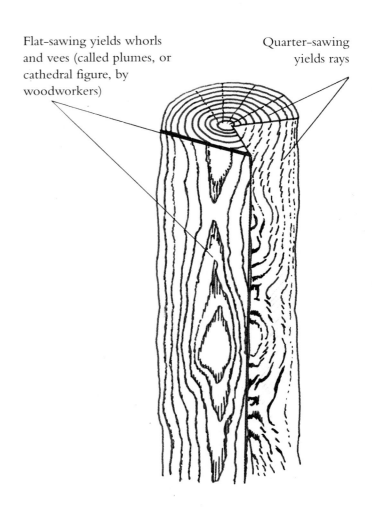

Flat-sawing yields whorls and vees (called plumes, or cathedral figure, by woodworkers)

Quarter-sawing yields rays

The grain of the upper part of the trunk is knottier, because it is there that the branches originate. The many varieties of knots are mainly of interest to those who work with real wood; we look at them only to imitate them.

Growth and cut, as well as disease and stress, indelibly mark the flesh of a tree. These scars, curiously, can very often serve to decorate the wood. Burls (on ashes, elms, and other trees) are good examples. The base of the burl, near the roots of the tree, resembles a cluster of knots where branches originate.

Woodworkers choose boards, once they have been cut, according to the purpose for which they are intended. A good piece of flecked ray, vee grain, or burl will be the centerpiece of a project. Simpler, more subdued straight-grained pieces will surround and complement the showier center.

Similarly, in the woodworking craft of marquetry, the decorative motif determines the choice of wood. Rosewood or violet wood cut straight yields a chevron pattern. Cut on the bias, the woodworker gets a butterfly-wing pattern. The decorative painter's imitations must follow suit, or the trompe l'œil will not be convincing.

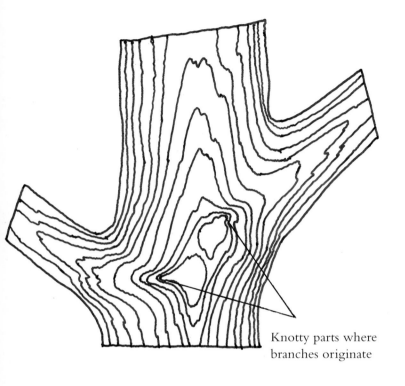

Knotty parts where branches originate

COLOR

The heartwood of the tree, unlike its bark, is generally of light and gentle tones. Its more forceful brilliance in furniture comes from products applied to it along the way. Cabinetmakers obtain this brilliance by tinting the wood to give it a ruddier and warmer tone. Some woods are lightened, others darkened, depending on how they are employed. In marquetry, pear wood, for example, is darkened to substitute for more costly ebony. Woodworkers sometimes radically change the color of wood for pictorial purposes, in still lifes, for example, or in specialized decoration of furniture. In these cases, wood may be green, blue, mauve, or whatever the design calls for. Again, the painter has the same latitude.

In painted decoration, color is the most important factor. The decorator's choice may well diverge from that of the cabinetmaker or carpenter.

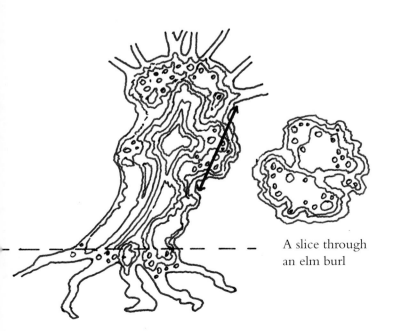

A slice through an elm burl

THE WOODS

Walnut

Since the Renaissance the walnut tree has rivaled the oak on every continent for fabrication of larger pieces of furniture and for sculpture. Walnut is tough and fairly hard, with a tight, fine grain. Rendering its warm tones and brilliant burnish is of paramount importance when imitating walnut. Walnut wood often has small squiggles at the tip of its plumes.

Ash

The ash tree prefers temperate climates. A light-colored wood, with yellow and pink nuances, its grain is more or less straight, gently undulating at the junctions of its plumes, its knots, and its shimmering moiré patterns.

Burl

Burls are excrescent beauty marks on the flesh of a tree. Sometimes as much as three feet in diameter, their grain is marked by many banded knots and unpredictable shapes. Any trees can have burls, but those of the elm, oak, and ash are most notable.

Sycamore

The sycamore, a member of the maple family, has been used since the time of the ancient Egyptians. Moiré ripples and "speckles" set off the delicate waves marking the wood. Its light and pearly color varies from white to pale yellow. The sycamore is prized in cabinetry and marquetry for its markings and color, whether natural, tinted, or outright changed (gray, blue, green).

Pitch Pine

While the pitch pine is related to the fir, its reddish-veined yellow wood, with its rougher figure, is clearly more decorative than that of its cousin, which is used for more mundane constructions like paneling. Since the markings of the pitch pine are a veritable decoration unto themselves, the wood serves more appropriately as centerpiece than accompaniment.

Lemon Wood

The pale gold wood of the lemon tree, with its relatively understated grain, is used for luxury cabinetry.

Amaranth

The amaranth is a variety of mahogany from Cayenne, in Guyana. Its purplish-red wood is prized in marquetry to set off lighter woods.

Maple

While the maple tree is confined to temperate regions, it comes in boundless varieties, from the delicate Japanese dwarves to the giants of the forest like the sycamore and the Canadian maple (whence both maple syrup and the country's maple-leaf emblem). Its leaves beautify autumn with their vivid reds and darker bronzes shading into tender greens.

Rosewood

Exotic rosewood, blush toned and straight grained, is named for its fragrance and not its color. It is rather more the latter that concerns the painter.

Macassar Ebony

Hard, dense ebony wood is very dark, with brown or white veins. Rare because it must be transported from its native Africa and because it has been overharvested, ebony is often replaced by less expensive dyed pear in marquetry. It is best to confine faux ebony to small-scale works.

Brazilian Rosewood

The tones of the straight-grained Brazilian rosewood, which we call violet wood, are darker than those of its relatives. And while it may smell of violets, once again, its dark hue and purple reflections are more important to us. Rosewood is often used in marquetry.

Palisander

The brown wood of the South American palisander has deep purple reflections. Its robust yet elegant dark grain is often displayed in symmetrical composition for the resulting decorative contrast.

Oak

The familiar oak, present across Europe and North America, can grow as tall as 120 feet (40 m). Its beautiful lobed leaves have been the model for many ornamental forms.

Elm

Elm trees can grow sixty to ninety feet (20–30 m) high. The solid wood of the elm is used in carpentry and cabinetry. Its burls yield wood with a superb knotty turbulence. Unfortunately, elms are often prey to disease, and diseased trees must be cut down and destroyed. The value of elm has risen as the tree becomes more rare.

Yew

The hardy yew, with its red berries, numbers in the millions across temperate regions. These conifers can adapt to almost any terrain. Some are stunted, others stand up majestically. Some are shaped like balls, others are cylindrical, conical, or bushy. They can reach forty-five feet (15 m) in height, and some live more than three hundred years. The markings are wavy. The wood is used in classical and contemporary furniture.

Cherry

Prunus padus is the wild cherry; *Prunus avium* is European bird cherry, not to be confused with the wild cherry, despite their common genus and similar wood. The wood of the wild cherry is warmly honey colored, with delicate darker veins.

Thuja

The thuja (or arborvitae) is a conical conifer present in many varieties in temperate regions. Some grow to remarkable heights, like the giant thuja.

Fir

The northern fir, the Christmas tree, is the most familiar of the firs. It is also one of the most useful, providing wood for a variety of everyday furnishings. Its wood is very light-colored, almost white but for a faint yellowish tinge. The figure is very simple, with fairly regular concentric growth rings around a knot.

Mahogany

The hard wood of the mahogany, beautiful when polished, is very much sought after in cabinetry for its warm and glowing decorative effects.

BASIC METHOD

Refer to chapter 1 for the preparation of the support, brushes, and materials.

There are two ways to render grain (here we show walnut). The traditional method is to flog over a satin-finish enamel with distemper, which is water-based, using Cassel earth pigment mixed with dextrin or stale beer (a medium that binds the pigment). If you work on this immediately with water-based media, you risk diluting the foundation. It is essential, therefore, to apply an isolating coat of varnish or oil glaze to protect the foundation. You must allow at least twelve hours drying time before you continue working.

Our method, demonstrated here, employs half the modern acrylic, half traditional oil glaze, starting with a layer of waterproof liquid acrylic. For walnut, shown here and on the following four pages, the acrylic is tinted with yellow ochre.

Acrylic

The modern method of graining (for both walnut and mahogany) is to flog with Cassel-earth-tinted liquid acrylic, which takes only one hour to dry, over the dry oil base coat. Apply the acrylic quickly and forcefully with a spalter. Before it dries, flog to produce the vertical grain. The movement is like drumming.

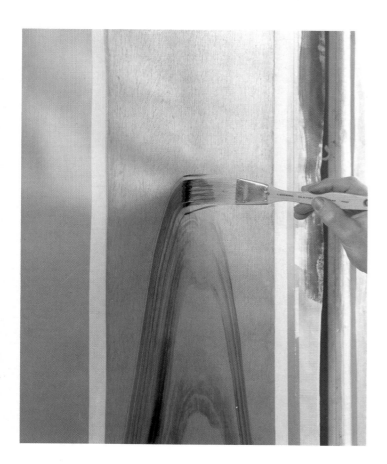

Then, with acrylic of equal parts burnt sienna and burnt umber, using a synthetic spalter, form the whorls of the vee-grain. Complete the figure with a water-moistened synthetic square sponge, and use a badger blender to soften.

A few minutes later, your work will be dry. Soak a graining brush in black acrylic slightly diluted with water, and touch up the top of the whorl. Soften with the badger blender. Then treat the bottom of the whorl the same way.

Use a spalter with different colors of acrylic (burnt sienna, burnt umber, black) to add bands of varying widths around the sides of the figure. Then detail these, first with a square sponge, and then with the graining brush.

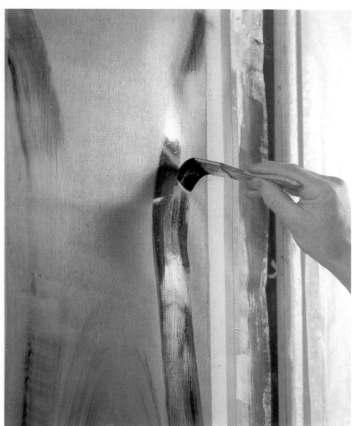

Finally, finish off the acrylic work by using a pointed brush to emphasize some rings and to detail the figure.

Let dry for fifteen minutes.

Oil Glaze

Cover the whole surface with a dark oil glaze (for composition, see page 13), tinted with burnt sienna and black from tubes. Then, wrapping your index finger in a soft, dry rag, remove glaze by wiping gaps into the markings previously rendered. By getting back to the base color here, you form the lighter parts of the figure.

Note that you can also remove the glaze with a graining brush soaked in turpentine or oil glaze. In this case, go over the bare, wiped parts with the badger blender. Do the same to the sides of the figure.

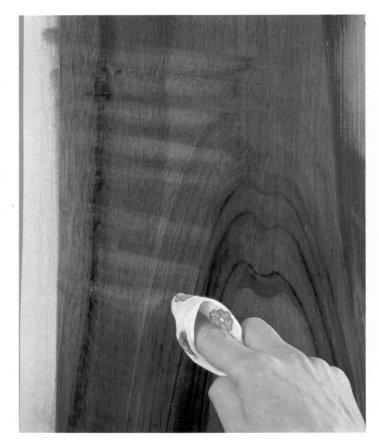

With rag or brush, in the same way, wipe the glaze horizontally to simulate the shimmering moirés and undulations of the wood.

Finish by lightly flogging over the fresh glaze. This final touch enhances the realism of the figure.

You will use this technique—first acrylic, then oil glaze—to render all of the woods that follow.

WALNUT

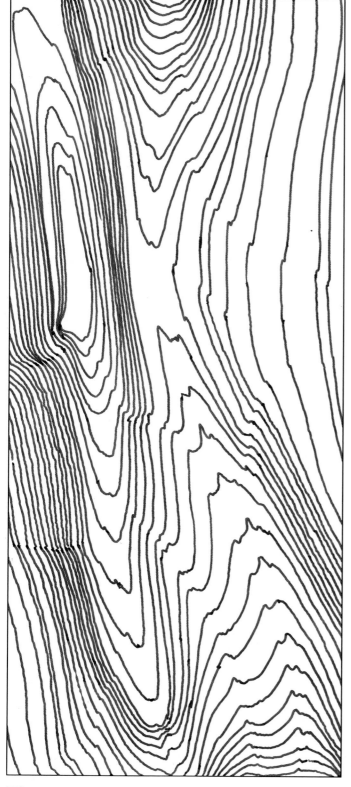

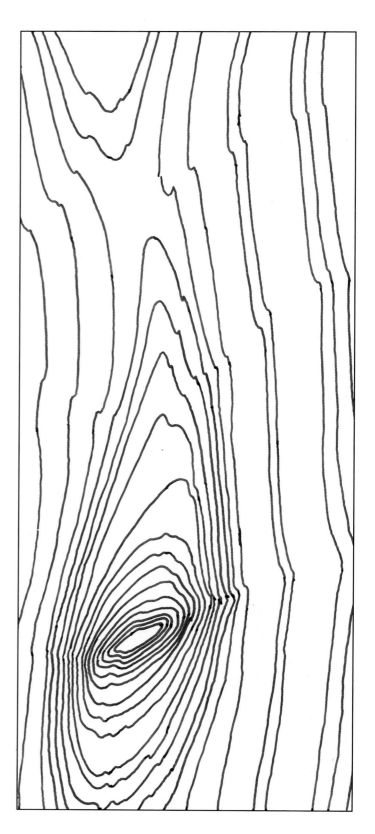

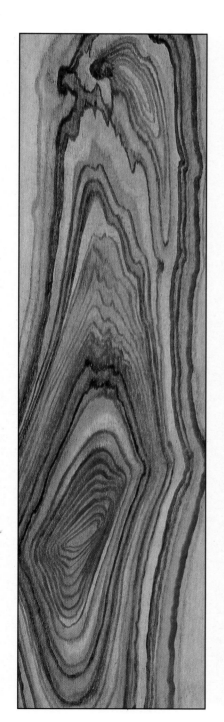

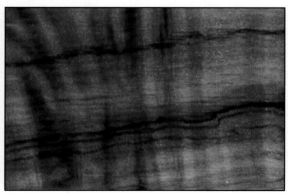

Walnut panel with molding
75 in × 31½ in
(1.90 m × .80 m)

*Walnut panel
on ash marquetry
with walnut burl
border
75 in × 30½ in
(1.90 m × .80 m)*

ASH

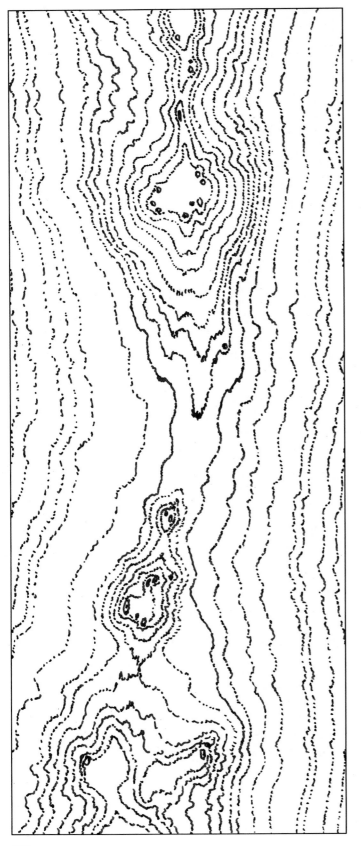

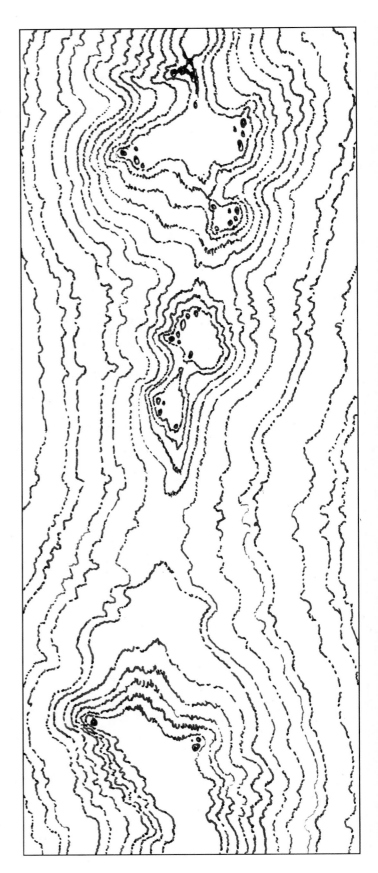

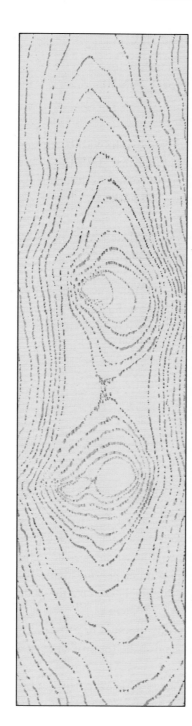

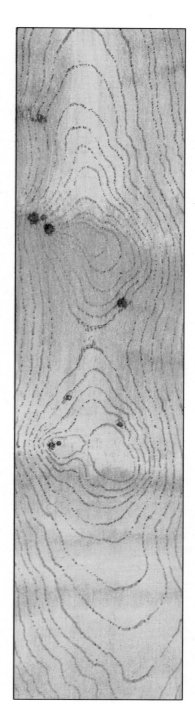

Base coat: luminous yellow (chrome yellow deep + yellow ochre + white)

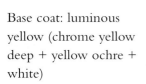

Acrylic

Using a pointed brush, with raw sienna, lightly draw the contours of the figure.

With a mixture of burnt sienna and burnt umber, form the small knots.

A few minutes later, using a spalter, with raw sienna, glaze the whole panel.

Again with the spalter, wipe the wet acrylic to produce the shimmering moiré effect. Ash grain can shimmer and undulate markedly.

Oil Glaze

Using a spalter, with a mixture of raw sienna and burnt sienna, apply a very thin glaze over the whole panel.

Use a soft rag to wipe bare spots in the glaze.

Soften with the badger blender.

Using a pointed brush, with a mixture of burnt sienna and burnt umber, retrace the tips of the figure and the fine shadings of the knots.

Finally, with a dry spalter, flog lightly over the whole.

WALNUT BURL

Base coat: orange ochre
(yellow ochre + cadmium orange + white)

Acrylic

Using a pointed brush, with burnt sienna, draw the grain of the burl. Note that this formation is larger than most burls, in fact somewhere between the size of a vee-grain figure and a normal burl.

Using the pointed brush, with black acrylic, retouch some lines of the markings.

With a square brush and a mixture of burnt sienna and burnt umber, form the knotty interior parts.

Oil Glaze

With a spalter and a glaze of burnt umber and burnt sienna, cover the whole surface. Then, with a graining brush dipped in turpentine, wipe bare spots inside and around the figure. These give the grain movement.

In black, with a pointed brush, detail some of the lines of the figure, and shade the space between the rings.

Using a square brush, with burnt umber, make the moiré pattern of the burl. Wipe lightly with a rag to nuance by lightening the shading more or less.

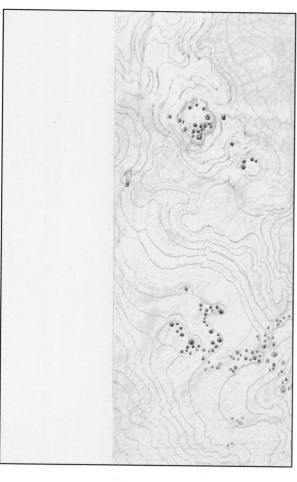

ASH BURL

Base coat: luminous yellow
(yellow ochre + chrome yellow + white)

Acrylic

In raw sienna, with a square brush, render the "eyes" of the burl.

This burl is less unusual and more compact than that of the walnut.

On the fresh acrylic of the eyes, use a small square sponge to wipe bare spots; these give the burl shading and grain.

Using a pointed brush, with a mixture of burnt sienna and raw sienna, give tight, sharp detail to some of the little eyes, so as to capture the sinuousness of the markings. Then, using a square brush with its bristles spaced (to serve as a graining brush), with raw sienna, make a series of irregularly spaced lines around and following the placement of the eyes.

With a mixture of burnt sienna and burnt umber and a pointed brush, render the small knots that cluster in the interior of the eyes.

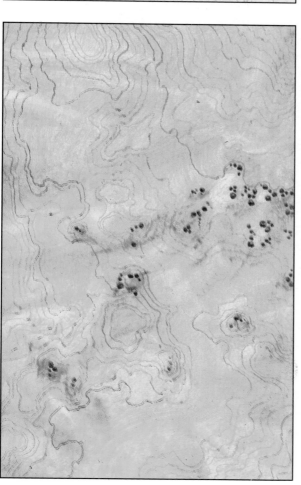

Oil Glaze

Glaze the whole surface with a raw sienna glaze.

Wipe with a rag around the eyes to render the shimmer of the grain.

With burnt sienna and raw sienna, using a pointed brush, retouch and retrace so as to emphasize these lighter shimmers.

Soften lightly with the badger blender.

Using a pointed brush, with a mixture of burnt sienna and raw sienna, retrace some lines of the grain and some knots.

Walnut burl surrounded by ash burl
39 in × 27½ in (1 m × .70 m)

Walnut panel on a pitch-pine background, with maple border
31½ in × 31½ in (.80 m × .80 m)

181

SYCAMORE

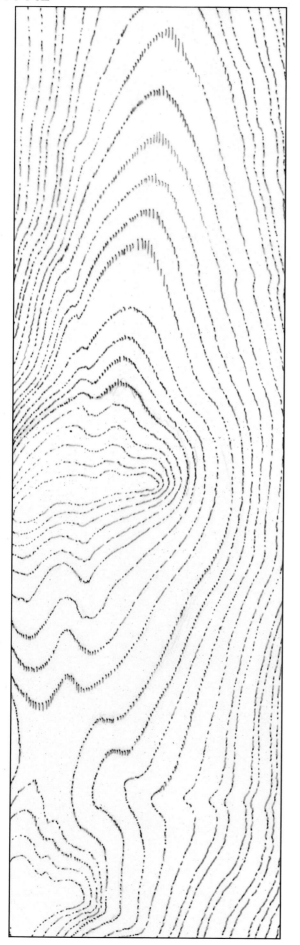
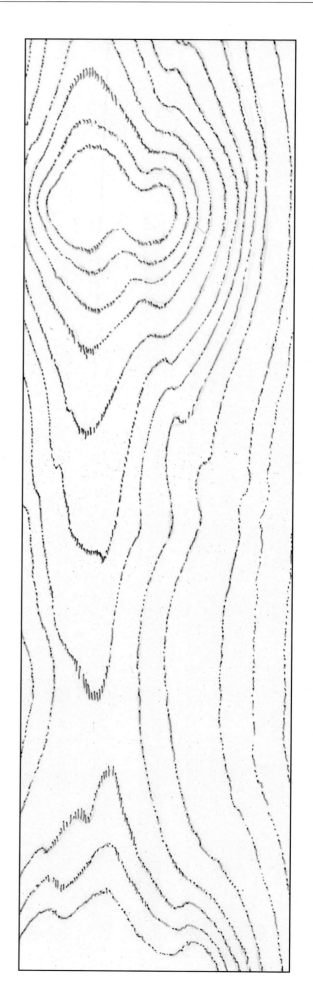

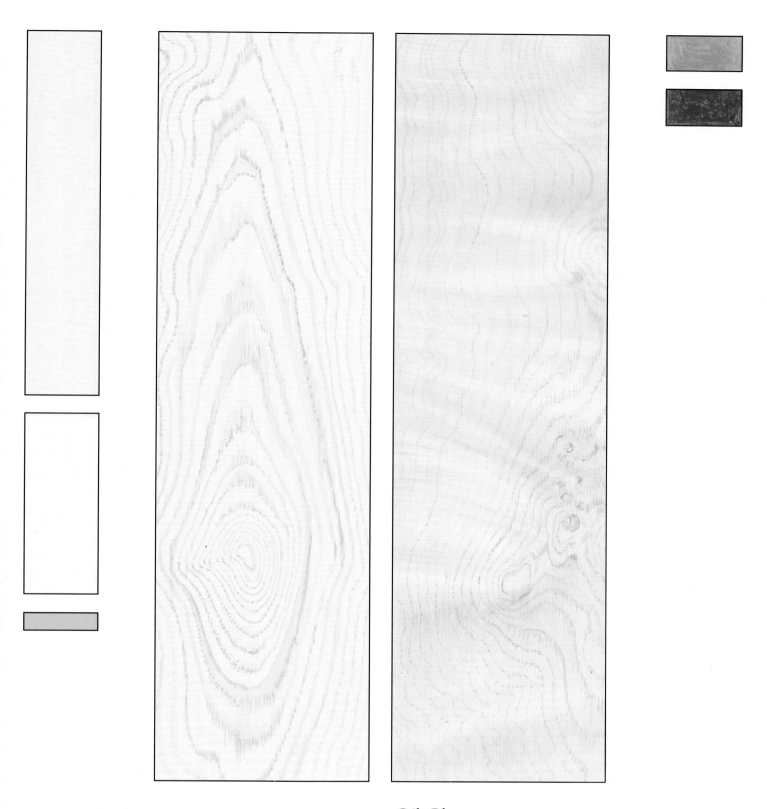

Base coat: pale yellow (white + a dot of yellow ochre)

Acrylic

Use a pointed brush and very dilute yellow ink to draw the grain, which should be drawn out and light.

Soften lightly with the badger blender.

Oil Glaze

Use a spalter to apply a glaze lightly tinted with raw sienna and burnt sienna. With a rag, wipe shimmers; then smooth over the whole forcefully with the badger blender.

Finally, using a pointed brush with burnt sienna mixed with a bit of raw sienna, retouch the figure.

PITCH PINE

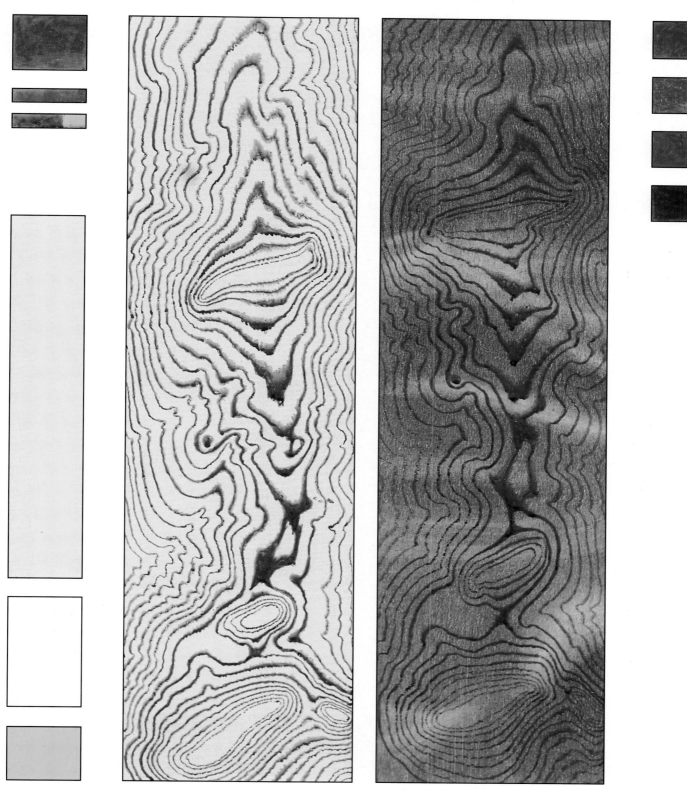

Base coat: medium yellow (white + chrome yellow deep)

Acrylic

With a mixture of burnt sienna and burnt umber, use a pointed brush to draw the grain. The curves should be tortuous, but still precise.

Soften lightly with a badger blender.

Oil Glaze

Using a spalter, apply a glaze tinted with burnt sienna, crimson lake, ultramarine, and a dot of burnt umber.

Wipe with a rag to produce the shimmers; then soften with the badger blender, accentuating the undulation.

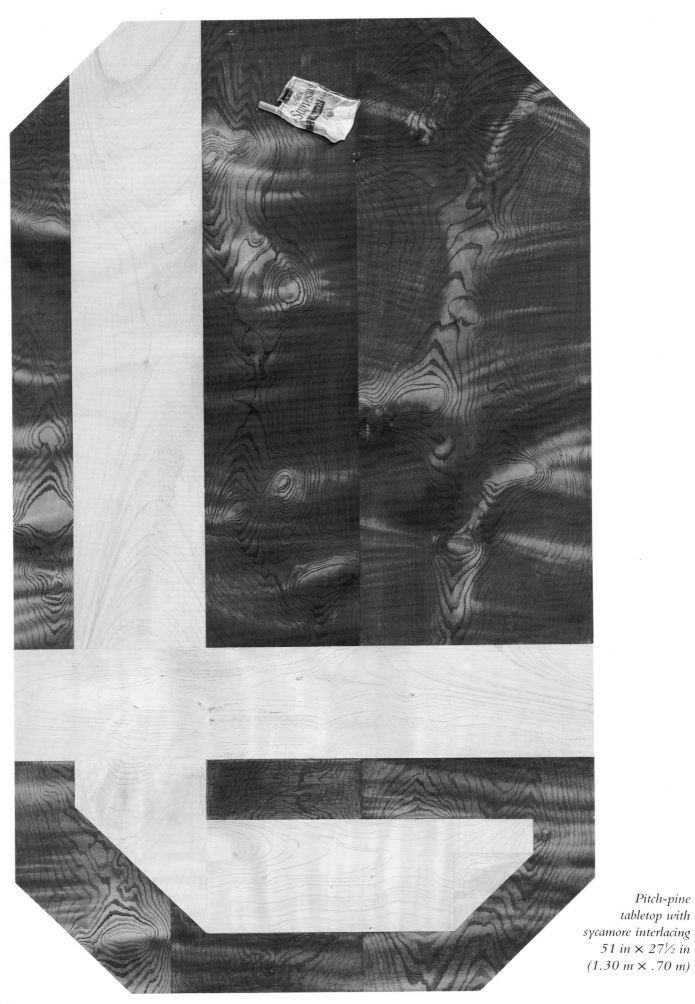

*Pitch-pine
tabletop with
sycamore interlacing
51 in × 27½ in
(1.30 m × .70 m)*

MARQUETRY

Marquetry is a very old technique that was rediscovered in the mid-fifteenth century. It consists of removing parts of a smooth surface and replacing them with other materials:

- ❖ all types and colors of wood
- ❖ precious or common metals: silver, gold, tin, copper, and so forth
- ❖ semiprecious or common stones
- ❖ certain animal products: ivory, shell, mother-of-pearl, galuchat (shagreen)

Many elements come into play in marquetry. A few such components, specific to wood, offer an almost infinite variety of decorative possibilities when combined:

- ❖ the particular type and markings (plumes, rays, burls) of the wood
- ❖ the cut (transverse, longitudinal, or diagonal)
- ❖ the design yielded by the cut (vees, butterfly wings) and the method of matching the pieces, often based on geometry or perspective
- ❖ the color of the wood, natural or tinted, colored or bleached

From the seventeenth century to the days of art deco, marquetry furniture was highly valued, and the cost of the finest examples today is stunning. Marquetry is becoming rarer and rarer; there are even fewer artisans who practice the technique than there are clients to purchase their work.

Fortunately, however, trompe l'œil marquetry can give the same results, while taking a much smaller toll on pocketbooks, forests, and animal species.

In trompe l'œil marquetry, you obviously must take care to keep the wood and its arrangement in harmony. Do not forget the "cut lines" when you are painting. It is helpful to mark these with removable tape.

Remember, too, that the pieces of wood you are painting must be small, not much bigger than 8 inches (20 cm) wide and about 30 inches (80 cm) long. If the main figure is too imposing, you can tone it down, and increase the decorative effect, by splitting it up symmetrically.

After applying the last coat of varnish to trompe l'œil marquetry, go over the "cut marks" with a thin pen line of black ink.

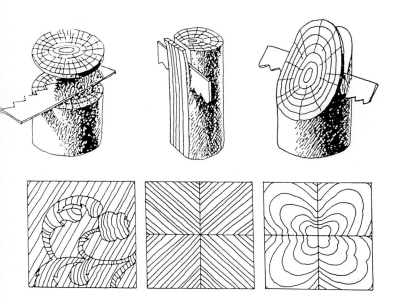

Half-moon of (from center to perimeter): ash burl, Brazilian rosewood, ivory, rosewood, ivory, ash burl, tortoiseshell, and Brazilian rosewood 47½ in (1.20 m) diameter

Marquetry of precious woods: lemon wood, Brazilian rosewood, Macassar ebony, maple, amaranth, rosewood 39 in × 27½ in (1 m × .70 m)

189

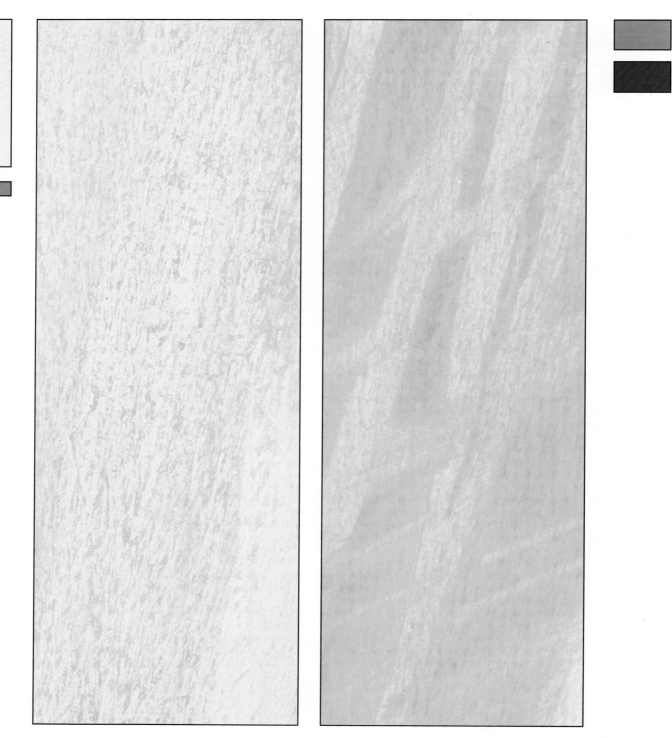

LEMON WOOD

Base coat: warm ochre (yellow ochre + white + red ochre)

Acrylic

With a very dilute mixture of yellow ochre acrylic, lightly stripe the surface with a square sponge; then immediately flog. Using a square brush, with acrylic of yellow ochre and a drop of sanguine, make a series of parallel bands of varying widths.

Using the square sponge, wipe short transverse strokes across the preceding work, to reveal the lighter shade of the base coat.

Flog across the whole surface.

With a pointed brush and very dilute sanguine, go over the darker stripes; then use the flogger across the surface.

Oil Glaze

Use a spalter to glaze the whole panel with raw sienna.

With a dry square brush, remove glaze from a few areas with varying pressure; these will become the luminous parts of the panel.

Flog across the whole surface.

190

AMARANTH

Base coat: rose ochre (white + red ochre + yellow ochre)

Acrylic

Step 1: Using a spalter, with dilute burnt sienna acrylic, cover the whole. Grain by striping with a square sponge, and flog.

Step 2: With a mixture of burnt sienna and burnt umber and the spalter, cover the whole surface; then remove glaze with the sponge to render the light grain. Using a square brush, with burnt umber, stripe some parts; then flog again.

Oil Glaze

Use the spalter to apply a darkening glaze of ultramarine, crimson lake, and burnt umber or Van Dyck brown. Wiping with a rag moistened with a little clear glaze, remove some glaze in striping strokes to bring out the lighter base.

Using a square brush, with a mixture of burnt umber and ultramarine, strengthen some of the grain lines. Then flog over the whole surface to finish.

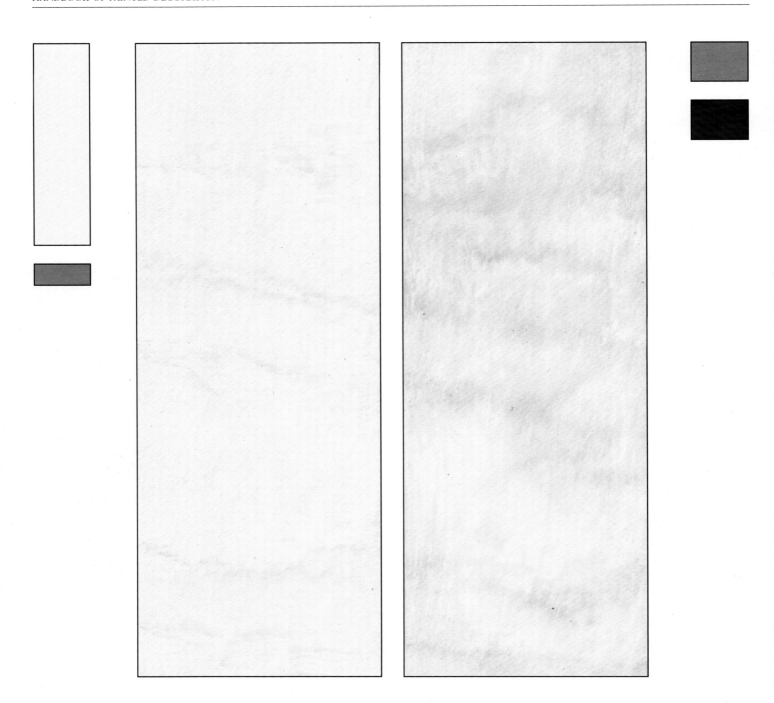

MAPLE

Base coat: sand (white + a drop of yellow ochre + a drop of red ochre)

Acrylic

Step 1: With dilute raw sienna, use a spalter to cover the whole surface; then, using a square sponge, wipe in a few places to render the first shimmers. Soften with the badger blender.

Step 2: Using a square brush, with very dilute raw sienna acrylic, accentuate the shimmers. Then, with moist fingertips, tap subtle spots of color across the maple. They should be very faint.

Step 3: Using a pointed brush, with raw sienna, surround the spots with a web of very fine undulating lines. Soften with the badger blender. To produce the effect of depth, go over the heart of the figure lightly in raw sienna with the pointed brush, and again use your fingers to intensify some spots.

Oil Glaze

Lightly glaze the whole using a spalter with raw sienna and a drop of burnt umber. Use a rag wrapped around your index finger to wipe in a few shimmers. Finally, with a square brush and a little burnt umber and raw sienna, liven up some shimmers.

Soften with the badger blender.

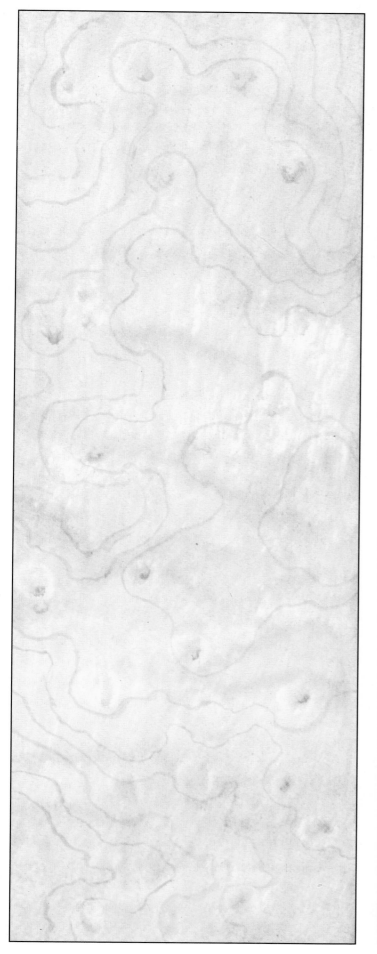
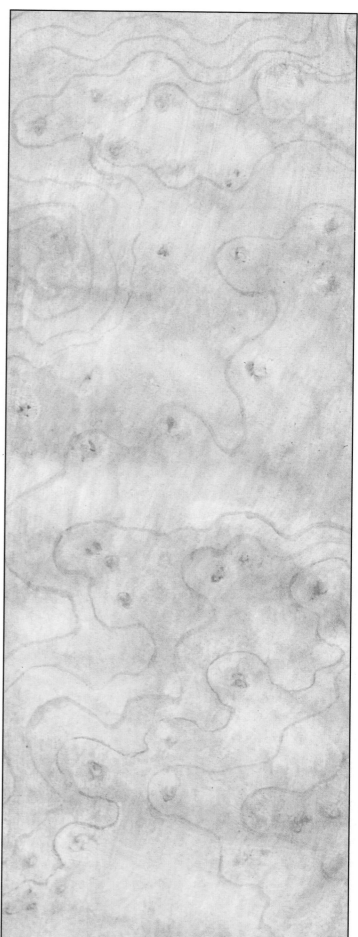

ROSEWOOD

Base coat: pale yellow (white + chrome yellow)

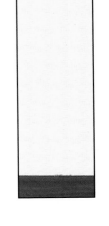

Acrylic

Step 1: Cover the whole surface, using a spalter, with dilute burnt sienna acrylic; then grain with the square sponge, varying the pressure to obtain lighter and darker parts.

Flog across the whole before it dries.

Step 2: Using a square brush, with burnt sienna, go over the stripes to emphasize some areas of the grain.

Flog once more to unify.

Oil Glaze

Using a spalter, with a glaze of burnt sienna, crimson lake, and black, cover the whole surface. Using a square brush, with a mixture of black and crimson lake, enhance the darker parts.

Wipe with a rag to bring out the light parts.

Using the square brush, again darken a few lines with burnt sienna

Flog across the whole surface once more.

MACASSAR EBONY

Base coat: slightly reddish medium yellow (yellow ochre + red ochre + white)

Acrylic

Step 1: Using a spalter, with sanguine-tinted acrylic, cover the base; then immediately grain with a small square sponge, varying the width of the bands and letting the base coat show through sometimes. Flog and let dry well.

Step 2: With dilute black acrylic, use the pointed or square brush to retrace the previous markings and make somewhat jagged lines in the darker parts. Flog before letting dry.

Step 3: With a slightly flared square brush, draw fine lines in black acrylic across the whole piece.

Oil Glaze

Glaze the whole panel with burnt umber; then intensify the darker areas with the pointed brush and dilute ivory black. Using a square brush, with transparent glaze, lighten some of the grain.

Flog over the whole.

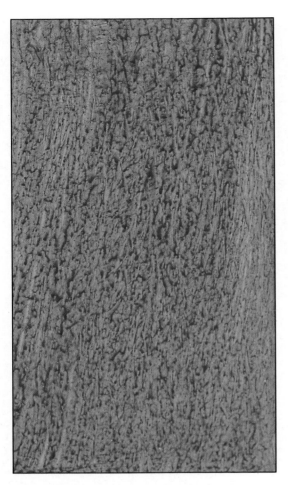

BRAZILIAN ROSEWOOD

Base coat: red ochre (Mars red + yellow ochre + white + chrome yellow)

Acrylic

Step 1: Cover the whole panel with sepia acrylic using a spalter. Flog immediately.

Step 2: Using a pointed brush, with a mixture of black and magenta acrylic, render the small jagged markings of the figure (some can be very dark, others are brighter and redder). With the same brush and acrylic, form the markings of the wood grain. This grain should include some dark stripes that are closely spaced and others that are spaced so the red base shows through.

Oil Glaze

Use a spalter to glaze the panel with a mixture of Van Dyck brown, ultramarine blue, and crimson lake.

Using a pointed brush, with black and a drop of ultramarine, retrace the darkest tips of the rings of the figure.

Flog across the whole surface.

PALISANDER

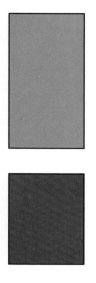

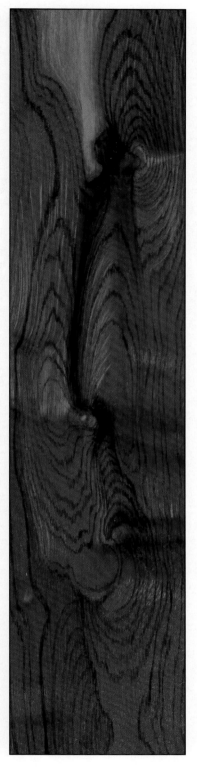

Unlike the other woods, palisander is not rendered with acrylic on a satin-finish foundation.

Base coat: "tarnished" orange (vivid orange with a little yellow ochre, 70 percent satin and 30 percent matte/flat enamel)

On this semi-matte base, using a spalter, apply a colorless oil glaze. In the wet glaze, draw the figure with a Conté crayon. Lightly soften.

Using the spalter, glaze with a mixture of crimson lake, burnt sienna, black, and burnt umber.

With black and crimson lake, use the square brush to emphasize some parts of the grain. Wipe some areas with a rag to produce the lighter areas that give an undulating effect.

Finish the surface by softening with a badger blender.

Palisander tabletop inlaid with ivory and galuchat 47½ in × 27½ in (1.20 m × .70 m)

Oak-ray panel with faux molding 43 in × 31½ in (1.10 m × .80 m)

204

OAK

The hard wood of the oak is used mostly for sturdy construction. Lighter oak furniture is usually built with veneer to reduce the cost. Young oak is light-colored; middle-aged oak, darker; old oak, dark: only the tones, and not the method, change when graining the wood.

For graining oak, you will need to have a supply of corks, their edges beveled with a knife blade, in addition to the customary equipment.

Base Coat

Light oak: pale yellow (yellow ochre + chrome yellow + white)

Medium oak: stronger yellow (yellow ochre + raw sienna + chrome yellow + white)

Older oak: aged ochre (raw sienna + red ochre + burnt umber + white)

Acrylic Layer

Light oak: bluish-black acrylic, diluted 75 percent

Medium oak: bluish-black acrylic, diluted 50 percent

Older oak: bluish-black acrylic, undiluted

Oil Glaze

Light oak: raw sienna + raw umber + burnt umber

Medium oak: raw sienna + burnt umber

Older oak: burnt umber

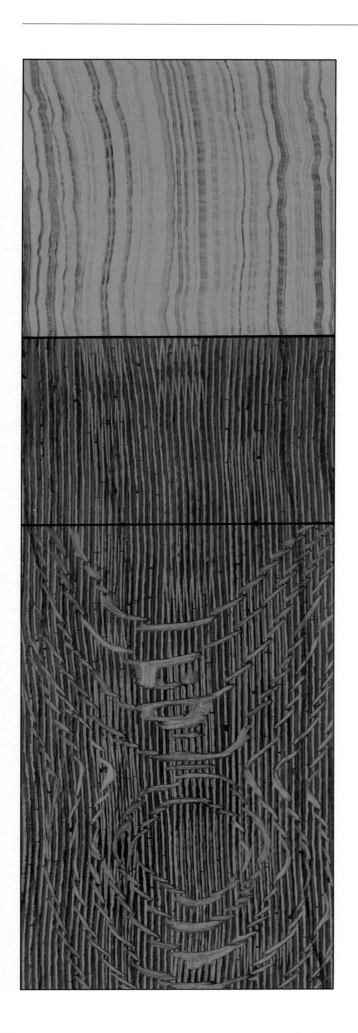

MEDIUM OAK

Our graining technique is almost identical to that of the old master decorators, but a lot quicker, yielding in minutes results that used to take fifteen hours to obtain. For a really nice finish, glaze twice over the acrylic. Using the modern water-based technique plus oil glazing requires two days, as against four by the old system.

Acrylic

Use a graining brush with bluish-black acrylic to grain the panel with a slightly wavy pattern of lines. These markings will show through at the end, giving a realistic effect.

Oil Glaze

Spread the raw sienna and burnt umber glaze over the panel with a spalter or graining brush. Let it sit for a few minutes; it will be easier to remove the glaze.

With a medium steel comb, comb the whole panel to accentuate the grain. Using a rag, wipe the glaze, following the course of the undulations. Apply more or less pressure to remove more or less.

In order to make a harmonious and convincing design for the ray markings, you should of course study the pattern before rendering it. Use a beveled cork covered by a soft rag held between your thumb and forefinger, and use it to wipe the lines of the the ray markings.

Lightly soften with the spalter.

With a rolled-up rag, wipe the glaze away to make some small bare spots in the empty space of the rays. Then comb lightly.

For the best results, wait a day before glazing again.

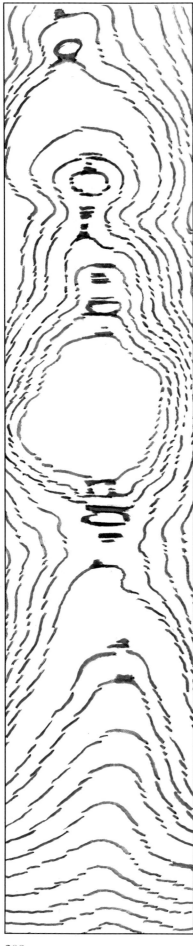
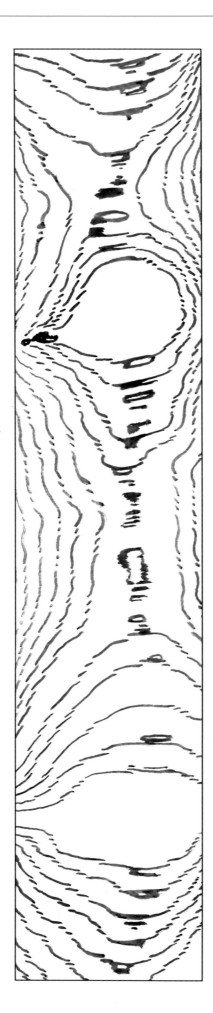

Reglazing

Reglaze the panel with glaze lightly tinted with burnt umber; then use a rag to remove glaze to suggest the kinetic effect of the grain.

Use a pointed sable to make dark strokes with burnt umber.

Using a graining brush dipped in clear glaze or turpentine, make wavy lines (following those of the first acrylic layer) at the heart of the rays.

Delicately soften the whole with a badger blender.

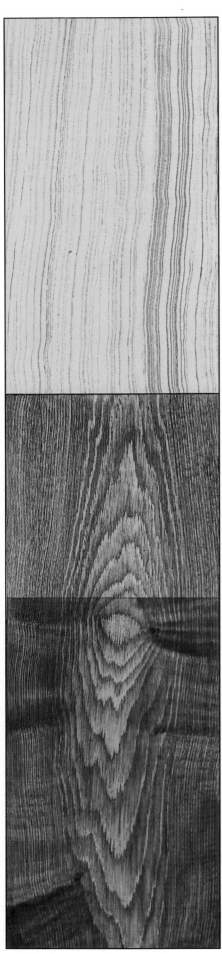

VEE-GRAIN

Acrylic

Grain the panel with a slightly wavy pattern of lines.

Oil Glaze

With another beveled cork wrapped in a rag, render the vee. Start with the heart and make the surrounding rings with a hatching motion. Use a rag to form the bands of the figure by wiping delicately over the rings.

Then with an ⅜-inch (8 mm) square sable brush, use a hatching motion to pull down the glaze from one ring to the one below it.

Grain around the figure with a medium comb, and grain the heart with a fine comb.

Reglazing

Glaze the panel with glaze tinted with burnt umber.

Wipe the heart of the figure and around it so as to capture its shimmer and undulation. Use a few strokes of burnt umber for emphasis; lightly smooth with a spalter. You can also add a few of these strokes around the heart to give it a nice sense of movement.

Model for a Renaissance case, showing preliminary drawing
39 in × 39 in (1 m × 1 m)

Renaissance case in oak, with ash burl rosette, ivory border, and molding 51 in × 51 in (1.30 m × 1.30 m)

A very high level of work, the oak imitation in the piece shown overleaf is very elaborate. The central panel includes a lower section with one vee figure and two ray boards placed vertically, and an upper section with four ray and straight-grain boards placed horizontally. Numerous small, tight retouching strokes made with a pointed sable simulate the grain and pores of the wood. The simple fleuret ornamentation on the vertical boards was made by shading on the finished oak rendering; the sculpted and molded effects were rendered on a light oak background, to enhance the relief effect.

Central panel of a Regency-style triptych. Work for the Gold Medal competition of the Meilleurs Ouvriers de France (Best Craftsmen of France) 51 in × 82½ in (1.30 m × 2.10 m)

Bookmatched yew bordered with elm burl, with four yew medallions in the corners 47½ in × 31½ in (1.20 m × .80 m)

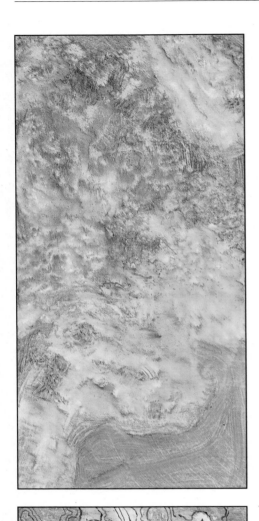

ELM BURL

Base coat: honey (yellow ochre + white + a drop of red ochre)

Acrylic

Step 1: With a spalter, cover the whole surface with dilute raw sienna acrylic.

Using a square sponge, wipe bare spots, and soften with a badger blender.

Step 2: With the square brush and a mixture of burnt sienna and burnt umber, emphasize some darker areas; then use the badger blender to soften.

With the same colors and a pointed brush, trace delicate webs around those small and medium-sized areas that will later become clusters of knots.

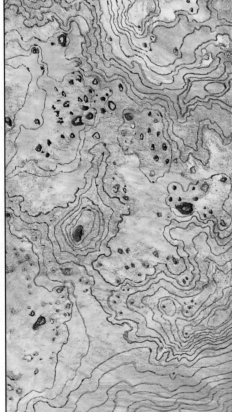

Oil Glaze

Using a spalter, glaze the whole surface with a mixture of burnt umber, black, and burnt sienna.

With the pointed brush, go over the hearts of the knots and parts of the surrounding network with black.

Wipe glaze away to make some lighter areas, and then use the badger blender to soften the whole.

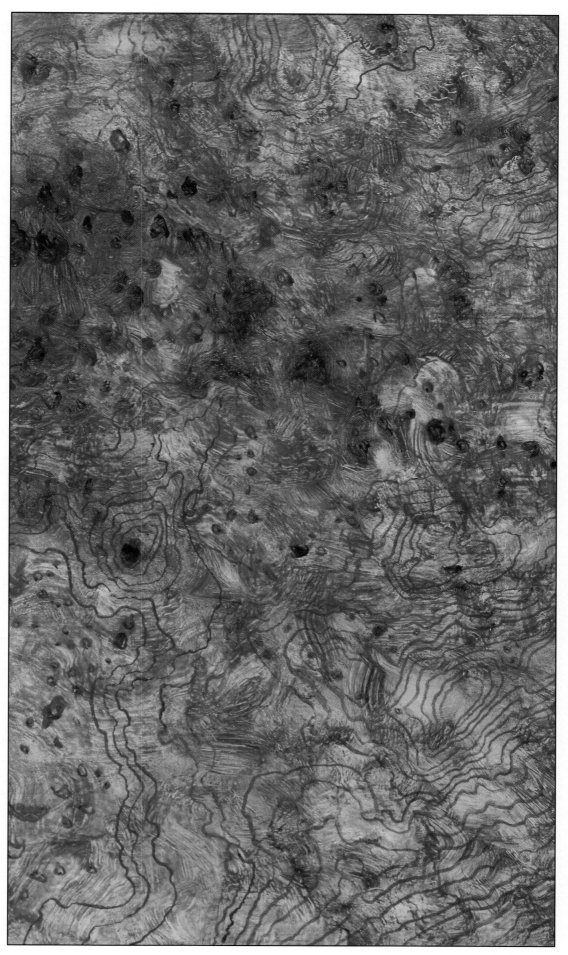

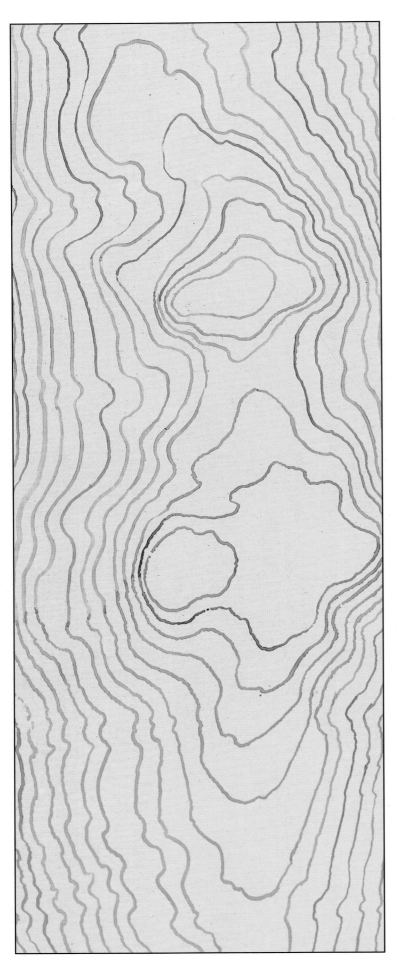

YEW

Base coat: pale yellow (yellow ochre + chrome yellow + white)

Acrylic

Using a pointed brush, with raw sienna and a drop of black, render the sinuous network of the figure.

Oil Glaze

With a glaze lightly tinted burnt sienna and chrome yellow, use a spalter to cover the whole surface; then use a rag to wipe lighter areas to get the shimmers and undulation. Emphasize the darker areas using a square brush, with burnt sienna. Then soften with the badger blender.

Make small knots in the heart of the figure with burnt umber, using a pointed brush, and soften with the badger blender.

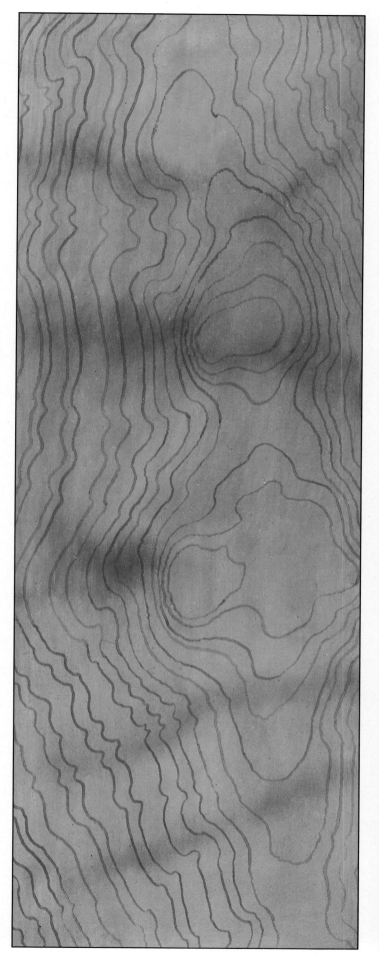
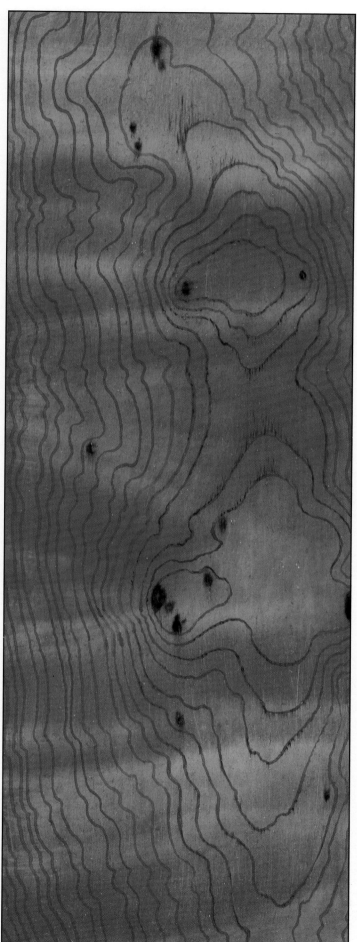

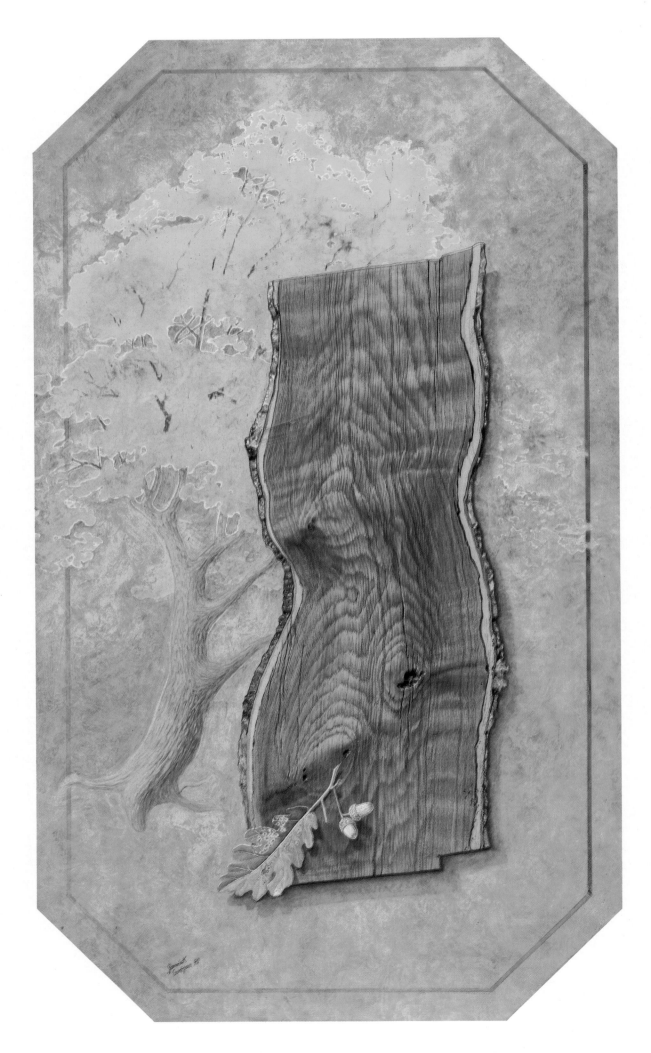

Tabletop with oak plume on patina, with leaf and acorn
47½ in × 31½ in (1.20 m × .70 m)

Model for a screen panel (see page 301); leaves and frame are
bird cherry, base is thuja burl, and leaf undersides are green oak
43 in × 31½ in (1.10 m × .80 m)

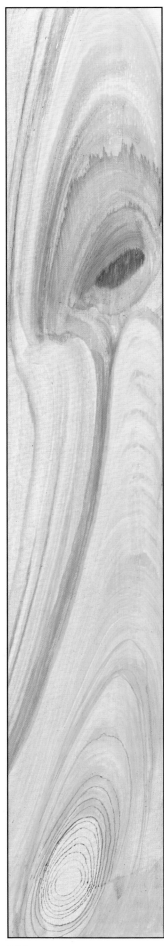

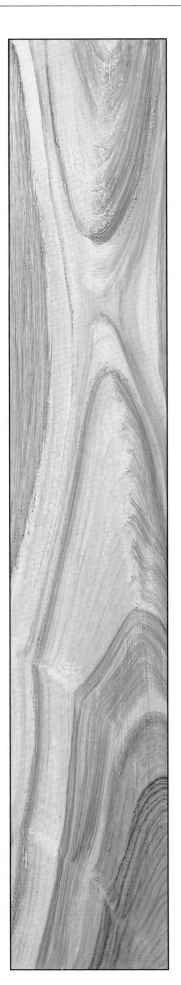

CHERRY

Base coat: straw yellow (chrome yellow + white)

Acrylic

Using a square brush with burnt sienna, raw sienna, burnt umber, black, and ultramarine blue, render the main figure.

Glaze the whole surface with very dilute burnt sienna.

Immediately use a damp square sponge to wipe some bare spots, following the shape of the plume.

Soften lightly with the badger blender.

Oil Glaze

With a glaze tinted burnt umber and burnt sienna, go over a few of the rings of the figure.

Soften with the badger blender.

Add touches of burnt umber in places to emphasize the shimmers.

Finally, soften once more.

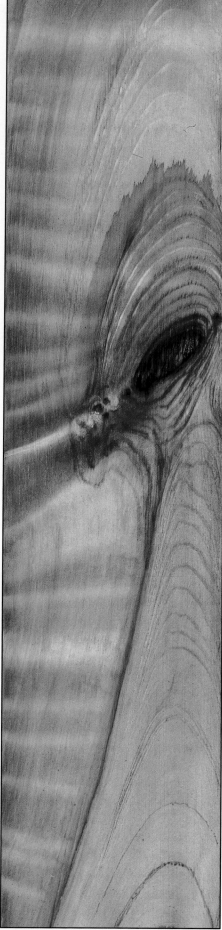

THUJA

Base coat: vivid orange (cadmium orange)

Acrylic

Step 1: With a mixture of yellow ochre, a drop of red, and a drop of black, use a spalter to cover the whole. Then, using the square sponge or a rag, wipe some parts to lighten.

Soften with a badger blender.

Step 2: With the same colors and a pointed brush, dab small spots on the knotty parts and surround them with a very delicate web of lines.

Go over the whole again with the badger blender.

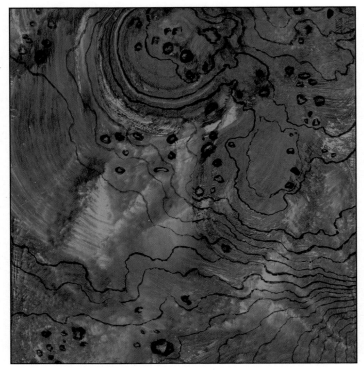

Oil Glaze

Using a spalter, apply a glaze tinted with crimson lake and burnt umber; wipe with a rag to render shimmer and undulation.

With a soft rag wet with clear glaze, wipe little spots in the hearts of the knots.

Then go over the whole surface lightly with the badger blender.

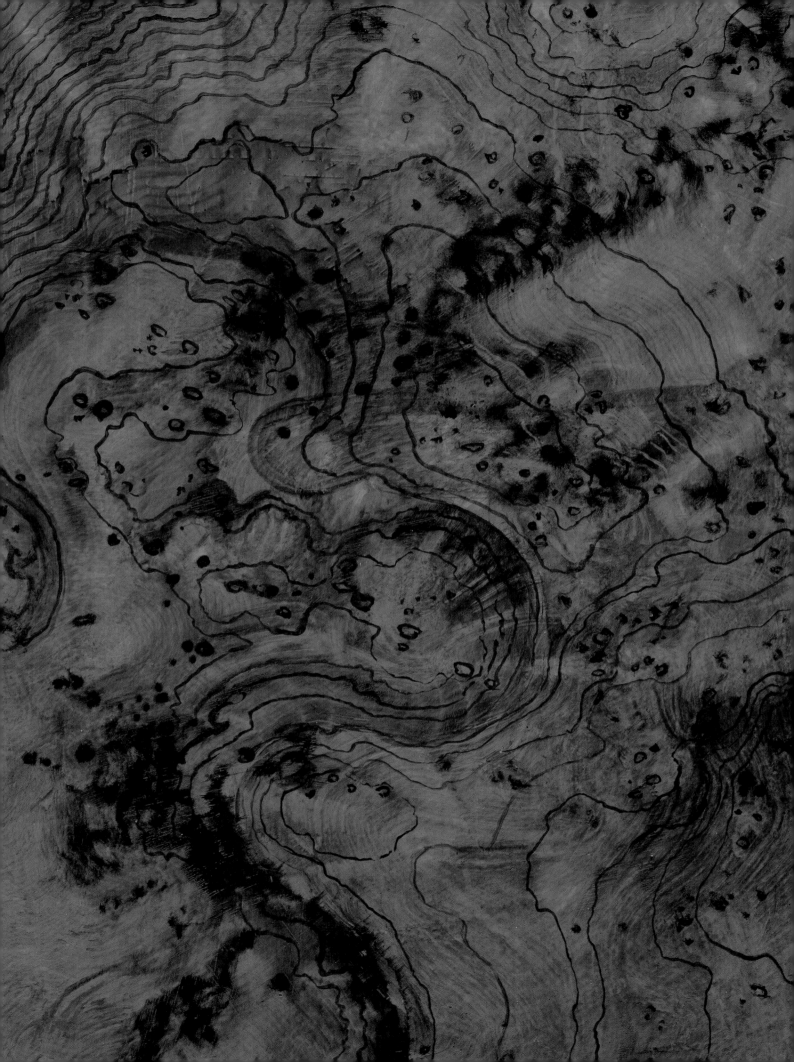

FIR

Base coat: sandy yellow (white + yellow ochre)

Acrylic

Step 1: With a mixture of undiluted raw sienna and a drop of burnt sienna, use a square brush to draw the markings of the fir.

Each element of the figure must be softened with a badger blender immediately.

Step 2: With the same tints, use a pointed brush to touch up the tips of the figure; soften with the badger blender.

Step 3: Using the pointed brush, with burnt sienna, form the knots of the fir. Then, with the square brush, render the surrounding grain.

Oil Glaze

Use a spalter to cover the panel with a glaze lightly tinted with Cassel earth.

With a rag, render the shimmers around the figure.

Retouch the knots and the edges of the figure using the pointed brush, with Cassel earth. Soften lightly with the badger blender.

Composition of fir on a maple foundation
39 in × 39 in (1 m × 1 m)

MAHOGANY

Even though mahogany has become synonymous with red, there is also a pale mahogany, which makes for equally sumptuous, and softer, furniture. Often associated with the Empire style, mahogany goes beautifully with different materials in different combinations (wood, marble, ivory, plain or richly decorated fabrics).

This noble wood comes in three varieties:

❖ Understated smooth mahogany, made up of plumes, lines, and straight grain, is mostly used to complement other woods.

❖ Flamboyant shimmering crotch mahogany, whose superb figure shoots out like a burst of flame, obviously demands to be the centerpiece of a work.

❖ Spotted mahogany, very different from the other patterns, even as it combines their elements, is notable for the maculations on its reddish foundation. It is used in marquetry either as centerpiece or as complement to other elements of the design.

There is not a strict dividing line between these three patterns, and they need to be carefully studied and rendered with finesse.

There are many modern techniques for rendering mahogany. As with the other woods (notably walnut), you can use the traditional and time-consuming distemper method, mixing the pigments in beer or vinegar. But our method has the advantage, besides its quick drying time, of conveying the transparency of the wood much better than distemper.

Empire-style door in crotch mahogany and ash burl
82½ in × 25 in (2.10 m × .63 m)

228

CROTCH MAHOGANY

Base coat: bright orange (cadmium orange)

Acrylic

Step 1: With Cassel earth acrylic, use the flogger to flog over the foundation. Let dry for an hour.

Sketch the markings of the figure with a dark, powdery (pastel) chalk.

Working in stages, glaze what you have drawn with a mixture of red and black acrylic. Work quickly and carefully to prevent runs.

With a moist square sponge, wipe bare a spot in the middle of what will become the figure. Then soften with the badger blender. Let dry.

Steps 2 and 3: Render the second and third stages of the figure in the same way.

A few minutes after finishing, retouch the heart with a mixture of black and red acrylic, either with a spalter or brush.

Soften with the badger blender before drying.

Half an hour later, you can reglaze in oil or acrylic.

Reglazing with Oil

Glaze the surface with a thin, even coat of glaze tinted with crimson lake, black, and sepia to darken the panel.

Using a small spalter, with black, form the crotch grain markings in the heart of the figure. Soften lightly with the badger blender.

With a graining brush soaked in clear glaze, wipe bare spots in the colored glaze.

Or

Reglazing with Acrylic

Work quickly, so as not to get caught by quick-drying acrylics, and proceed in steps (usually three), as with the first acrylic work. Use the same process and same colors with acrylics as with oils.

It is preferable to finish mahogany with a gloss varnish and then polish.

SPOTTED MAHOGANY

Base coat: bright orange

Acrylic

Cover the panel with a dilute mixture of burnt umber, black, and crimson lake; then flog to grain.

Oil Glaze

Using a spalter, cover the whole surface with a glaze tinted with black and crimson lake. With the square brush lightly draw, in black, a figure with the characteristic rounded spots. To finish, soften with the badger blender; then flog while the surface is still wet.

Arrangement of mahogany on base of copper leaf
oxidized with vinegar

*Empire-style half-moon of crotch mahogany with
ivory frieze and narrow jade border around
Imperador marble center
47½ in (1.20 m) diameter*

*Empire-style tabletop in Mediterranean Green
marble with malachite border, surrounded by
spotted mahogany and gold leaf
71 in × 47½ in (1.80 m × 1.20 m)*

*Empire-style tabletop of symmetrically cut pale
mahogany, with border of thuja burl, surrounded by
porphyry Greek frieze, on a Griotte marble base
71 in × 47½ in (1.80 m × 1.20 m)*

231

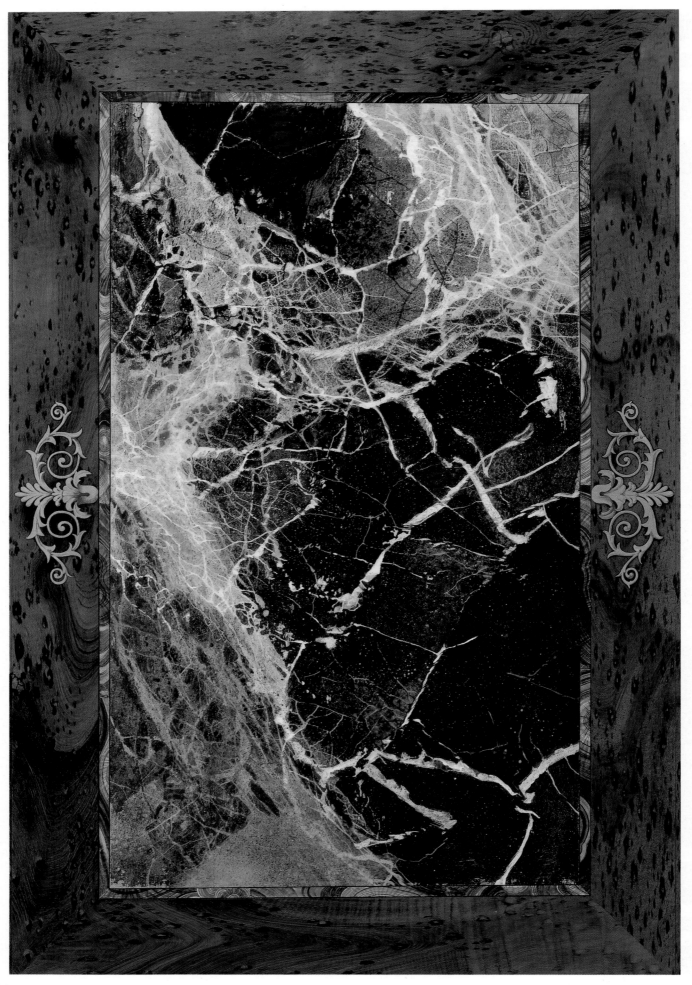

5

FRIEZES AND ORNAMENTS

INTRODUCTION

Even the most brilliantly executed faux wood or marble panel can be enhanced by ornament. Ornament gives character, style, and life to faux materials. Open your eyes to your surroundings and you will discover myriad themes: people, animals, plants, the sky, and so on. The history of art offers inspiration in the form of the basic motifs that have been adapted, stylized, and combined in trompe l'œil through the centuries. For example, ancient Egyptian art greatly influenced French Empire and Art Deco; Greek art was the source of many Gothic and Renaissance motifs. Although we draw principally on these traditions for the examples in this chapter, Islamic and Asian art also offer many decorative motifs for trompe l'œil painting.

The examples in this chapter employ one or more of the techniques previously covered, and introduce a few new ones.

Geometric and floral friezes mainly serve as accompaniment to other decoration. Among the possible designs are sawtooth zigzags, chevrons, interlacement bands, squares, diamonds, circles, hearts, ovals, flowers, leaves, and so on.

In ornamentation we use the same motifs as in friezes, but in this case they are generally enlarged, and rendered in greater detail. Some common examples are:

❖ The acanthus leaf, certainly the most popular subject since the Middle Ages; but also oak, vine, bay, holly, ivy, clover, and palm leaves

❖ Flowers, alone or in garlands; most notably the lily, but also the chrysanthemum and the rose (whence the rosette), very often used as a central motif

❖ Fruits, in garlands or cornucopias

❖ Realistic or fanciful shells

❖ Scrolled motifs—ribbons, cartouches, parchment roll

❖ Human and animal figures—representational, grotesque, fantastic

The play of contrasts is very important in ornamentation. Depending on the background to which it is applied, a simple ornament can become exceptional. Invariably, the more care and polish that go into the foundation, the more vigorous and beautiful the ornamentation—and thus the whole decor as well.

Even a monochrome motif, using light and shadow, can yield a startling trompe-l'œil effect, as can be seen in many works from the Louis XIV period. These fool the eye to such an extent that the hand wants to touch the reliefs—which are not there. So striking is the effect sometimes that only an expert eye can distinguish the real from the imitation.

Like our predecessors, we can still play with reality today, but the modern techniques we employ allow us to create trompe-l'œil ornamentation more quickly and easily than they did.

Ornamentation has its own grammar, given voice and form in furniture and sculpture. Various motifs can be combined in myriad ways to realize any number of decorative effects.

233

5

FRIEZES AND ORNAMENTS

INTRODUCTION

Even the most brilliantly executed faux wood or marble panel can be enhanced by ornament. Ornament gives character, style, and life to faux materials. Open your eyes to your surroundings and you will discover myriad themes: people, animals, plants, the sky, and so on. The history of art offers inspiration in the form of the basic motifs that have been adapted, stylized, and combined in trompe l'œil through the centuries. For example, ancient Egyptian art greatly influenced French Empire and Art Deco; Greek art was the source of many Gothic and Renaissance motifs. Although we draw principally on these traditions for the examples in this chapter, Islamic and Asian art also offer many decorative motifs for trompe l'œil painting.

The examples in this chapter employ one or more of the techniques previously covered, and introduce a few new ones.

Geometric and floral friezes mainly serve as accompaniment to other decoration. Among the possible designs are sawtooth zigzags, chevrons, interlacement bands, squares, diamonds, circles, hearts, ovals, flowers, leaves, and so on.

In ornamentation we use the same motifs as in friezes, but in this case they are generally enlarged, and rendered in greater detail. Some common examples are:

❖ The acanthus leaf, certainly the most popular subject since the Middle Ages; but also oak, vine, bay, holly, ivy, clover, and palm leaves

❖ Flowers, alone or in garlands; most notably the lily, but also the chrysanthemum and the rose (whence the rosette), very often used as a central motif

❖ Fruits, in garlands or cornucopias

❖ Realistic or fanciful shells

❖ Scrolled motifs—ribbons, cartouches, parchment roll

❖ Human and animal figures—representational, grotesque, fantastic

The play of contrasts is very important in ornamentation. Depending on the background to which it is applied, a simple ornament can become exceptional. Invariably, the more care and polish that go into the foundation, the more vigorous and beautiful the ornamentation—and thus the whole decor as well.

Even a monochrome motif, using light and shadow, can yield a startling trompe-l'œil effect, as can be seen in many works from the Louis XIV period. These fool the eye to such an extent that the hand wants to touch the reliefs—which are not there. So striking is the effect sometimes that only an expert eye can distinguish the real from the imitation.

Like our predecessors, we can still play with reality today, but the modern techniques we employ allow us to create trompe-l'œil ornamentation more quickly and easily than they did.

Ornamentation has its own grammar, given voice and form in furniture and sculpture. Various motifs can be combined in myriad ways to realize any number of decorative effects.

LAYOUT

Laying out your design before you start to paint is imperative. You cannot produce perfect trompe l'œil friezes and ornament without tight layout—whether this will be simple or elaborate depends on the style and shape of the desired result.

Even if you have a sure hand with a pencil, it is absolutely necessary to use a ruler, T-square, and compasses to get well-balanced layouts. With this basic equipment, you can construct all the geometric motifs: squares, rectangles, diamonds, triangles, and circles. All ornament is inscribed within one or a combination of these figures.

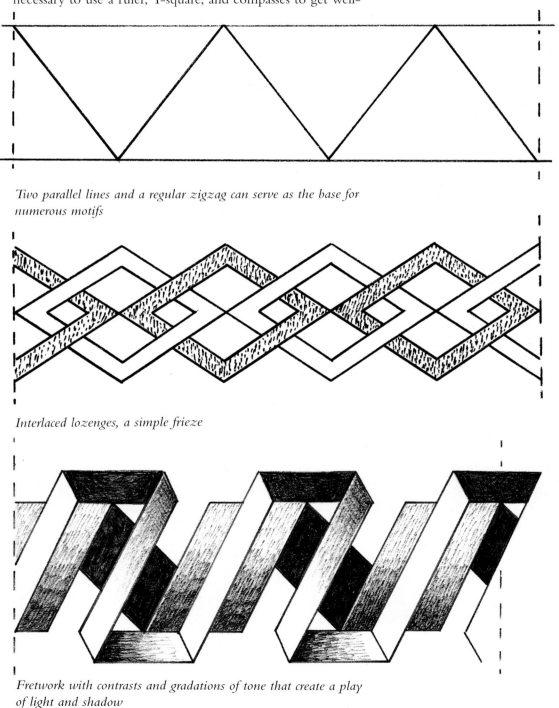

Two parallel lines and a regular zigzag can serve as the base for numerous motifs

Interlaced lozenges, a simple frieze

Fretwork with contrasts and gradations of tone that create a play of light and shadow

Art-deco-style ornamentation

Note the use of squares, rectangles, diamonds, circles, and
parallel lines in the underlying layout.

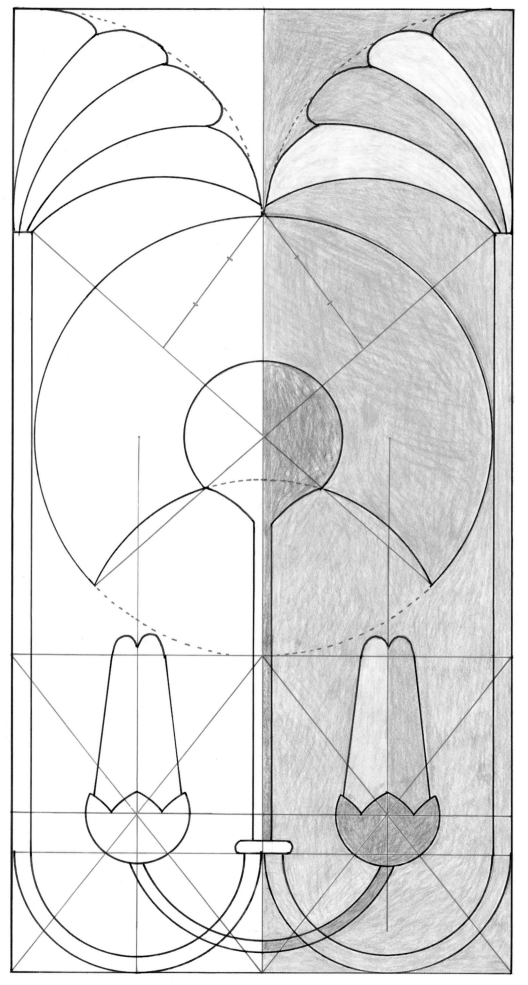

237

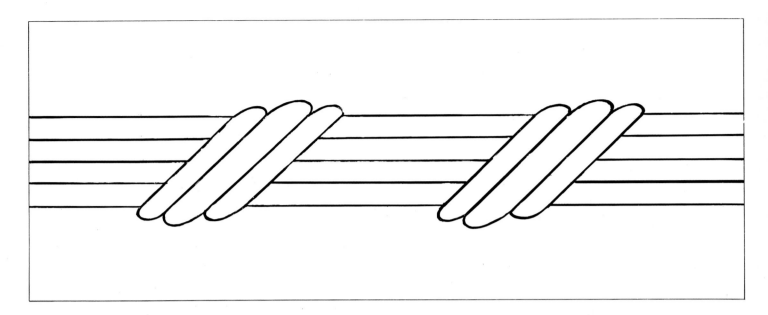

STENCILING: A TIED MOLDING

Stenciling makes it easier to get an accurate layout onto the surface to be decorated. Draw the design in pencil on sturdy tracing paper (preferably made of polyester). Using a needle, punch holes about ¹/₁₆ inch (2 mm) apart along the outlines of the figure.

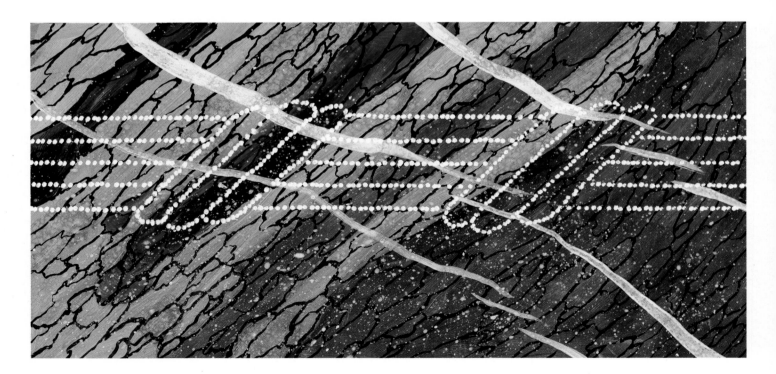

Affix the stencil to the surface you are decorating and dust over it with a pounce bag (a small cloth bag filled with paint pigment). You might use white on a dark foundation or, conversely, a darker color on a light foundation. Avoid especially strong colors like crimson lake, ultramarine blue, or Prussian blue, since they will be difficult to remove later. Lightly tap over the stencil with the pounce bag so that the holes of the stencil fill with powder. Carefully remove the stencil and retrace the motif, following the dots of powder.

Shadows

Choose the color for the shadows according to the tones of the
foundation. A mixture of oil paints (chrome green light + a
drop of black + a drop of raw umber) suits this Campan mar‑
ble. Using an edging tool, such as a straightedge, and a medium
sable brush, apply the color. Then, using a small *rondin* or the
equivalent, lightly grade (shade) the bands.

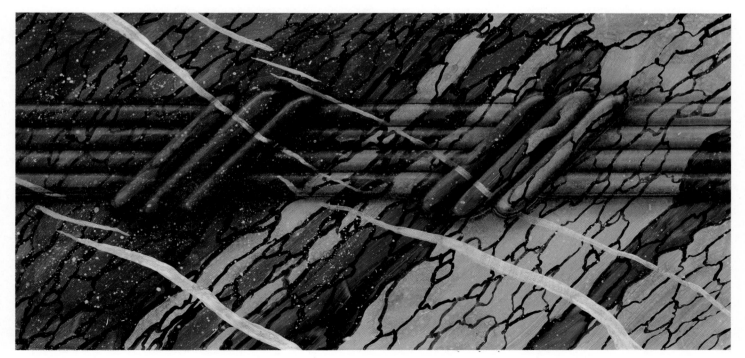

Highlights

Repeat the same operation with a lighter color (chrome green
light + a drop of white + a drop of raw umber).

Louis XV–style tied molding, on Campan Mélangé
23½ in × 35 in (60 cm × 90 cm)

240

METALLIC LEAF

Metallic leaf—whether rich real karat gold and silver or the less costly copper, aluminum, or others—makes a wonderful foundation for trompe l'œil. Leaf comes in two forms: "books" of loose leaf, and transfer (sheets and rolls), backed with tissue. Illustrated below is the application of metal leaf with twelve-hour gilding size, a kind of varnish that allows the leaf to stick to the support. Depending on the temperature, it takes eight to fourteen hours to dry—whence, more or less, its name. A three-hour size, called quick size, is used for retouching. Size must be applied to a nonporous base (satin finish, for example). Because the gilding size is transparent, it is a good idea to tint it with yellow oil paint, to avoid missing spots.

Using a gilder's tip, a special rectangular brush made for the purpose, apply the first leaf—gold, silver, copper, or aluminum—onto the mixture. The tip holds the leaf on the way to the support. It is customary to stroke the brush against hair or apply a little Vaseline to it so the leaf will adhere to it. (The gilder's tip shown here is double: it consists of two tips side by side.)

Position the leaves starting at the lower left. Press very gently on the leaf so it adheres to the support, and brush out air bubbles, proceeding from the center toward the perimeter. The brush shown here is a soft sable held in a quill.

Work carefully: metallic leaf is fragile and tears easily. Once it is adhered, it cannot be shifted.

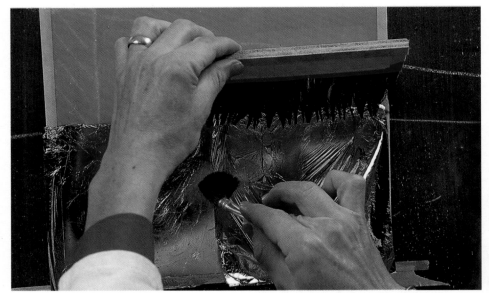

When the first row of leaf is in place, continue in the same fashion for the second row. Overlap the leaves a fraction of an inch, to avoid leaving blank spots. Remove any misplaced scraps of leaf.

Apply all the squares this same way, from left to right, row after row, until all the leaf is in place.

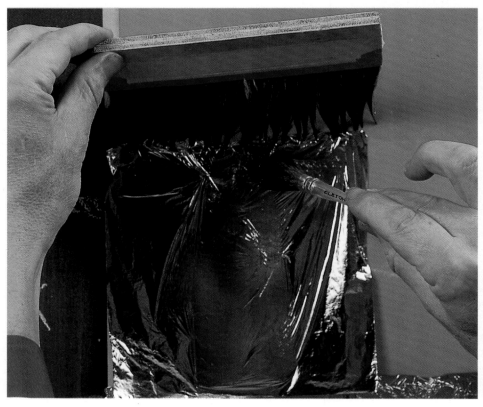

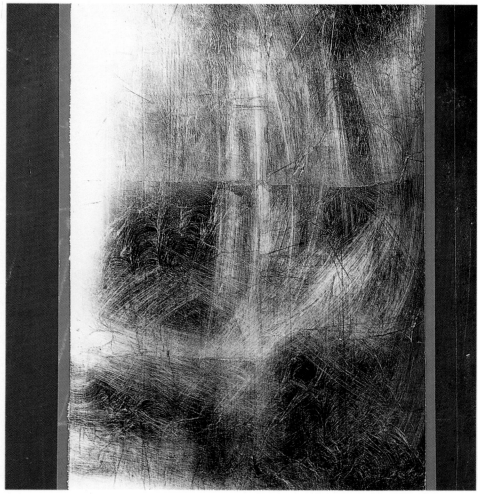

Use a soft brush to remove, very delicately, the excess leaf. For a uniform surface, wipe very lightly with a soft rag, taking care not to scratch the surface.

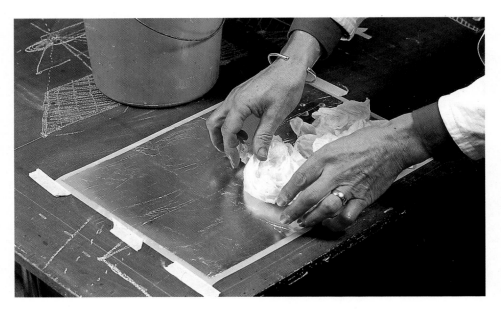

OXIDATION

Oxidizing a metallic ground yields still another group of effects.

With the surface to be oxidized lying flat, place crumpled, vinegar-soaked tissue or paper toweling on the metal leaf. The thickness of the tissue, the amount and concentration of the vinegar, and the duration of the treatment, from a few hours to overnight, all influence the look of the oxidation. The corrosive action of the vinegar produces a very decorative verdigris (gray-green), more or less pronounced depending on the application time. After oxidation, protect the surface with a layer of satin or gloss varnish.

TWO-TONE OXIDATION

You can produce spectacular oxidation effects by varying the color of the base coat underneath the metal, as demonstrated here with copper leaf.

On a light-colored satin-finish foundation, oxidized copper is gray-green. On a dark foundation, like dark green, the base color will show through the holes made by the oxidation, mixed in with the grayish-green. You can also use a strong red, brown, or black base.

Another possibility: replace the base coat of paint with a layer of aluminum or silver leaf. Apply another coat of gilding size and then the copper leaf. The result is magnificent, but costly. Save it for important small-scale projects.

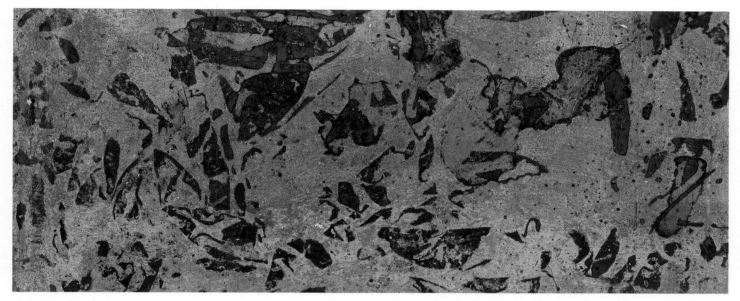

Garnet-colored base coat

Bluish-silver base coat

Black base coat

Almond-colored base coat

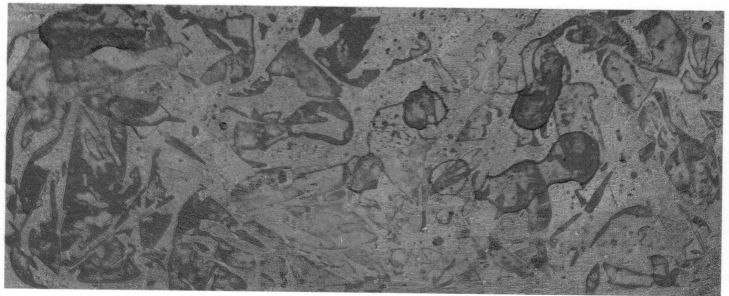

Orange base coat

246

Hunter-green base coat

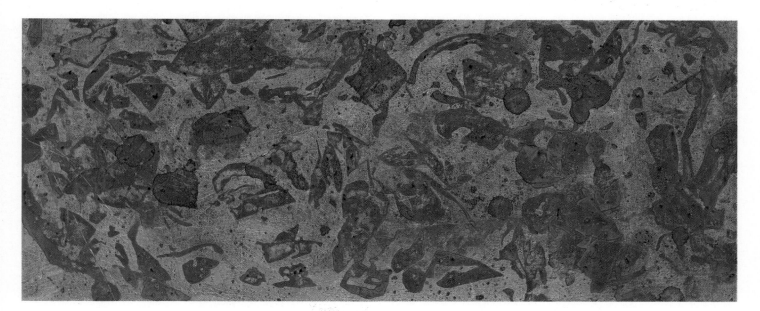

Violet base coat

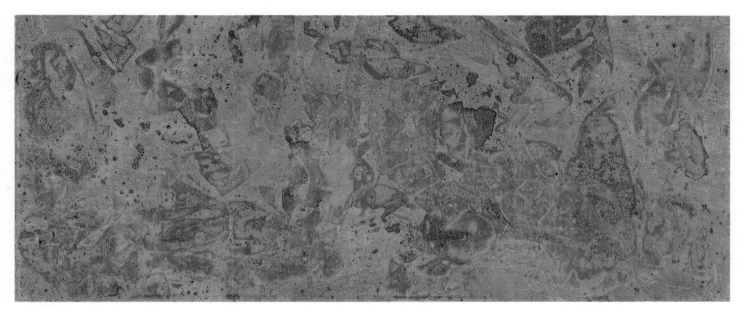

Green base coat

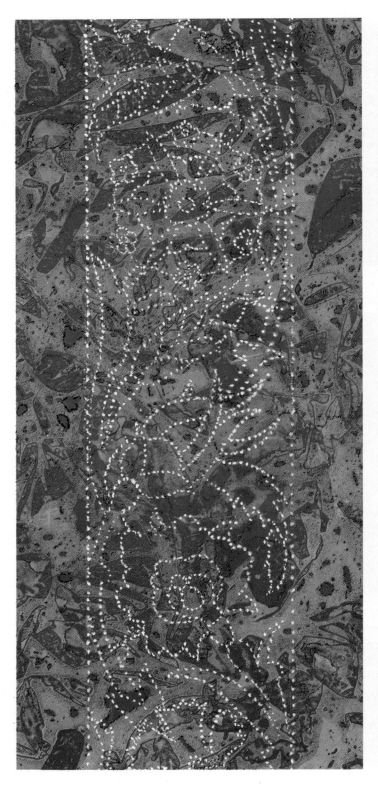

PERSIAN-STYLE FRIEZE ON OXIDIZED METAL

The base coat is satin-finish, oil-based brick-color enamel to which metal leaf has been applied and oxidized with vinegar. Make a stencil (see page 24) and transfer the design to this foundation.

Metal-leaf the stenciled elements of the frieze with aluminum, copper, and gold. Use black acrylic or oil-based enamel for the background of the frieze.

The finished Persian-style frieze on oxidized metal leaf
35 in × 10 in (90 cm × 25 cm)

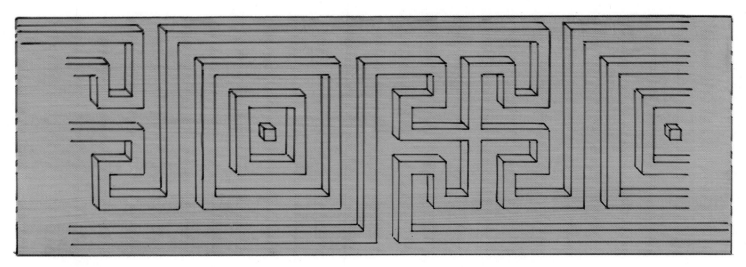

GREEK FRIEZE

Base coat: ochre satin-finish oil-based enamel.

Lay out the frieze on a faux stone background (see chapter 2).

Ultramarine blue + a drop of white + a drop of raw umber.

The shadows: tube oil paint diluted in glaze (raw sienna + raw umber) and
the highlights (white + a drop of raw sienna).

MOLDINGS

Simple geometric motifs with well-placed light and shadow yield relief here.

GREEK FRIEZE
This fret-molding frieze is easy to execute, and very decorative.

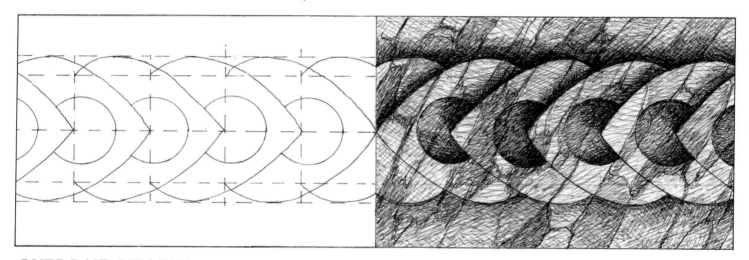

OVERLAID HEARTS
Shadows go in the interior circles and in the lower parts of the heart-shapes.

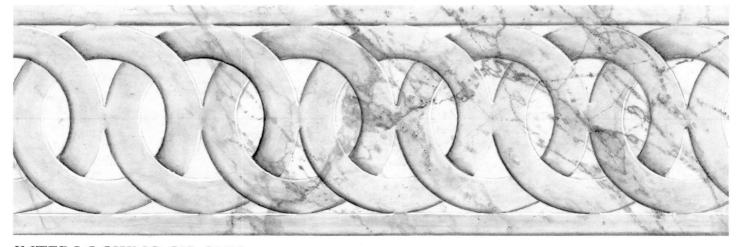

INTERLOCKING CIRCLES
The placement of the shadows gives the appearance of an interlocked chain.

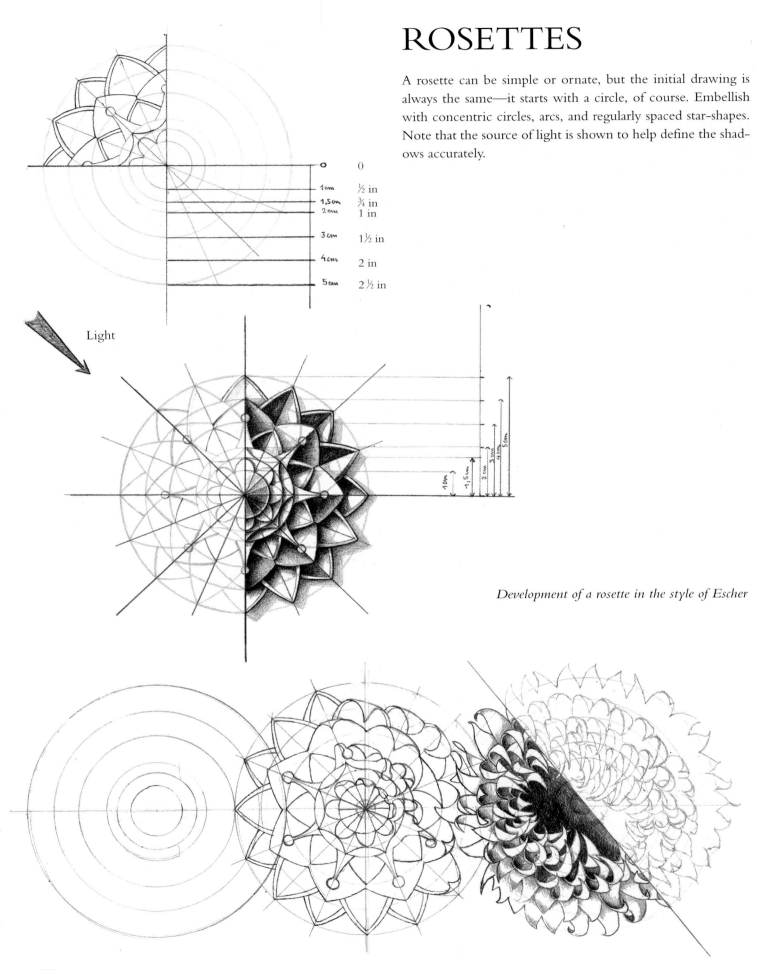

ROSETTES

A rosette can be simple or ornate, but the initial drawing is always the same—it starts with a circle, of course. Embellish with concentric circles, arcs, and regularly spaced star-shapes. Note that the source of light is shown to help define the shadows accurately.

0	0
1cm	½ in
1,5cm	¾ in
2cm	1 in
3cm	1½ in
4cm	2 in
5cm	2½ in

Light

Development of a rosette in the style of Escher

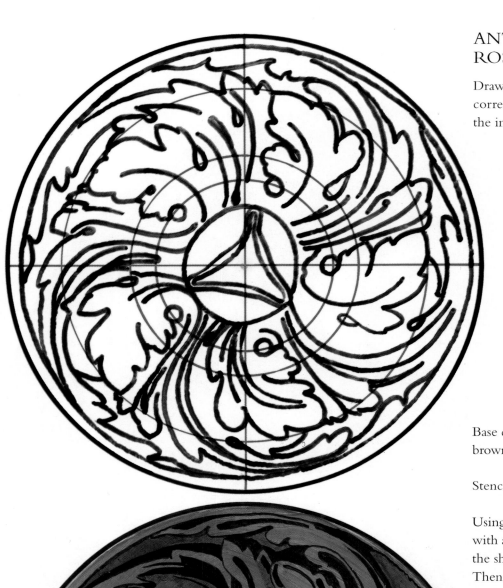

ANTIQUE BRONZE ROSETTE

Draw concentric circles as a guide for the correct placement of the acanthus leaves in the initial layout.

Base coat: basque red (Mars red + Van Dyck brown) acrylic

Stencil the design on the base coat.

Using a synthetic brush, place the shadows with acrylic (emerald green + white). Grade the shadows with the tip of the damp brush. Then make the highlights with lighter green and white in the same way.

Acanthus-leaf rosette in antique bronze
19½ in × 26 in (50 cm × 65 cm)

Overlapping circles and interlaced hearts, with rosette and moldings 19½ in × 26 in (50 cm × 65 cm)

Moldings, egg-and-dart frieze, and facetted shapes on canvas 19½ in × 26 in (50 cm × 65 cm)

256

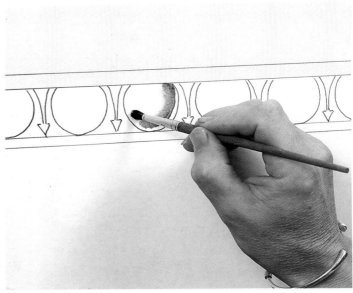

EGG-AND-DART

A monochrome frieze.

Draw the egg-and-dart frieze on tracing paper, and color using a fine-pointed sable brush, with Prussian blue oil paint.

Delicately grade with a mixture of Prussian blue and a drop of black.

Below, the frieze on tracing paper with base coat of liquid acrylic (dilute ultramarine blue), with alcohol spatters.

Add a little more white to the mixture to render highlights.

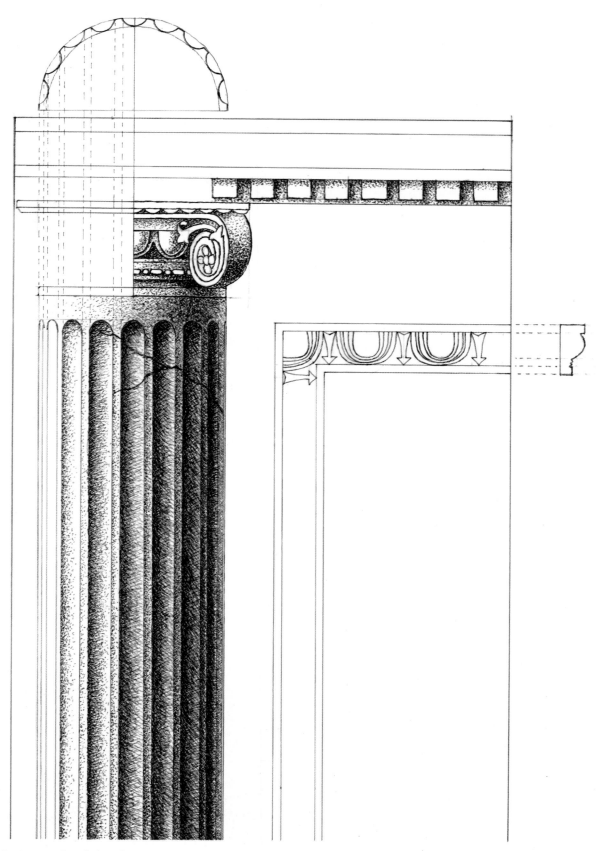

Column with Ionic capital and dentillation, with cyma-and-ovolo band, pearl, olive, flower, and scrolled acanthus-leaf ornamentation

Model for a fluted column and molding in Sarrancolin marble on tracing paper 11½ in × 16½ in (30 cm × 42 cm)

Make the edging with ruler and edging brush, then delicately grade. Use oil paints: a mixture of black, raw umber, and a drop of raw sienna for shadows; white diluted in glaze (for transparency) for highlights.

259

This piece is the base of a wall with the corner of a panel and half a column, in Louis XIV style. It was painted with a brush on a Yellow Sienna marble ground (see page 160) with oil paints (raw sienna + a drop of black) for shading and white diluted in glaze (for transparency) for highlights. The edging, molding, and ornamentation were airbrushed with waterproof liquid acrylic.

Fluted column, molding, and rosette in Yellow Sienna marble
90½ in × 39 in (2.3 m × 1 m)

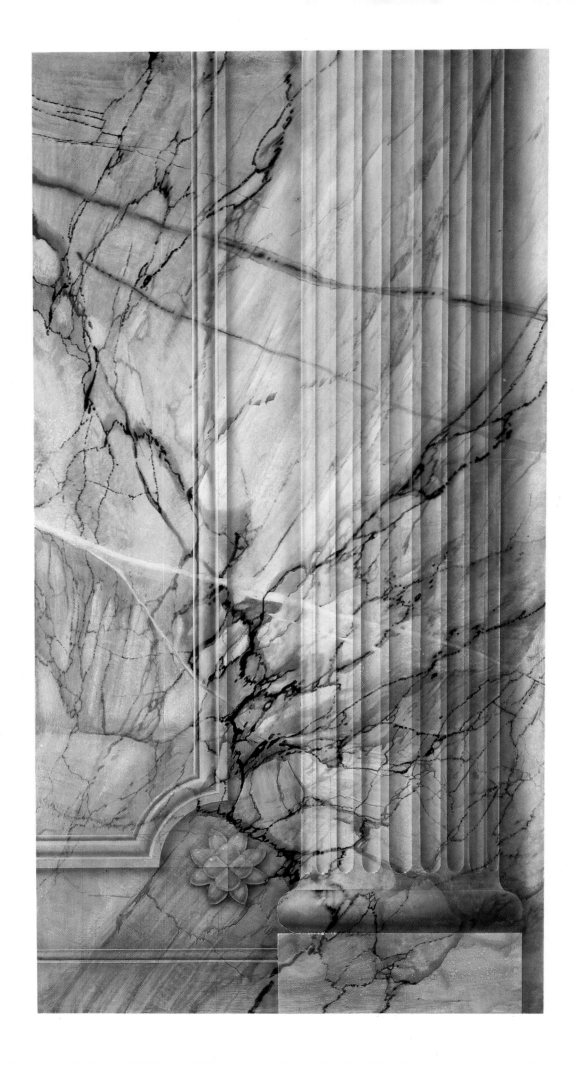

261

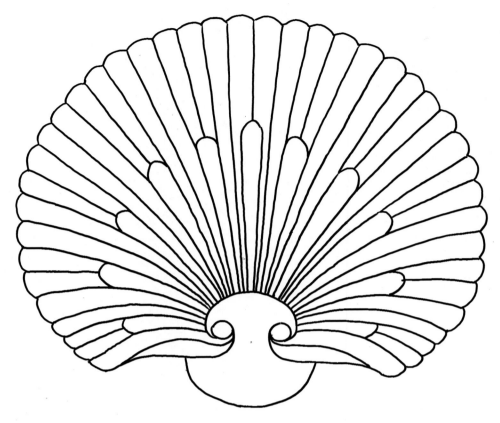

SHELL AND ACANTHUS LEAVES

Shells and acanthus leaves have been used as decorative motifs since antiquity. The exuberant rocaille style of the seventeenth and eighteenth centuries, with its taste for natural forms, exalted these motifs.

Precise layout of a classical shell-and-acanthus-leaf motif

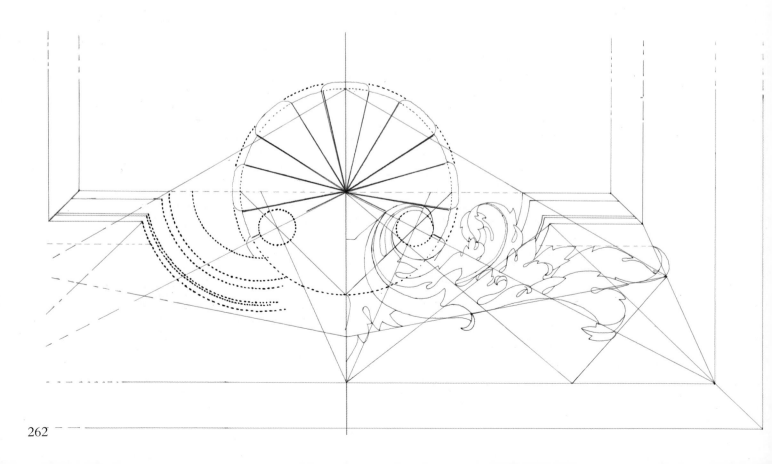

Study for gold leaf on Mediterranean Green marble

Eight varieties of gold leaf applied with twelve-hour gilding size. From left to right, top to bottom:
White
Green
½ Lemon
½ Yellow
A.D. (the initials of the famous French gold worker who created this color)
Versailles
Superieur
Red

Note: This sample shows gold leaf made by Dauvet, a French manufacturer. Dauvet leaf as well as many other brands are available from suppliers of gilding materials.

Below: Rocaille design composed of acanthus leaves and a classical shell

Lay out the whole design on polyester tracing paper and stencil it onto the gold leaf. The shell will be in red gold, the acanthus leaves in Versailles gold.

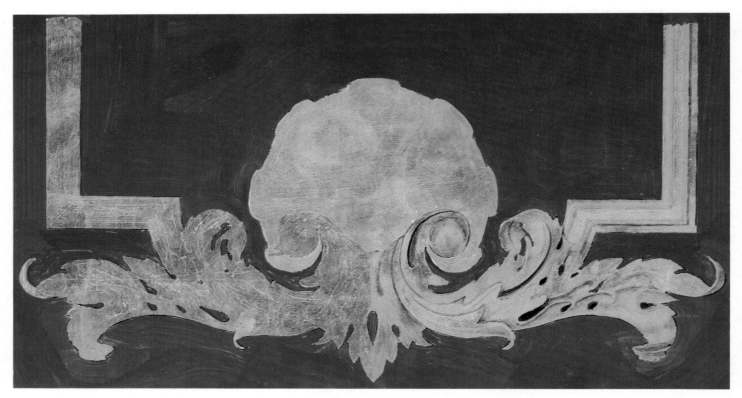

Using a fine sable brush and an oil glaze, add the shadows. For the acanthus leaves use a mixture of Van Dyck brown, burnt umber, and burnt sienna. Delicately grade.

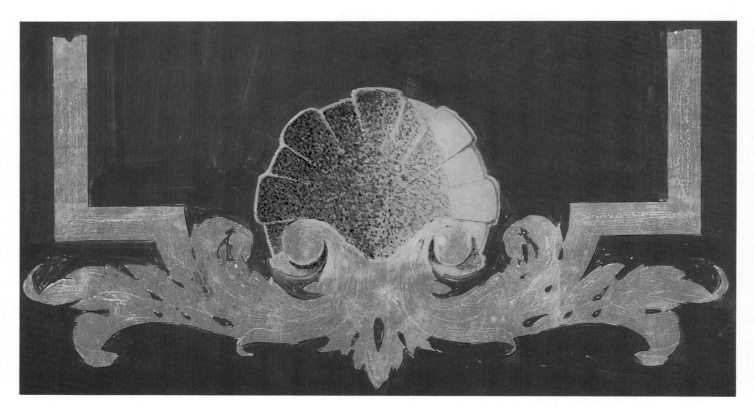

Place the shadows on the shell with burnt sienna and burnt umber, and stipple with the fine sable brush. The unpainted gold forms the highlights.

Apply the gilding size to a marbled foundation. Dust talc over the whole surface to avoid unwanted adhesion of gold scraps; apply gilding size to the area to be gold-leafed. Remove excess leaf with a soft brush; wipe with a soft rag or cotton.

Louis XV–style rocaille, gold on Mediterranean Green
39 in × 19½ in (1m × .50 m)

264

265

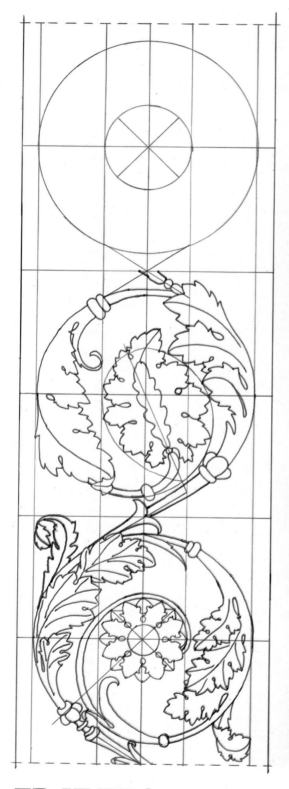

Schematic drawing of coiled acanthus leaves. Using a grid of circles and parallel lines allows a perfectly balanced arrangement

The background colors are waterproof liquid acrylic

FRIEZES

RENAISSANCE FRIEZE

Blue base coat: Prussian blue + a few drops of raw umber + a few drops of white

Yellow base coat: yellow ochre + white + a few drops of orange

Use a fine pointed synthetic brush to make the shadows, then delicately grade, with the tip of the brush slighly dampened. Add highlights with the yellow foundation color mixed with a few more drops of white. The yellow shadows are raw umber + white + yellow ochre. The blue leaves are Prussian blue + a drop of white + a drop of raw umber.

266

Renaissance frieze in ochre monochrome
15½ in × 4 in (40 cm ×
10 cm)

EGYPTIAN FRIEZE

Draw a heron, and repeat it to make a stencil.

Transfer the design onto a red granite foundation by pouncing; then fill in the herons with a base coat of pure white acrylic. Let dry.

Using a synthetic brush with acrylic over the white base, color the herons turquoise (cobalt blue + viridian + white).

With a pointed sable brush, form the shadows with oil (raw umber + black); then delicately grade inward.

Now add the highlights, less emphatic than the shadows, with an oil mixture of white and a drop of raw umber.

Then return to the shadows to sculpt the forms. Outline the herons with ivory black oil paint, using a pointed sable.

The resulting effect is spectacular: the herons seem carved in granite. For the crowning touch, use the pointed sable to place a fine line around the edges of the herons with oils (white + red ochre + yellow ochre) to simulate the reflection of light.

Egyptian frieze: turquoise herons on red granite

PALMETTE FRIEZE

Sketch of a faux-mosaic table, with palmette frieze at bottom, on polyester tracing paper.

The palmette is a palm-leaf-shaped ornament; the lotus flower is also cited as a source of the design. Whether from the palm or the lotus, this stylized form, often fan-shaped, is very widespread in Greek antiquity, where it was used to great effect in friezes. The palmette also works well with more varied forms, such as the acanthus, or flames.

Layout of the mosaic palmette frieze on tracing paper.

Using a square brush, apply acrylic colors on a white base coat: green + raw umber; green + raw umber + white; orange + burnt sienna; orange + burnt sienna + white; ultramarine + white; ultramarine + cobalt blue + white; vivid yellow + a drop of white.

Render the joints in gray with a pointed brush.
Some of the mosaic tesserae are gold leaf on gilding size.

Stipple the whole surface using a natural sponge with a mixture
of white + a drop of black.

272

The finished faux-mosaic table, inspired by the design on a Greek krater
51 in (1.3 m) diameter

Faux mosaic inspired by the mythical Medusa
11½ in (30 cm) diameter

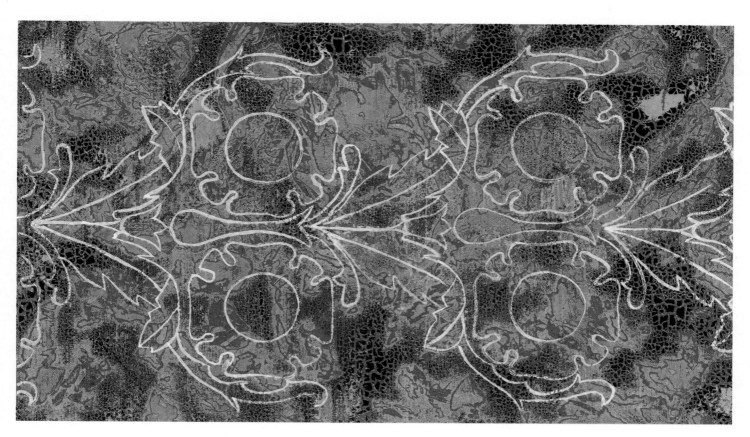

ANTIQUE-STYLE POMPEIIAN FRIEZE

Base coat: oil-based brilliant red
Apply copper leaf over gilding size, and oxidize with vinegar. Protect the oxidation with a coat of varnish. "Age" the work with a mixture of raw umber and phthalocyanine green acrylic. Make a stencil and transfer the frieze design onto this background.

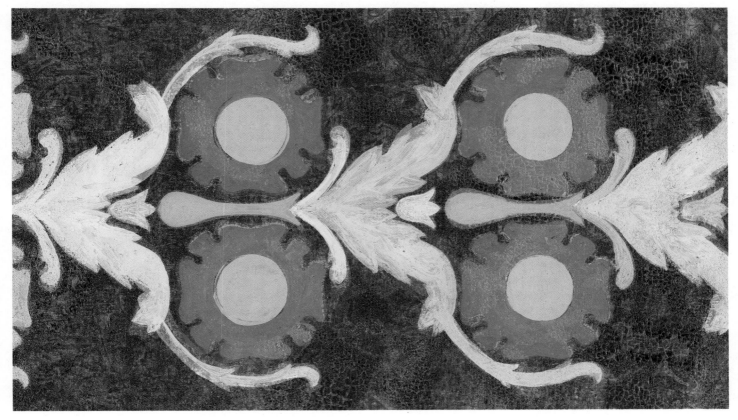

Using a synthetic brush, paint the leaves with a mixture of emerald green and white acrylic, the centers of the flowers with Mars yellow, and the petals with Mars red.

Shadows

Render shadows and highlights with dilute acrylics using a synthetic brush.

Leaves: phthalo green + burnt umber. Petals: burnt umber. Central criss-crosses: red ochre + yellow ochre.

Highlights

Leaves: viridian + a drop of white.
Petals: Mars red + a drop of white.
Centers: chrome yellow + a drop of white.

When dry, sand very lightly with fine sandpaper to give the colors a realistic effect of wear.

Frieze on Pompeiian-style painting, inspired by a work found at Herculaneum

frieze: 39 in × 11½ in (1 m × .3 m); entire fresco: 51 in × 98½ in (1.3 m × 2.5 m)

TAPESTRY WITH ANTIQUE-OAK BORDER

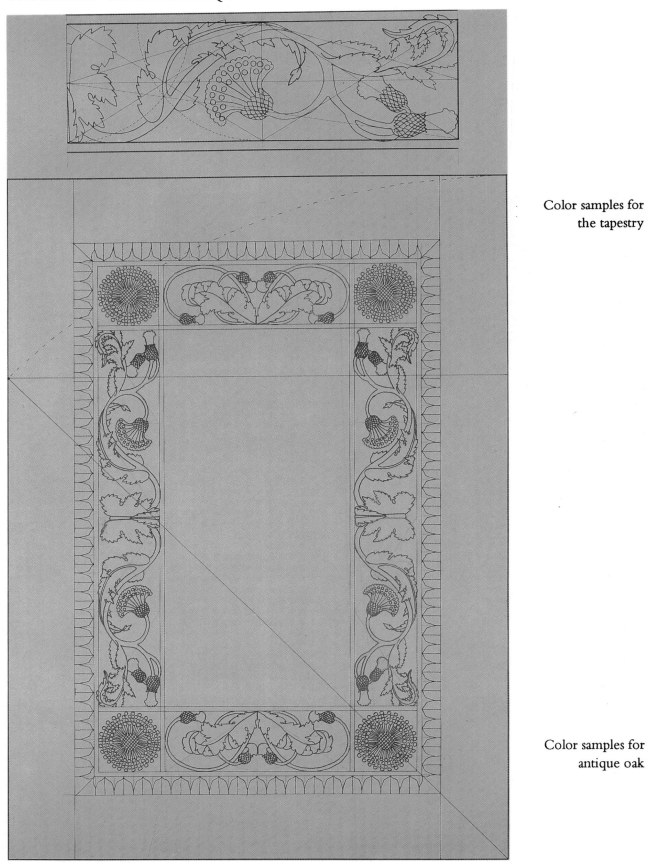

Color samples for
the tapestry

Color samples for
antique oak

Layout of the tapestry, with detail of the frieze, on polyester tracing paper

Tapestry Frieze

Apply a thick base coat of satin-finish oil-based enamel, ochre- or putty-colored depending on the tones of your tapestry, to the support. This example is ochre (raw sienna + white).

After about an hour, comb horizontally with a medium metal comb. Press the comb into the paint firmly, and allow the lines to undulate gently. Let dry.

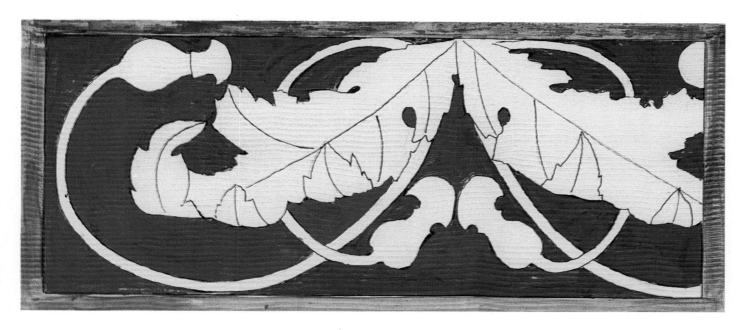

Sketch the design directly on the base coat or stencil it on. Using acrylic paints, toned down a little with a drop of white and a drop of raw umber, block in the colors of the background and border (above) and the floral elements (below).

Apply the colors mainly in the direction of the combed lines. When finished, let dry and apply a coat of matte varnish.

279

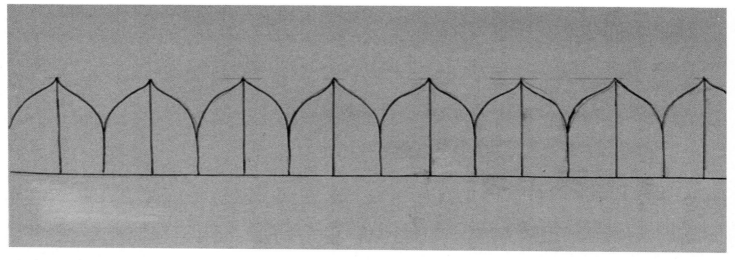

Oak Border

Base coat (old oak): burnt siena + Van Dyck brown + white
Sketch the design or pounce using a tracing-paper stencil.
Grain in oak tone (see chapter 4).

With a pointed sable, add the shadows with an oil mixture of
Van Dyck brown and black. Then grade.

Add highlights the same way, with Van Dyck brown + white.

Corner of the tapestry framed in faux oak

ORNAMENT

MARQUETRY

This is a complex project, requiring the rendering of many different faux materials. The layout on polyester tracing paper shows, on the bottom half, the basic geometric grid; at top, the arrangement of the various inlay designs.

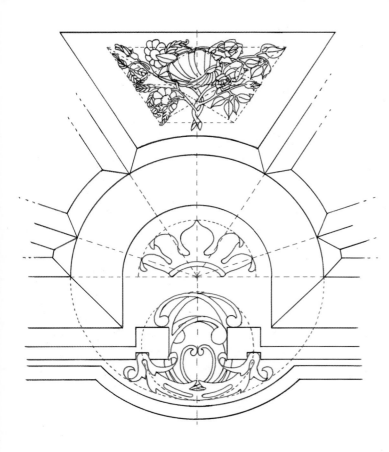

At left, detail of the principal motif; below, left, the base coats of the main sections. The marquetry is as follows:

Wild cherry: chrome yellow deep + a drop of burnt sienna + a drop of white (oil-based satin-finish enamel). Grain as described on page 222.

Base for tortoiseshell inlay: copper leaf on gilding size, protected with varnish. Render as described on page 90.

Walnut: red ochre + yellow ochre + a drop of burnt umber + white (satin-finish oil-based enamel). Grain as described on pages 172–173.

Golden tortoiseshell (page 90): acrylic, reglazed with oil (burnt sienna + burnt umber).

Blue wood inlays: ultramarine blue acrylic.

Add the shiny black borders with high-gloss oil-based black enamel.

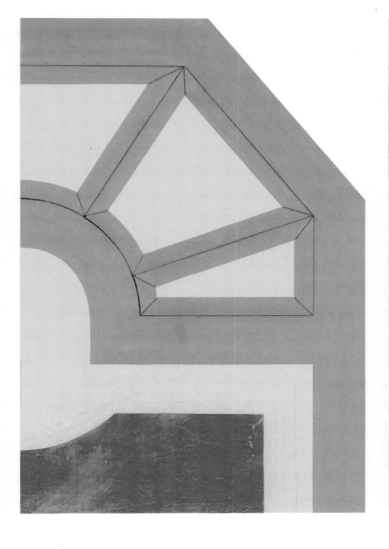

283

Stencil the small inlays; then give them a base coat of white acrylic.

The little figurative inlays are trompe l'œil jade, mother-of-pearl, and lapis lazuli.

Seventeenth-century-style marquetry—wood, tortoiseshell,
ivory, and semi-precious stone

284

285

EMPIRE-STYLE GILDED BRONZE

Stenciled design on tracing paper, to be transferred onto mahogany-grained background.

Sprinkle talc over the surface. Apply gilding size to the design. Place gold leaf on gilding size. Dust and polish to remove sur-plus leaf.

Using a pointed sable brush, with a mixture of oils (burnt sienna + burnt umber), add shadows on the gold. Lightly shade. The bare gold represents the highlights. There is no need to varnish.

FRUIT BOWL

In baskets, bowls, cornucopias, and bunches, fruits have symbolized *joie de vivre* since antiquity. The grapes of Bacchus, a very well-known motif, stand for joy and intoxication. Oranges, figs, apples, and cherries, with their rounded forms, harmoniously fill any composition.

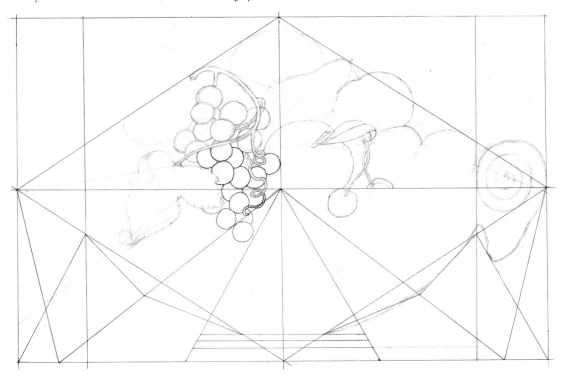

As always, a precise layout is indispensable for a balanced composition and to situate the many forms properly. The drawing should include details and shadows.

Transfer the design onto a foundation of red porphyry (see page 111 for porphyry).

Shadows

Using a pointed sable brush, render the shadows in mono-chrome oil tones (Van Dyck brown + English red + a drop of black), to harmonize with the porphyry. Lightly grade.

Highlights

Repeat as for shadows, with English red and a drop of white.

Eighteenth-century-style porphyry fruit bowl

To achieve this polished and lustrous final finish, rework the piece with a rondin; for a perfect imitation, add a few splinters of light, with pure white. Then varnish with a high-gloss oil-based varnish.

Model for Renaissance polychrome ornament inspired by a tapestry
in very different colors 10 in × 13½ in (25 cm × 35 cm)

RENAISSANCE POLYCHROME

Layout on tracing paper. The acanthus-leaf frame is symmetrical.

The base coat colors are waterproof liquid acrylic.

For the center and the bird: ultramarine blue + white

For the foliage: ochre (burnt siena + raw sienna + raw umber); green (phthalo green + white)

For the fruits: monochrome pink (crimson lake + English red + chrome yellow + white)

Background for the
ornament: gold leaf

Shadows

Shade each part with its base-coat color (except for the white bird).

For the fruits, use a synthetic brush with a mixture of carmine red, English red, and burnt umber acrylic colors. Delicately shade with the lightly moistened tip of the brush.

Highlights

Like the shadows, but use white in place of the burnt umber.

LEAF-MOTIF MOLDING WITH SARRANCOLIN MARBLE

Sketch of the design with ink colors roughed in.

Base coat of the frame: copper leaf over gilding size with a coat of protective varnish

Transfer the design by stenciling.

Stipple the shadows with oil paint, using a pointed sable brush. The leaves and ribbon are shaded with chrome green deep and burnt umber; the molding with burnt umber, burnt sienna, and a drop of chrome yellow. Grade lightly.

Add highlights in the same way: for the leaves and ribbon use chrome yellow and a drop of English green. For the molding: chrome yellow diluted in glaze.

For an impeccable finish, apply several coats of varnish.

Marble the interior panel as described on page 132.

Finished leaf-motif panel
39 in × 59 in (1 m × 1.5 m)

EGYPTIAN BAS RELIEF

Base coat: putty-colored oil-based enamel (raw umber + raw sienna + white)

Shadows and Highlights

Render the shadows using a pointed sable brush with an oil mixture of raw umber, raw sienna, and a drop of burnt sienna. Delicately grade. For the highlights, use a pointed sable with a mixture of oil colors: raw sienna + white.

Trompe l'œil inspired by an Egyptian bas relief
16 ½ in × 23 ½ in (30 cm × 42 cm)

CARTOUCHE

Cartouches are ornaments usually placed at the top and center of a design to frame such elements as a coat of arms, armorial bearings, an emblem, a grotesque face, a plant form, or a simple inscription.

Stencil the design on a blue-gray (Prussian blue + black + white) acrylic base coat.

Render the shadows using a pointed sable brush, with Prussian blue and a drop of raw umber. Lightly stipple to grade.

*Sixteenth- or seventeenth-century-style cartouche,
with "grotesques"
16½ in × 23½ in (30 cm × 42 cm)*

*Sketches on tracing paper
each 4 ¾ in × 12 ½ in (12 cm × 32 cm)*

ART DECO SCREEN

Lay out on polyester tracing paper.

The leaves and framing are wild–cherry grain (see page 222); the background is a thuja–burl checkerboard (see page 224).

The parrots are painted on a background of aluminum leaf on gilding size and detailed with a pointed brush and a mixture of oil colors: ultramarine blue + chrome yellow + white, lightly graded.

Finish the whole screen with satin varnish.

The finished screen
each panel 43 in × 31½ in (1.10 m × .80 m)

Regency-style shell on marble
10 in (25 cm) diameter

After the initial layout was stenciled on a marbled foundation, the shell was airbrushed with acrylic.

Depending on the distance from which a design is to be seen, it is sometimes necessary to exaggerate the illusionistic elements. In this case, the highlights and edge of the shell were intentionally accentuated. Up close, the light line outlining the shell seems overdone, but at the correct distance, it makes the shell appear three-dimensional.

Bay-laurel branch on
Campan marble
35 in × 79 in
(90 cm × 2 m)

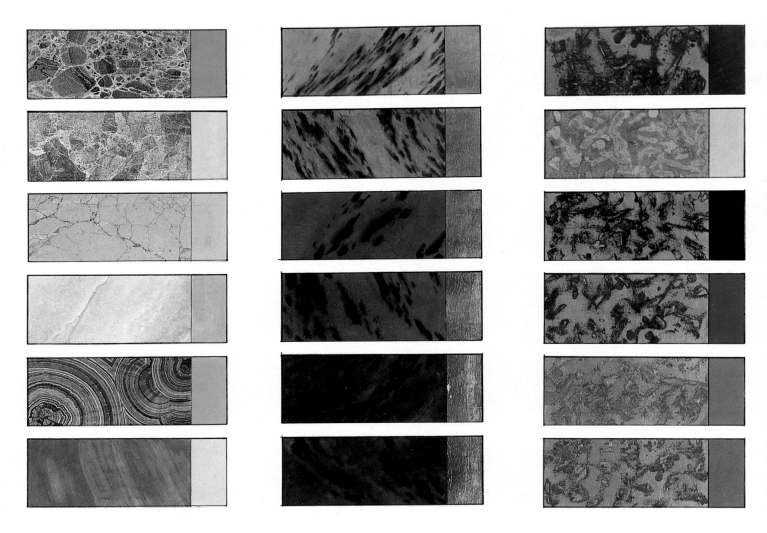

These samples suggest a range of effects you can try.

SOME DECORATIVE FINISHES

Corsican green jasper
Imperador marble
Turquoise
Alabaster
Malachite
Coral

Golden tortoiseshell
Brown tortoiseshell
Red tortoiseshell
Red tortoiseshell
Green tortoiseshell
Blue tortoiseshell

Oxidation, Van Dyck brown base
Oxidation, yellow base
Oxidation, black base
Oxidation, blue base
Oxidation, green base
Oxidation, red base

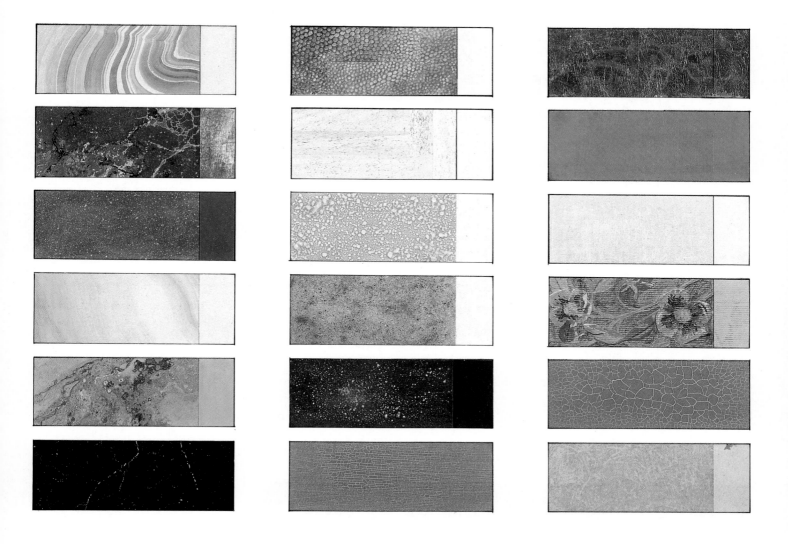

Agate
Lapis lazuli
Porphyry
Chalcedony
Jade
Belgian Black

Galuchat (shagreen)
Ivory
Wiped patina
Rag-rolled patina
Patina with gold powder
Crackled patina

Oxidation, flamed
Aged patina—green base
Aged patina—white base
Imitation tapestry
Crackled paint
Ochre patina

6

DRAPERY

INTRODUCTION

In this chapter we will start with a little history and a look at some great paintings, for there we find inspiration for trompe l'œil drapery. From the most ancient times, artists have enjoyed painting all the wealth of ornament of the applied arts. The paintings reconstruct for us, generally, the lives of princes and the bourgeois, but they also reveal the technical progress of everyday life. Around the main subject of a paint-

ing, therefore, we often see architecture, furniture, precious objects, and textiles, all showing us the best artisanry of the period. The paintings of the celebrated fifteenth-century Flemish painters (such as Van Eyck) offer magnificent examples. The excellent work of Hans Memling reproduced here is one. It combines all the great art of figural painting—and that of trompe l'œil. You may be more or less moved by the

Hans Memling (1433–1494),
The Mystic Marriage of
Saint Catherine *(1475–1479)*
(Hôpital Saint-Jean, Bruges)

characters and content of the painting, but it is impossible to remain unaffected by Memling's rendering of materials—marble, stone, metal, and above all fabric, from the shepherd's simple robe to the velvets, tapestries, and Saint Catherine's brocade.

We cannot help but emerge humbled and impressed by Memling's vision: it takes genius, indeed, to fool the eye with a few brushstrokes that render only the essential.

This painting shows the importance of drapery in the Middle Ages. The very conventionalized representation of cloth allows us readily to distinguish the high dignitary (as much social as spiritual) of the group.

Let us look briefly at textiles in history. Technical and technological progress have become so humdrum that we tend to think that everything is very simple. The computer has so revolutionized and simplified the rendering of things that nothing surprises us, and we become, sometimes, difficult and demanding. But let us go back and imagine the artisans of Egyptian antiquity with their rudimentary methods. We might envy them that everything was theirs to create—including the very fundamentals of their craft and method—in order to master and realize their art.

Weavers appeared very early, capable of composing with surprising deftness the first textiles, first by hand, and then on primitive looms. Over time, machinery and method progressed, and from simple homogeneous weaving, interlacing weft and warp, weavers graduated to artistic fabrics, richly ornamented with various motifs and even precious metals. (If weavers learned to make these precious fabrics, it was not without the help of painters and decorators, who very often made the cartoons, or drawings, underlying the decoration.)

Thus practical everyday cloth, embellished, became an artistic element in its own right. As motifs were transmitted from generation to generation, rules of style developed and themselves evolved. Ancient themes and motifs were reinterpreted in each century. Today we are in the middle of a neoclassical period again. The revival of trompe l'œil has given us a new taste for the ancient, with its frescos, panoramas, columns—and drapery. The creators of antiquity remain our teachers, and we only borrow their inspiration. But to perpetuate their mastery, we must analyze it, copy it, and hand it down.

MOTIFS AND DECORATION

The necessity of clothing was the point of departure for an elementary production of handwoven everyday consumer items, without complex weaving or great artistic aspiration. Ancient Greek pottery shows that women knew how to spin and weave the clothing necessary for the family, as well as curtains, and that they wove on large looms. The simplicity of their work, often with conventional motifs, lacks neither nobility nor distinction, thanks to its balance of proportions.

Production at the time was limited to plain cloth, of wool, linen, or silk; in white or vivid colors, often bordered with brocaded or appliquéd decoration. These were most often composed of simple narrow or wide stripes, embellished with dots, squares, ovals, chevrons, fretwork, palmettes, and the like. Textiles were too fragile to survive across the ages, leaving pottery, mosaics, and frescos (Egyptian, Greek, or Roman) to reveal to us the importance of the frieze-decorated and orna-

Lyre Player
*Fresco from the tomb of
Triclinium, Tarquinia, Italy*

mented cloths that would in fact become the basis of all classical art. These archaeological treasures, belatedly discovered, help the art historian to understand stylistic evolution, as their themes and motifs are found again and again throughout history, and up to the present.

In time came mechanization. To mass-produced plain fabrics would be added more ornate ones, tied to religion. Thus ornament, governed by a particular grammar, assumed a very large place in traditional art.

Regulated by the laws of a well-established society, this often forced ornament nevertheless evolved. Weavers competed in ingenuity, to make more and more elaborate fabrics. The most extraordinary (and most exclusive) were made for dignitaries. The costly fabrics, covered with ornament (with repeated motifs or more elaborate decoration worked in gold thread with precious stones), were used for luxurious garments, draperies, and hangings, and for religious objects.

Works from the Middle Ages underline the importance of religion. If the Flemish artists bore witness to their time, we should not forget that the Italian painters and weavers were the precursors of textile art. At that time, the great cities of Italy waged among themselves an economic and artistic war without mercy. This rivalry contributed to the development of velvets and extremely precious brocades.

To the ancient (then classical) and religious foundations would be added Oriental themes from the precious fabrics and silks brought back from long voyages to the Near and Far East.

Artists mixed these elements to create a particular style. Design, liberated from the traditional geometry, turned toward more

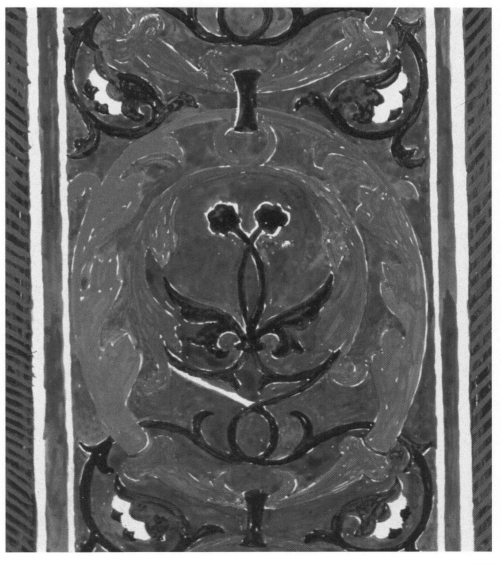

Twelfth-century motif

representational animal and plant forms: deer, rabbits, birds, vine shoots and leaves, and so on.

But Italian workmanship established itself at the pinnacle, provoking a response all across Europe. Commercial competition obliged each state (and notably France) to have one or several textile centers, where methods and decorative motifs were the object of carefully protected study.

At the end of the Middle Ages and the beginning of the Renaissance, motifs became more vigorous. Decorative elements came together to form a well-structured design where a central plant theme is set against a contrasting (in texture as well as in color) foundation—for example, the pomegranate, which lends its name to a whole related set of fruits (pineapple, thistle, etc.).

Too numerous in their own land, the Italian masters emigrated, notably to France and Spain. Their culture was assimilated to that of their adopted homes. Thus Moorish Spanish art and Gothic French art adapted to the tendencies of the Renaissance.

Although appreciative of Italian wealth, as shown in their paintings, the more spare northern countries were content to imitate the luxurious materials in a rougher fashion: common fabrics (linen, wool, hemp) bordered with trimmings, imitation velvet (by flocking), imitation brocade with printed gold and silver.

Through the history of art, we may notice, every ornamental theme follows the same evolution: first simple representation; then the motif expands, almost to excess, in numerous varia-

One of many interpretations of the pomegranate

tions. Thus the vine shoot, for example: the initial design becomes larger, and joins with the opposite shoot to form an oval medallion, in the middle of which is a central motif. The well-arranged repetition of this motif gives these works a strong unity, leading in the sixteenth century to a new generation of textiles, like Genoan velvets, damasks, matching-toned lampas, whether opposing shiny and matte or two contrasting tones in relief. These motifs were reduced for clothing, and enlarged for hangings.

Around 1650 the silk industry in Lyons and Tours developed rapidly, assuring France a high station in European commerce. The wealth and great variety of designs showed the high quality of these French artists: from lace lampas, usually with symmetrical motifs, to the more freely decorated bazaar silkwares.

Subjects became more free, in an exuberance of flowers and fruits mixed with gold and silver thread. Plain foundations also evolved, with shadings for a more impressive effect. And again,

overabundance bordered on excess, some designs growing to more than a yard (meter). The wild luxury of the court and style bound manufacturers to considerable production, with continuous turnover.

Around the middle of the eighteenth century, rural cloths and tapestries rivalled paintings in their great richness of shadings. French ornamental painters spurred foreign competition, and their designs were very often copied. Thus it was decided to stamp each work, and in Lyons the first specialized design school was opened.

Like all styles, the rococo brought new arrangements of motifs: parallel bands decorated with flowered and ribbonned garlands, chinoiserie, playlets depicting achievements (such as balloon flights).

If brocaded textiles maintained a certain superiority, beautifully printed cottons and superb wallpapers (printed, like the calicos

Damask pattern

of the same period) grew popular as well. After the French Revolution, however, Lyons underwent a certain decline. Textiles of great artistic worth are still produced there, but they are of a decidedly more restrained character.

The Napoleonic era was equally restrained, though still no less "imperial" for the restraint. The return of the taste for the "antique" considerably influenced, if only for a short period, the ornamentation of upholstery and feminine clothing.

Around 1820, the Jacquard loom marked an important turn in the evolution of weaving. This technological advance allowed,

in addition to greater ease of placement and realization of large-scale textiles, access to a much larger audience.

By the end of the nineteenth century, with the new technological revolutions adapted to and adopted, the restraints of both the traditional artisanship and the past centuries' figural grammar were unloosed. New tendencies in modern art appeared: small solitary motifs, sharp and precise, very stylized, to form their own unity. This modernist current was not limited to textile art; it influenced the whole of artistic and artisanal thought in general: painting, architecture, furniture. The age of precious silks and brocaded velvets had passed.

Art-nouveau (or moderne) design

DRAPERY IN FINE ART

Let us start by looking at drapery in paintings. Interpretations are as different as they are numerous, on easel or fresco. They come in innumerable styles, each master bringing a personal touch, character, and sensibility to the representation of drapery, whether as subtle accompaniment to another theme or as the main subject of the work.

In trompe l'œil painting, the artist sets out to reproduce as closely as possible that which nature sets forth. (If Van Eyck was the first "known" master of trompe l'œil in oils, the artists of antiquity were the masters of the trompe l'œil fresco). But in fine art and in decorative painting, from primitivism to modernism, the artist's interpretation remains free of such constraint, devoted instead to the taste of the work's future owners.

We cannot study here each and every style and fashion of rendering a given detail. Rather, we list a few outstanding painters whose representations, though different, are of particular interest to students of cloth and drapery. We have grouped these by type of textile: the fine, transparent voiles; the rougher wools; the delicate silks; laces, embroidery, and jewel-encrusted materials; and the heavy velvets and furs.

Voiles

Anonymous Egyptian, Etruscan, and Pompeiian paintings
Botticelli (1445–1510), *Primavera*
François Gérard (1770–1837), *Cupid and Psyche*
Edward Burne-Jones (1833–1898), *Pygmalion and the Statue*
Edgar Dégas (1834–1917), *Dancer with Bouquet*

Botticelli,
Primavera
(1478)
(Uffizi Gallery,
Florence)

Wool and Other Fibers

Stiff Byzantine mosaics from Ravenna:

Empress Theodora and her Court, before 547

The Bayeux Tapestry (1073–1083)

Drapery studies by Leonardo da Vinci (1452–1519)

Caravaggio (1571–1610), *Bacchus*

The Le Nain brothers' *Woman with Five Children,* or *The Snack*
    (1642)

Gauguin (1848–1903), *Tahitian Women*

David Ligare, *The Spoils of War* (painted between 1978 and
    1986)

The brothers Le Nain (Antoine, Louis, Mathieu), detail, Woman with Five Children *or* The Snack, *oil on copper (National Gallery, London)*

Silk

Giotto, Detail,
The Kiss of Judas, *fresco*
(1304–1306)
(Scrovegni Chapel, Padua)

Lace and Embellished Fabric

Marc Gheeraerts (1561–c.1635), *Portrait of Elizabeth I*

El Greco (1541–1614), *Portrait of a Gentleman with Hand on Breast*

Sir Joshua Reynolds (1723–1792), *Suzanna Beckford*

Holman Hunt (1827–1910), *The Awakened Conscience*

Auguste Renoir (1841–1919), *Pink and Blue*

Claude Monet (1840–1926), *Women in the Garden*

Heavy Draperies, Velvets, and Furs

Jean Fouquet (c. 1420–c. 1480), *Guillaume Jouvenal des Ursins*

Jan Van Eyck (c. 1400–1441), *Giovanni Arnolfini and his Bride*

Peter Paul Rubens (1577–1640), *Portrait of Suzanne Fourment*

Jan Vermeer (1632–1675), *Women Playing a Guitar*

Philippe de Champaigne (1602–1674), *Portrait of Richelieu*

Dominique Ingres (1780–1867), *Napoleon in his Coronation Robes*

El Greco,
Portrait of a Gentleman with
Hand on Breast *(1577–1584),*
oil on canvas
(El Prado, Madrid)

After a look at even these few works, we must grant that it is impossible to choose between one or another master, between one or another masterpiece. We can simply note that interpretive style, from the simplest to the nearly photographically perfect, is a function of the particular artist's thoughts, gifts, faith, and era.

Jean Auguste Dominique Ingres, Napoleon in his Coronation Robes *(Musée de l'armée, Paris)*

PREPARATORY STUDIES

In this chapter we consider several types of cloth, looking at different interpretations, techniques, and styles, from simple drapery in the Greek style in an elaborate Pompeiian fresco to silks and velvets of various periods. We start with sketches and layouts, and progress to large-scale details and more ambitious plans. As always, you must think out your design, and prepare with sketches or more detailed models. Whatever the function of the drapery—central subject or accompaniment, drawn or painted—get the folds right. Arrange the fabric, as still life, garment, or hanging, then draw it freehand. Light it well to get a noticeable play of light and shadow, for maximum depth. This way of proceeding is "artistic," but it also requires a quick and expert hand. A simpler method is to photograph the layout, allowing more leisurely freehand drawing, or to draw from an overhead projection.

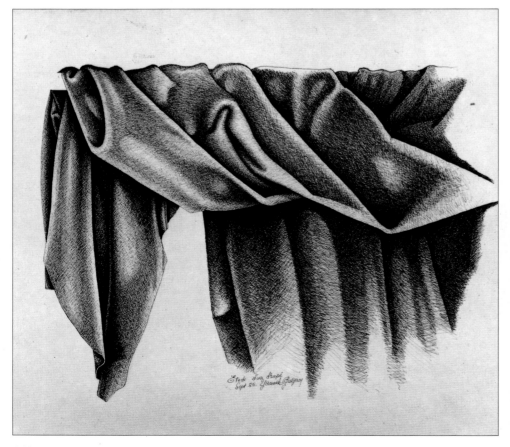

Antique-style drapery study
Pen and ink on drawing paper
27½ in × 23½ in (70 cm × 60 cm)

In this study of heavy fabric, the folds are rounded by the weight of the material. Shadows are exaggerated to better show off highlights (formed by the base tone of the paper).

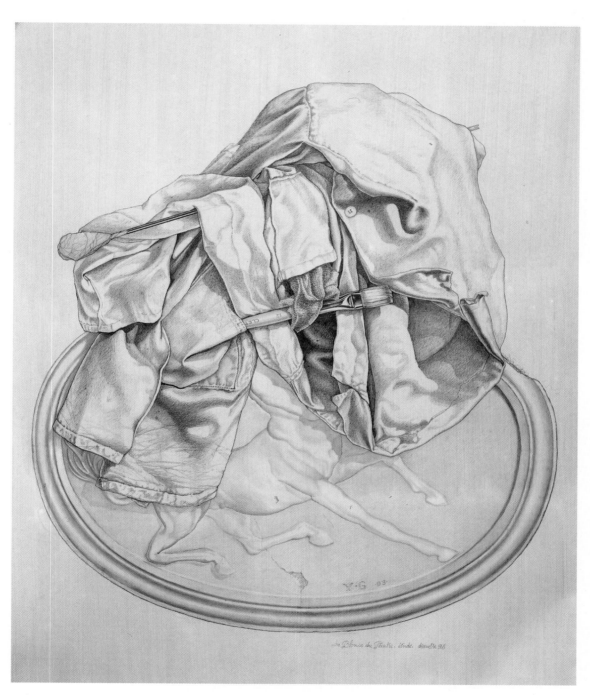

The Painter's Smock
Black pencil on polyester tracing paper
29½ in × 31½ in (75 cm × 80 cm)

Model for The Painter's Smock

Evolution of The Painter's Smock

White-on-white elements are a challenge. The play of shadows must be more intense, differentiated, to capture the oppositions of the material: the mahlstick is finely penciled with varying intensity, while the cotton fabric is worked only in shadow, leaving untouched spaces for the highlights.

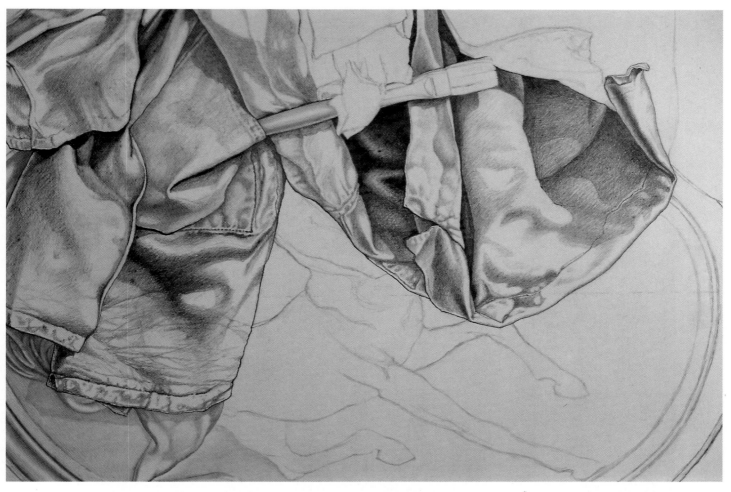

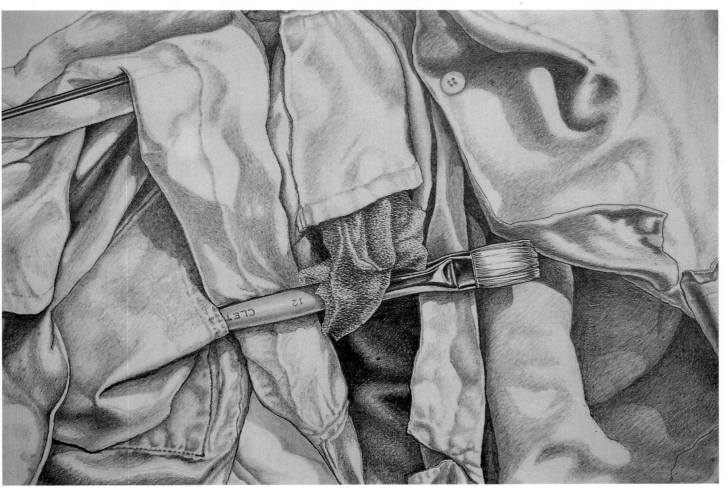

321

Draped Young Woman
Acrylic and oil on tracing paper, with fine-pointed brush
11½ in × 16½ in (30 cm × 42 cm)
Study of drapery for August 23 at Stabies *(see page 326)*

Starched linen
Acrylic on polyester tracing paper
23½ in ×11 in (60 cm × 29 cm)
A study in exaggerated light and shadow

The model for this study was soaked in starch, and placed on a thin rod; when it dried it became rigid, its folds permanent. Changing the lighting allows different studies in light and shadow. When the natural folds of cloth do not give a strong feeling of depth, it may be necessary to exaggerate reality with shadows and highlights, or even by metallizing (as for *Homage to Horus,* page 344), to make the three-dimensional effect apparent from a distance.

Empire-style drapery with Fleur de Pecher marble
Study on tracing paper
11 in × 16½ in (29 cm × 42 cm)

The drapery harmonizes with the marble. The light-colored curtain, bordered with a simple Greek frieze, is set off by a Roman-style festoon and gold satin lining (burnt sienna and raw umber) that gives richness to the fabric and echoes the Yellow Sienna marble accents.

The design was first rendered with light pencil lines to establish placement of the various elements. Then gold leaf was applied on the upper drape. The shadows of the white folds were hatched and stippled using a pen and deep purple acrylic.

LIGHT FABRICS

SHEER VOILES

When the preliminary studies are completed, the elements that remain to be done (depending on the level of decoration) are: the background—opaque or transparent, plain, striped, or with motifs—and the highlights and shadows.

Antiqua
Acrylic on tracing paper
27½ in × 94 in (.70 m × 2.40 m)

Interpretation of a Pompeiian fresco, bordered by two Greek-style friezes. This figure, with its light, sheer drapery, is taken from a fresco

August 23, 79 at Stabies
Acrylic and oils on tracing paper, rendered with fine brush
11½ in × 16½ in (30 cm × 42 cm)

Green voile painted over antique-red clothing, with Van Dyck brown shadows.

The painting is intended to evoke the last hours of the ancient villages of the Bay of Naples, before the eruption of Vesuvius. For millennia before our time, the peoples of the Orient, Asia, and Egypt ornamented the fabric they used to make clothing and decorated interior spaces with fabric.

Voile
Acrylic and metal leaf on tracing paper
43 in × 88½ in (1.12 m × 2.25 m)
Decorated bronze railing, fine voile

Voile

1. On a background composed of a bronze railing on an oxidized base with trompe l'œil stone in a strong ochre (so as to show off the white voile), draw the contours and main folds of the voile in white chalk.

2. Using a synthetic spalter, apply a very dilute acrylic base coat in slightly ochred white (white + yellow ochre + a drop of raw umber), carefully following the outlines of the folds.

3. Once this work dries, make the initial highlights in the folds using the synthetic spalter and the square brush. For the strong highlights use undiluted white acrylic. For the soft highlights use white acrylic diluted with water so as to easily grade into the strong highlights.

4. The rapid drying of acrylic allows you to render the shadows a few minutes after the highlights. Make the first base layer of shadow in soft gray-blue (cobalt blue + a drop of black) lightly diluted with water.

5

6

7

8

5. The development of the folds through shadows and high-lights, in several more or less dilute coats, gives the relief effect without a loss of the transparency necessary to a rendering of voile.

6. All the shadowed and highlighted folds, and the decorative lace.

7. Detail of the lace. In a darker ochre, first tint the background of the part that will be decorated with lace. On this foundation, form the outlines of the lace in pure white acrylic with a synthetic pointed brush. When this drawing dries, retouch some spots with strong highlights, using several overlaid layers of pure white. To give the lace a relief effect, add some shadows in medium gray (black + a drop of cobalt blue) and in gray-black (black diluted with water).

8. The finished voile, with button, tie, and decorated rod, rendered with constant consideration of the direction of the light that creates the cast shadows. The shadows are made with very dilute ochre acrylic.

329

FINE SILKS AND SATINS
PLAIN AND STRIPED

Silk thread is secreted by the silkworm. This delicate and shiny thread yields the strikingly brilliant, fine, smooth precious fabric. Known since antiquity and originally from Asia, silk was very popular throughout the western world. All the European manufacturers (notably the French and the Italians) competed to produce still more beautiful and ornate silks. Since silk was a clear sign of wealth, churches and courtesans alike took to it, seeking to own the most beautiful material, sometimes enhanced with gold threads or precious stones. The variety of motifs contributed still more to the splendor of the fabrics.

Drawing for Empire-style hanging with festoon and cascades
Graphite on tracing paper
16½ in × 35 in (42 cm × 90 cm)

First study with strongly accentuated shadows, in preparation for development in paint

The discovery of Pompeii and Herculaneum in the mid-eighteenth century stimulated neoclassicism, still evident in the Empire style of early nineteenth-century France. This study was inspired by Empire hangings and painted wallpapers. Classical motifs for hangings were used in repetition to beautiful effect for wall decoration. The Château de Saché, where Balzac sojourned, houses some of the best examples.

Rendering for the hanging
Acrylics and oils on tracing paper
15½ in × 35 in (40 cm × 90 cm)

Narrow ultramarine-blue stripes on a
monochrome gray-blue foundation accentuate
the brilliance of the satin. The ornament and
trimmings are gold leaf.

EMPIRE-STYLE HANGING

Acrylic

1, 2

Make the layout of the folds with hard lead pencil, apply a light gray-blue base coat of transparent acrylic inks (white + a drop of ultramarine blue + a drop of black). For this panel, painted on an easel, use a square brush or 1-inch (2.5 cm) spalter. Make irregular strokes to cover the surface and form the first impressions of drapery.

On this first coat, with the pencil markings showing through, using the square brush, apply a dilute transparent layer of stronger blue (ultramarine blue + a drop of white + a drop of raw umber) to block in the shadows. Before it dries, lightly grade, with another square brush, very wet with water.

Make the first soft highlights the same way, in dilute white acrylic very lightly tinted with ultramarine blue.

Do not work with pure paint, but rather with numerous overlays of dilute coats to keep transparency. These dilute layers give a satiny shimmer as the work develops. The method lends a certain "coolness" to colors. It requires fine and quick work because the acrylic inks dry quickly.

A well-made work requires eight to ten layers. (The same work could be done with the traditional oils, but it would take as many days of drying as there were layers of color. If you have the time, that may be an option. Otherwise, take advantage of acrylics, which allow you to complete a very high quality rendering in one day.)

3, 4

Develop some areas of the deepest shadows with several layers of slightly less dilute ultramarine blue acrylic.

Similarly, exaggerate the brightest highlights with slightly less dilute white.

To increase the effect of brilliance, repeat these overlays, letting each coat dry before applying the next, gradually diluting less and less.

1

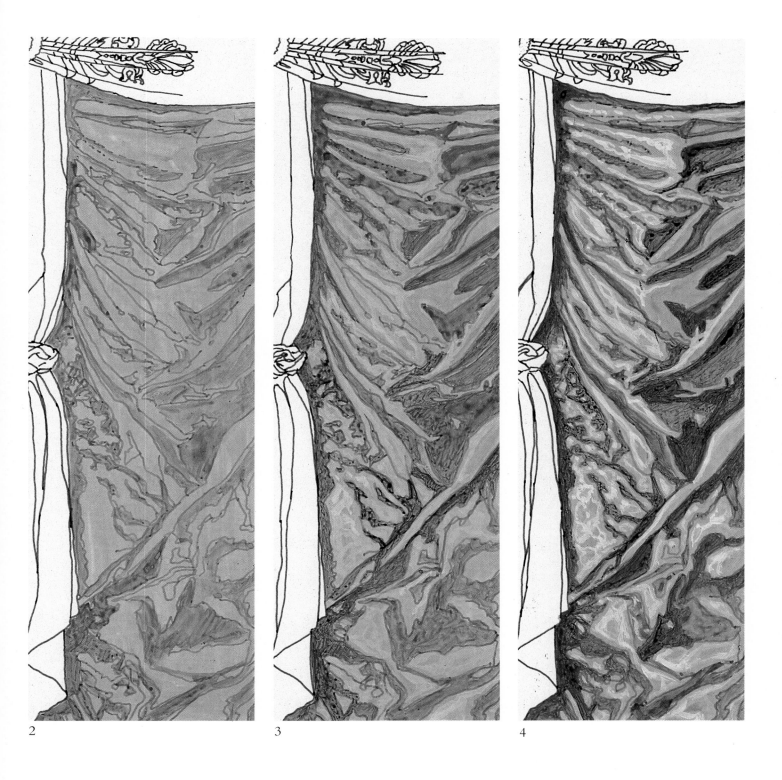

2   3   4

5

6

Oil Glaze

5, 6

The acrylic highlights and shadows give the satin a nice three-dimensional effect, but they look a little severe. You can soften the effect by smoothing with oils. To avoid the yellowing of traditional oil glaze, use turpentine with a drop of white satin enamel.

Apply, very thinly and evenly, the transparent, snowy white glaze over the body of the fabric. This glaze takes quickly, in about half an hour. Before it dries, in the semiwet glaze, using a square brush, reinforce the strongest highlights of the satin with the same white satin enamel, applied a little more thickly (that is, less diluted with turpentine).

Finish this delicate satin with satin varnish (acrylic, to avoid yellowing) applied with a spalter, and smooth.

CASCADE

Acrylic

Draw the outlines of the folds and stripes. Make the light-blue stripes with bluish-gray acrylic (white + ultramarine blue + black), lightly diluted to more easily edge the stripes.

Make the dark blue stripes in the same way (with lightly diluted ultramarine blue acrylic).

Finish with satin acrylic varnish.

Oil Glaze

Make an ultramarine-blue oil glaze. Apply this transparent glaze over the whole surface for a uniform base. In a thick dark blue tone (ultramarine blue + black), make shadows with the square brush, and grade with a *rondin* or the equivalent.

To make striking highlights for this brilliant fabric, use white satin enamel mixed with a very little bit of turpentine.

Finish with a satin acrylic varnish.

For the gilt ornament at the top, use three different colors of gold leaf: green gold, yellow Versailles gold, and red gold (see page 263). The shadows are oil, burnt sienna.

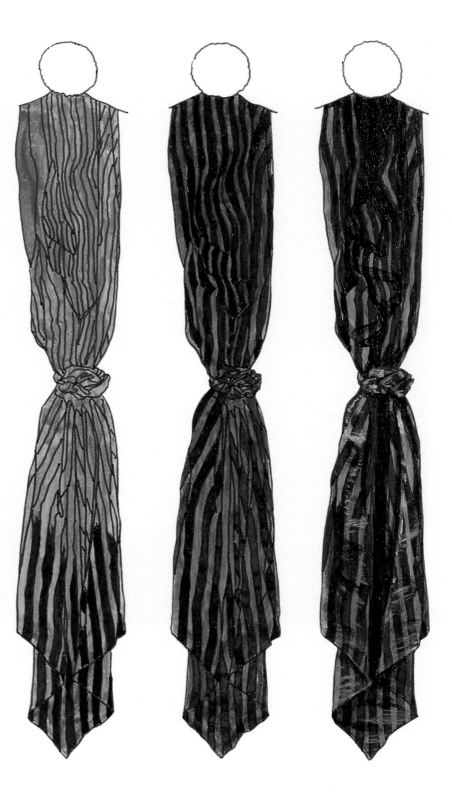

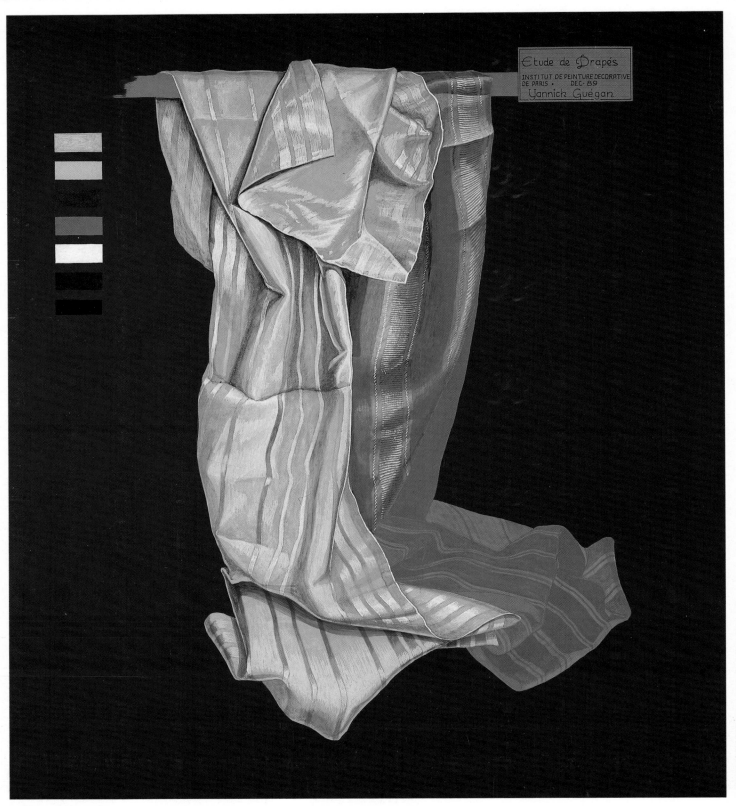

Silk scarves, study
Acrylics on tracing paper
27½ in × 31½ in (70 cm × 80 cm)

The hardest part of this piece is rendering the sheen of the stripes and the monochrome silk fabric. For the yellow scarf, saffron yellow was applied to a white base coat with a fine brush. The yellow was lightened with white and chrome yellow to render the shine; highlights were rendered with white. Shadows were made with burnt sienna and a drop of Van Dyck brown for the darkest parts. The palette is shown in the upper left.

FINE PATTERNED SILKS

Stippling the shadows and highlights intensifies the shine of the fabric. The stylized pineapple motif on the fabric echoes the real fruit, rendered like a still life. The goal was to harmonize the tones of the drapery with the colors of the fruit: the strong yellow monochrome dominates, while the background color contains an echo of the bunch of purple-black grapes.

Still life with pineapples
Acrylic on tracing paper
13½ in × 21 in (35 cm × 53 cm)

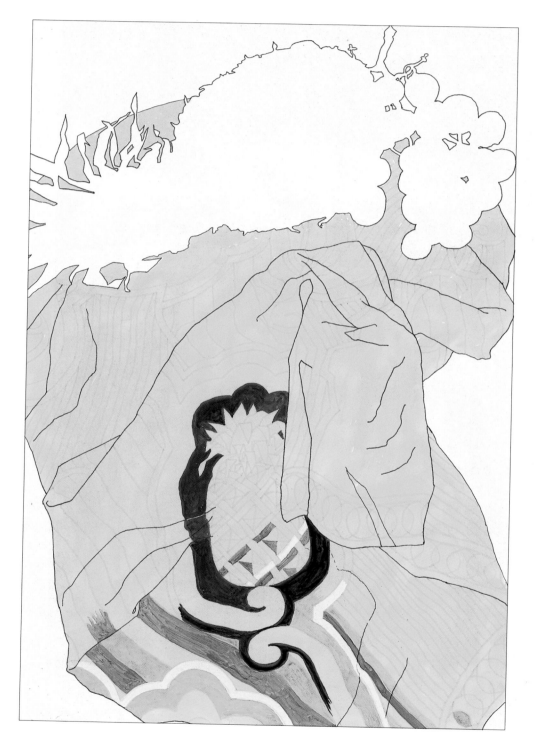

This piece is done with overlaid coats of acrylic alone to get the very silken effect.

Over a lightly pencilled sketch, apply a coat of dilute luminous yellow acrylic (vivid yellow), so that the motif shows through. Five different tones of yellow are required: vivid yellow, antique yellow (with raw sienna), chrome yellow deep, vivid yellow mixed with red ochre and raw umber, and a pale yellow made of vivid yellow and white. Use a pointed brush and acrylics, lightly diluted to edge the stripes and motifs more easily. The outline of the pineapple motif is Van Dyck brown, in harmony with the grapes.

Render the shadows with several overlays of color (raw umber + chrome yellow deep + red ochre), then stipple in the same color to accentuate the effect.

Repeat for the highlights, using white.

Finish with satin acrylic varnish.

HEAVY FABRICS

There are many types of heavy fabric, and the particular character of each influences how you render it. Thick cotton, linen, hemp, and wool are treated differently from velvets, plain or brocaded silks, and tapestries. What varies is the size of the folds. Fine fabric has narrow folds; thick fabric has wider folds that fall more heavily. Thus, highlights and shadows are applied over larger areas for heavy fabrics. Highlights are delicate on draperies, velvets, and tapestries, and much more brilliant on silks.

Study—form draped in heavy cloth
Drawing on tracing paper
11 in × 16½ in (29 cm × 42 cm)

Black acrylic for shadows, set off by highlights in white oil pastel; shaded blue acrylic base worked on the reverse of the paper.

Second study of form draped in heavy cloth
Acrylics and oils on tracing paper
31½ in × 71 in (.80 m × 1.80 m)

An interpretation of three different kinds of fabric: satin velvet, satin, and uncut velvet.

Silk drapery

Wool drapery

Toga
Acrylic on tracing paper
25 in × 59 in (.63 m × 1.50 m)

The key to this rendering is a harmonious placement of the folds, Roman-toga style. The easiest way to get it right is to photograph a draped model, which "freezes" the drapery.

Homage To Horus
Acrylics on tracing paper, marouflaged on wood
(see chapter 7 for the marouflage technique)
59 in × 96½ in (1.50 m × 2.45 m)

An elaborate scene that recalls a procession in homage to the Egyptian god Horus. The drapery is only one element.

Details of the drapery: the folds of the priest's robe and the festooned hanging. An aluminum-leaf foundation produces the shine, which varies with the lighting.

345

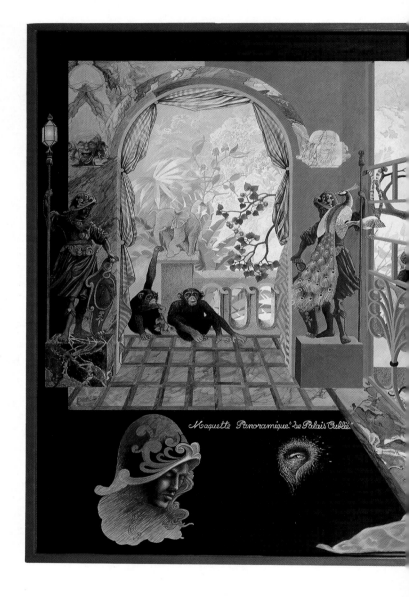

Study for The Forgotten Palace
Acrylic on tracing paper
94 in × 59 in (2.40 m × 1.50 m)

*The two sculpted characters guarding the archway were inspired
by figures in the hall of the Chateau d'Anet in Eure-et-Loir.
This study for a large panorama also includes details: the head,
eye, birds, fountain, and drapery. These elements were worked
in the foreground here and moved to their final position in the
completed work.*

STRIPED FABRICS

The textiles on the preceding pages were striped silks (a light one on the left, a heavy one on the right). Their folds were more supple and rounded than this example. The "glazed" look of this fabric comes from a sharper, more rigid rendering of highlights, compared to softer and less sharply contrasted highlights in unglazed fabric.

The draping of stripes is interesting for the energy of the "broken" folds (note how many of the draped fabrics in these pages are striped). It is important to place stripes harmoniously and realistically. If possible, use real striped cloth as a model.

After drawing the stripes and folds, apply the first base color. When this dries, apply the second, opposing, color. Then proceed as for plain fabric, placing shadows and highlights according to the primary direction of the light: more or less strongly shading the parts in shadow, more or less strongly highlighting the parts in light.

Heavy striped glazed silk
Acrylics and oils on tracing paper
22 in × 45 in (.57 m × 1.15 m)

Light
Grisaille, acrylic on canvas
56 in × 85 in (1.43 m × 2.17 m)

*With heavy striped silk in the foreground, stripes in the same
tone as the foundation, this is a study in monochome.*

HEAVY PATTERNED FABRICS

A fabric with tapestry-style motifs, placed on a balcony to be seen as though from below.

The harmonious drape of a cloth does not come from thin air. When you plan a trompe l'œil fresco like this, with figures and other complex elements, it is much easier to use real models, light the scene as desired, and photograph the composition. Getting it right requires plenty of time.

FLORAL DRAPE

Acrylic

Sketch folds and the floral motif with a very fine indelible felt-tip pen, and apply a base coat of apricot-colored acrylic (yellow ochre + white + a drop of orange) for the flowered fabric, so as to lightly cover the sketch of the flowers.

Using a pointed brush, add the dark blue background of the fabric, with slightly diluted acrylics (Prussian blue + a drop of raw umber), taking care not to encroach on the flower motifs. Painstaking work is necessary for a good end result.

Depending on the hues of the real cloth, or your chosen colors, fill in the motifs with more dilute acrylics, to make their coloration and the edging of the outlines easier.

For a more finished look, apply an oil glaze over an isolating coat of varnish, which will also make it easier to apply the oil glaze.

Study for The Balcony
Acrylics and oils on tracing paper
23½ in × 27½ in (60 cm × 70 cm)

Oil Glaze

In this demonstration, only shadows are applied; this is heavy tapestry-style fabric, with no sheen.

Over acrylic matte varnish, apply a tinted oil glaze (Cassel earth + a drop of black) to lightly dull the whole surface. Soften with a patina brush.

Using a dry rag wrapped around your thumb, wipe highlights in the wet glaze.

Once again, grade the whole to avoid harshness between shadows and highlights.

Then, using a square brush, apply a dark oil tone (black + Cassel earth + a drop of Prussian blue) thickly—almost in a paste—over the shadowed folds.

Grade as before to soften.

Finish with acrylic or oil matte varnish.

SOLID-COLORED DRAPE

Acrylic

Using the square brush with acrylic, apply a coat of dark lilac (white + vivid red + ultramarine blue + a drop of yellow ochre). The application must be even in the vertical direction, following the fall of the fabric. After a few minutes drying time, cover with an isolating coat of satin acrylic varnish.

Oil Glaze

Apply a transparent purple-red oil glaze to the whole (ultramarine blue + crimson lake + a drop of black + a drop of Van Dyck brown). With a paste of this same tint, using the square brush, make the shadows, without highlights, as shown here. The surface has a feltlike, rather than a silky look. Soften with the patina brush or *rondin*.

Shade using a crumpled rag lightly soaked in glaze and "rolled" over the surface, and finish with a coat of varnish.

PLAIN AND PATTERNED BROCADES AND DAMASKS

Brocade is cloth decorated with patterns woven in silk, gold, or silver thread on a base fabric. With technical progress, decorative possibilities have become limitless, increasing the splendor of these fabrics. The Italian velvet relief brocades are a striking example.

Detail from study for The Musician
Acrylics and oils on tracing paper
60 in × 108 in (1.52 × 2.75m)

A character and perspective study for
a panorama with draped brocade.

PLAIN BROCADE

Oil over Oxidation

On a layout of the drapery, apply an antique-red base coat with oil-based satin enamel. Let dry and apply a layer of twelve-hour gilding size, and apply copper foil over the whole area of the cloth, as described in chapter 5.

Burnish the copper, and apply tissue paper soaked in vinegar to oxidize it. Let dry and cover with oil-based satin varnish.

Over the oxidized base, sketch the folds (following a photograph or model, if possible). Render the drapery step by step, breaking it up into sets of folds.

Using a ⅜-inch (1 cm) flat brush, render the shadows with boxcar-green oil (chrome green + burnt umber + Van Dyck brown + black), diluted in glaze. Shade with *rondins* (or the equivalent) in different sizes, depending on the width of the folds you are rendering.

Very delicately highlight with chrome yellow deep to produce the effect of gold. Protect with a shiny varnish to accentuate the effect of the gleaming brocade.

Make the next set of folds in the same way as the first, and so on until the drapery is finished.

PATTERNED BROCADE

This is rendered with overlays of dilute acrylics, using synthetic brushes.

Using a 1-inch (20 mm) synthetic spalter, apply a moss-green base (cinnabar green + yellow ochre + raw umber) with acrylic diluted with 20 percent extra water.

Draw the motifs with a pointed brush and very dilute white acrylic.

Apply a transparent raw umber tint using a synthetic square brush.

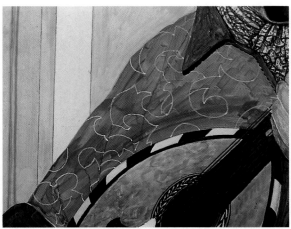

Apply small rounded dots with the pointed brush and undiluted dark green (cinnabar green, raw umber, yellow ochre, black). Be careful not to obscure the foundation.

Begin to lighten the areas that will be in full light, and darken the ones in shadow.

Using a pointed brush, with vivid yellow (chrome yellow number 3 + a drop of white), fill the areas of "gold" motifs with bright dots.

Stipple the motifs in shadow with a darker tone (yellow ochre + cinnabar green + raw umber + a little more black than in the bottom illustration opposite), so as to suggest the dynamic sheen of the fabric.

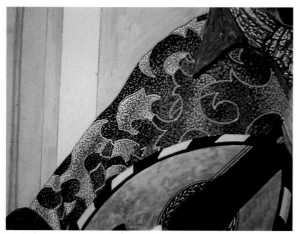

Intensify the very light area by retouching with white; retouch the shadows with a medium tone (yellow ochre + raw umber + a drop of white).

Still Life with Candy Jar and Damask Cloth
Acrylics and oils on tracing paper; the damask fabric was rendered entirely with acrylics
13½ in × 21 in (35 cm × 53 cm)
The damask motif is shown in detail on page 311.

DAMASK

Executing tone-on-tone damask is one of the most subtle feats of trompe l'œil. The difficulty is to render the motif so that it is in the same hue as the base, but is evident through the play of light and shadow. To figure out how to achieve these effects, especially if you are painting damask for the first time, you should work from a directionally lighted real damask model.

Using a pencil or a brush and pale, dilute acrylic, draw the main contours of the piece, and apply the base color in acrylic with a square brush.

Draw the damask motifs very lightly, so that the sketch will not show through the work to follow. The coloration has the qual-ity of a complex grisaille. Grisaille is monochrome decoration generally worked in three tones: the base color, the base color lightened, and the base color darkened.

For damask, these shadings are even more subtle because of the folds—gradually shadows become highlights and highlights, shadows, depending on the lighting and the arrangement of the cloth. To get it right you must maintain the same lighting and look at your model often over the course of rendering, so as to place the colors appropriately.

To imitate the structure of the fabric, apply the tint using a fine pointed brush, with little, tight, irregular hatching.

A thick velvet drape
The Painter's Entrance
Acrylic on wood flush door
35 in × 90½ in (.90 m × 2.30 m)

359

PLAIN VELVETS

Produced by a European technique that appeared around the thirteenth century, velvet is a fabric covered with very closely packed raised pile on one side. The pile is obtained by interlocking two chains of the desired depth. Leaving the knots as is yields uncut velvet pile; shearing them yields cut velvet pile. Since the Renaissance, Italian weavers (notably those of Venice and Genoa) have been renowned for their magnificent "rose velvet" silk velvets in matching tones, reliefs, and polychromes, set off with gold and silver thread.

Base coat: yellow ochre + chrome yellow

1. Lay out the composition in pencil on a yellow base coat, shaded with a quick and uneven application of color, as a first step toward the velvety effect that will develop over succeeding coats.

1

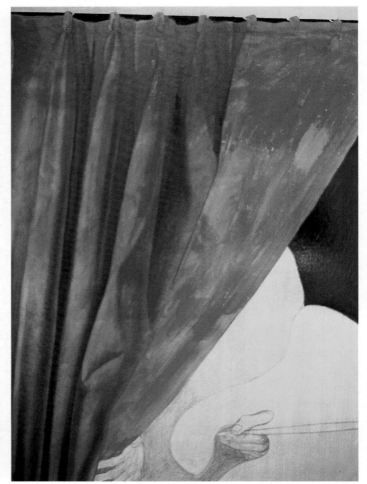

2

3

4

5

2 and 4. Using a spalter, apply the base color of the curtain, again in wide, uneven strokes, using acrylic (vivid red darkened with burnt umber) to increase the velvet effect.

It will be easier to render the shadows if you cover this acrylic base with an isolating coat of oil satin varnish, lightly cut with paint thinner.

The next day, apply (still more or less unevenly), an oil glaze tinted with burnt umber to further darken the base.

Work fold by fold.

Wipe the highest points of the folds and some highlights with a dry rag where they receive full light.

Smooth with a patina brush.

3 and 5. Using a small square brush lightly soaked in oil glaze, make the shadows with oil glaze tinted with burnt umber.

Very delicately smooth, using a *rondin* or the equivalent for narrow parts, a patina brush for wider parts.

6. The next day, add small strokes to make the highlights, using a fine square or pointed brush depending on the size of the area you are working. Do not make the contrasts too strong: light on velvet gives very soft coloration. Use a mixture of yellow ochre and a drop of chrome; and smooth with the *rondin* or the equivalent.

When the trompe l'œil is finished, apply a finish coat of satin oil varnish for protection.

EMPIRE-STYLE HANGINGS

Luxurious velvets play a large role in many styles, among them, notably, the Empire, as much in clothing as in decoration. With their color and texture, velvets gave warmth to the silks and gauzy fabrics that were also much prized at the time.

The ornament and motifs of the example below refer to the wealth and glory of Napoleon: the spear struck with an "N," holding the heavy velvet, the acorn tiebacks holding up the hanging, the laurel crowns on the satin.

The spear and velvet are painted on a metallized foundation, so the materials glow. The tieback is painted on a silver base, to accentuate and contrast the metallic coolness of the green with the warmer ochre and antique red of the drapery. The subtly striped silk in the background is rendered with a very light touch, in yellow monochrome.

Velvet and satin curtains
Acrylics and airbrush on wood, with red drape on copper-leaf base, yellow on normal foundation
236 in × 102 in (6 m × 2.6 m)

Detail of drapery in an Empire-style panorama.

Velvet drape with festoon from the same panorama
67 in × 102 in (1.70 m × 2.60 m)

More satiny than the example on the preceding page, the highlights and shadows of this velvet are in greater contrast. The burnt umber is accentuated with black, and the highlights in the same yellow tone are more hatched and less smoothed.

Hangings served to draft-proof openings and to warm cold moist walls in the great homes of the nobility. The textiles used were very beautiful in the Middle Ages, but starting in the Renaissance they became sumptuous decorative elements for walls, doorways, and beds. In the age of Louis XIV, the monarch's majesty encompassed all these elements. The recreated hangings in the chamber of the Sun King allow us to appreciate today the luxury of those regal cloths. The ones illustrated here are more simple.

Green velvet with striped festoon
Acrylics and oils on tracing paper
60 in × 108 in
(1.52 m × 2.75 m)

STRIPED VELVET

1

Striped velvet with hydrangea
Acrylics and oils on tracing paper
13½ in × 21 in (35 cm × 52 cm)

2

Bruges
Acrylics and oils on tracing paper
21½ in × 36½ in (55cm × 93cm)

The valance is red frisé velvet over a set of striped velvet curtains. In shape and color, this hanging suggests the end of the Renaissance and the beginning of the seventeenth century, a more austere period than the preceding one. Although quite elegant to twentieth-century eyes, the design is somewhat sober and restrained in its colors and materials. A handsome Flemish cityscape shows through the diamond-paned window, characteristic of the region.

Velvet hangings can be more decorative or more stately, depending on the choice of material (silk velvet), weave (reliefs, rose velvet, ribbed velvet), motifs (embroidered velvet, velvet brocaded with gold or silver), or colors (striped velvet). There are many varieties of stripe: single, double, triple, multi-toned, narrow, wide, and so forth. To increase the splendor of the hangings, the tops of the curtains are also ornamented with festoons, all sorts of valances, and cascades, chosen to suit the style of the interior.

365

3

1. Lightly sketch the layout in pencil. Using a synthetic spalter, apply an uneven "dirty putty" acrylic base coat (white + yellow ochre + raw umber + a drop of black + a drop of ultramarine blue) for a preliminary shading. Let dry.

2. Draw the folds and stripes; then color the stripes, again in acrylic with shading (green: dark green + raw umber; red: vivid red + raw umber).

Apply an isolating coat of satin oil varnish (or a varnish that dries more quickly, if time is a consideration) lightly tinted with burnt umber, to "age" the work.

3. After a few hours' drying time, even out the shadows with the fine square brush, in a tinted oil glaze (burnt umber + Van Dyck brown), and grade with a *rondin* or the equivalent. For highlights, use a light application of Naples yellow in oil.

Finish with a very dilute coat of satin oil varnish.

TIEBACKS

Ornamental tiebacks, braids, fringes, tassels, and pompons accentuate the decorative effect of drapery. You must be careful, however, not to overdo it (unless the decoration is for a ceremonial room meant to have the ambience of the chambers of Louis XIV or Marie Antoinette), or you risk losing the harmony of your design.

Gold tasseled tieback with Louis XIII velvet
Acrylics and oils on wood, brush and airbrush
39 in × 67 in (1 m × 1.70 m)

Study of a column with drapery. Note the rounded elements of the striped velvet and tieback, which break the rigid rectilinearity and soften the composition. The color of the cloth echoes the colors of the marble: the red of the Languedoc and the greenish veins of the Yellow Sienna. Gold metal leaf on the tieback gives the materials richness and brilliance. The stripes are worked lightly on the velvet and more strongly on the tiebacks, to accentuate the three-dimensional effect.

368

Tasseled tieback on oxidation
Study on tracing paper, acrylics and oils
15½ in × 23½ in (40 cm × 60 cm)

Study of tasseled tieback
Drawing on tracing paper, acrylics and oils
13½ in × 19½ in (35 cm × 50 cm)

Using a real model if possible, lightly sketch the composition in pencil. Sketch the tassel and cord carefully, working in the fine details of shadows and highlights.

Apply the colors using a fine brush with acrylics. Apply the contrasting base tones one after another. Add the next coats, smoothing the shading.

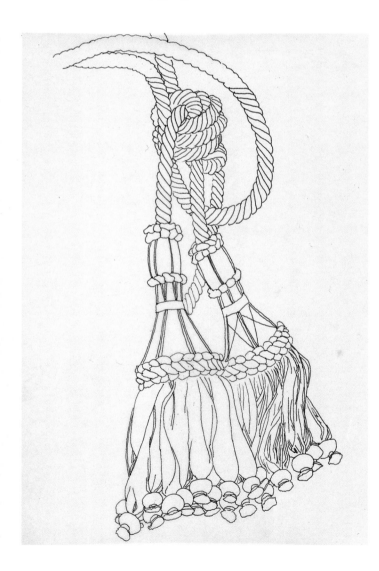

Render the fringes, thread by thread, in the foreground, and then the very finely detailed soft shadows.

Add touches of white acrylic for the highlights.

SCULPTED
DRAPERY

Grisaille
Oils on tracing paper
16½ in × 51 in
(.43 m × 1.30 m)

Study for a sculpture for a
panorama, inspired by a caryatid
from a Parisian building (engraved
by Lombard/Péjin). Softly worked
shadows and highlights on a gray
foundation.

drapé et grisaille. Versailles en Automne.
Institut Supérieur de Peinture décorative de Paris.
Nov. 88. Yannick Guégan.

Study for Versailles in the Fall
Acrylics on tracing paper
11 in × 16½ in
(29 cm × 42 cm)

The foreground element in a
panorama inspired by sculptures on
a garden path at Versailles in
autumn, the draped figure was
rendered in grisaille on an ochre
base coat, stippled with pen and
acrylic. Dark acrylic for shadows,
white acrylic for highlights. The
green cloth was rendered with a
brush, in smoother fashion.

Girl with Hoopoe
Acrylics and oils on wood
43 in × 71 in (1.10 m × 1.80 m)
Shadows and highlights on marbled foundation

7

*F*ORGOTTEN *T*ECHNIQUES

INTRODUCTION

This chapter assembles and describes various decorative techniques that are little practiced in our time, despite their enduring utility and accessibility; taken together, these methods represent a corner of traditional lore threatened by neglect and oblivion. Most of them are based on the old methods of signpainters and decorative painters, but they lend themselves to simple explanation, and thus are still within the range of any skilled and attentive professional or amateur today. No one is excused or excluded from giving these projects a try—the first step toward accomplishing them successfully.

In the execution itself, the difference between the professional and the amateur rests mainly on facility and ease of drawing freehand, painting edges accurately, and making clean, sharp, sure strokes without masking repeatedly.

We hope that in your hands these reliable traditional techniques, which require only simple equipment, will prove as valuable as the more familiar ones covered earlier in this book.

METALLIZATION UNDER GLASS

Use bronze powders (or the nontoxic, environmentally safe new mica powders) for ordinary work, and gold leaf for special projects. (You may want to refer to the sections on bronzing in chapter 2 and the handling of leaf in chapter 5.)

BRONZE POWDERS

Bronze powders come in various colors (pale gold, dark gold, silver, copper, etc.). Apply, mixed with oil glaze,

directly onto glass to paint edgings, small ornaments, and small areas of flat tone. On larger surfaces, visible brush marks tend to spoil the effect. In these cases, good-quality aerosols (and masking) produce a better result. Powders, sealed on the back by succeeding coats of paint, and isolated on the front by the glass, remain stable over time.

The procedure is the same for powders applied to canvas glued to glass (the marouflage technique described later in this chapter), providing you allow a short drying period before gluing.

GILDING

Because of the costly materials involved, gilding on glass is generally practiced by professionals who are experienced in the technique of manipulating and cutting loose gold leaf, skilled with the gilder's knife, and adept at using gilding size in edging, and other applications. Nevertheless, it is worthwhile to be familiar with the techniques, and our simplified description of the operations should allow you to try gilding on glass with metallic leaf if you wish.

There are two possible sheens: matte gold, applied with gilding size, and glossy gold, applied with gelatin size.

MATTE GOLD

Lay out the design on tracing paper.

Place the tracing paper on the back of the cleaned and degreased glass. Remember to reverse the design (the other side of the work will be seen through the glass).

Carefully apply a thin coat of gilding size to the parts to be gilded, edging along the outlines seen through the glass. (The adhesive should have no thickness).

Place the gold leaf on the size, past the boundaries of the design.

Press the leaf with cotton and let dry for a day. Then clean the edges by removing the loose pieces by dusting with a soft brush.

The protective finishing of this delicate work is accomplished on the back, with the succeeding coats of paint that complete the decoration of the glass.

GLOSSY GOLD

Draw the elements to be gilded on tracing paper, and make a stencil (for later use).

Place the reversed tracing paper on the back of the glass, or use it as a stencil.

Prop the glass up so it is on an incline on a table (1), and with a soft brush, moisten the parts to be gilded with a light solution of gelatin size; the excess will roll off the glass.

Gelatin Size

Dissolve a little ordinary gelatin in distilled water, a scant quarter-ounce (3 grams) to one quart (liter). To dissolve it quickly, heat the mixture in a very clean glass in a water bath.

To test the gelatin size: It is too strong if it leaves matte traces when it dries. Add a little bit of water, and test again. It is too weak if the gold leaf comes apart when burnished or dusted; add a little more gelatin, and test again. Kept cool, the mixture lasts for two or three days.

Apply the gold leaf over the moistened parts, going over the boundaries seen through the glass (2). Let dry for a day. Then apply a second layer of gold leaf with the same size. The gold used for this technique is usually 22-karat loose leaf applied with a gilder's knife, but you can also use transfer gold for your first attempts.

When it is dry, burnish the gold using cotton or a piece of velvet with very soft circular motions. The result should be a deep shine, like a gilt mirror.

Place the stencil on this fragile gilding, and transfer the reversed design.

Go over the transferred design, edging precisely, with slightly fluid gloss enamel or tinted varnish, so as to fix the previously applied gold (3).

When the fixative coat is dry, clean around the edges with moist cotton to remove loose pieces of leaf.

Now paint the desired design on the unpainted parts of the glass, as described on page 442. Do not worry about painting over the solidly gilded parts.

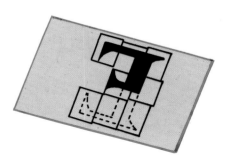

1
Inclined glass, with reversed design stencilled on the back of the glass.

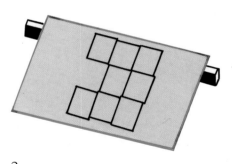

2
Gold leaf applied on glass wetted with gelatin size.

3
Application of the final fixative, following the stencilled outlines on the polished gold.

To save time and to avoid difficult edging, you can start by putting designs on the glass with a stencil cut from frisket film. This allows you to paint and design unmasked areas immediately and to apply gilding size or gelatin size directly to the glass, without the need for edging.

In the same way, a set of precut frisket stencils allows you to mask successively appropriate areas of the glass at appropriate times.

For gilding canvas under glass, see page 392. Areas gilded with leaf and size on canvas will not be affected when they are affixed to glass; the glue has no effect on their brilliance. They do need to be protected with an isolating coat of copal varnish.

FAUX ENGRAVED GLASS

Professionally engraved glass is a durable and high-quality material with many uses in interior design: translucent partitions, doors, mirror decoration, frescos on glass walls, cabinets, tables, and so on. Glass engraving, executed with a fine jet of sand, yields a whole range of effects, from light frosting to deep carving that produces veritable relief. Engraving with hydrofluoric acid is more limited and more dangerous, and is only rarely practiced.

Old-style engravings are characterized by the harmony of gradated frosted tones produced by varying the amount of sanding, carefully designated with masks. Despite a resurgence of interest in such old-style engraving, few craftsmen specialize in this work and the cost of their exquisite pieces is very high. The trompe l'œil painter can imitate sand-frosted glass in two ways:

❖ Adhesive Frosting Films. For several years, signpainters have used "frosted crystal" adhesive films for storefronts, inscriptions, and commercial signs.

  Advantages: Frosting films can be applied to exteriors. They are a reasonable approximation of sand-frosted glass. Although expensive, they are guaranteed to be durable, and they can be applied to the glass without removing it.

  Drawbacks: Cutting frosting films manually or with a machine and applying them without bubbles requires professional skills. Multitoned designs cannot be duplicated in frosting film.

❖ Dabbed Paint. Painted glass engraving produces a lower-quality result, but is less costly.

  Advantages: Painted glass engraving can be done without removing the glass. It accommodates almost any design, including multitoned effects.

  Drawbacks: Painted glass engraving can only be done indoors. It must be cleaned with water or alcohol, and is sensitive to detergents.

Real glass engravings
Frosted frieze and more deeply engraved
border around the edge of a glass table
(France Vitrail International)

Engraved glass from the front window of a restaurant
Early twentieth-century in style and design
(Boulevard Pereire, Paris)

Basic Method for Dabbed Paint

Cut masking film according to the layout, place on the glass, and paint the open spots of the glass with a very liquid white paint.

Immediately dab the paint with a rolled cotton cloth, finely stippling.

Imitation glass engraving with dabbed paint requires no prior experience. You need only work with precision and dexterity.

Layout

For straight lines, bands, and simple rectilinear patterns, use a fine felt-tip pen to draw guide lines on the back of the glass for placement of masking tape. For more complex decorative motifs, draw the design full scale on tracing paper, and transfer it, reversed, to the back of frisket film. If the design is symmetrical or composed of repeated elements, make one stencil for the basic motif and reposition it as needed on the final film. You can also use wrapping paper, as described on page 384.

Frosting

The only paint that will simulate frosting in one application is clear oil glaze (equal parts oil and turpentine, plus a little dryer) added to a small amount of zinc-, silver-, or titanium-oxide white tube oil paint.

Apply this very liquid paint smoothly and evenly over the design (the unmasked areas). Dab evenly over it with a small wad of cotton inside a scrap of cotton cloth.

For a more opaque frosting, more utilitarian than decorative, add about one part white satin alkyd to six of the above glaze.

A Simple Frosting

Make a tracing-paper rendering of half of the design, using a template to make the curves.

Transfer the whole design, repositioning the tracing paper as necessary, to the back of a sheet of frisket film and cut the stencil. Indicate the position of the stencil on the glass.

Place the stencil on the back of the glass, following the guide previously placed on the glass.

Frost, dabbing the fluid paint evenly. Let dry for 24 hours.

Remove the stencil, and carefully clean off smears with a rag wet with alcohol or with a razor blade.

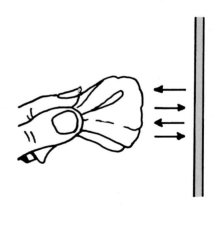

Template

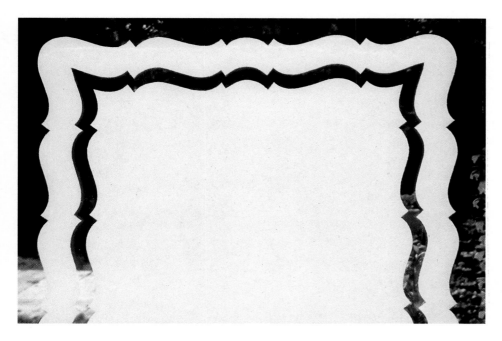

Glass partition

Example of simple frosting (upper part)
For the curves around the perimeter of a piece of glass, you can use separate masks for each side, with mitered cuts at the corners, to make the manipulation of the stencil easier.

Armoire window (detail)
Example of embellished frosting

The first step here is the same as for simple frosting. Follow with an application (using a sable brush) of a second, more opaque white glaze over the first glaze to produce the appearanced of relief carving. Paint over the first frosting without masking or dabbing.

MULTITONED FROSTING

By using successively more opaque glazes, you can simulate many tones of frosted glass in the same piece, as illustrated in the logo opposite (1).

Start with the moderately opaque parts (the central, lighter-toned areas of the logo opposite), by masking around them. Paint and let dry for a day. Next, carefully mask the more translucent parts. The work is done in this order because smudges of more transparent glaze on more opaque glaze show less than the other way around. The third, whitest, glaze can also be used (more sparingly) following the same procedure.

The sequence is as follows:
1. Mask around the middle tones, and frost.
2. Mask around the most translucent tones, and frost again.
3. Mask around the most opaque tones, and frost a last time.

In the classic design opposite (2), only the corners required stencils; the strips along the sides of the glass and the central panel were produced with masking tape, following a layout drawn on the exterior side of the glass. The fine line within the panel was made by removing glaze, while it was still wet, with a straightedge.

Checklist for Faux Glass Engraving

❖ Make sure the glass is clean before you start work. Clean with alcohol and a lint-free rag.

❖ Remember to reverse the tracing paper design, as it will be transferred to the back of the frisket film.

❖ Make sure your stencil is adhering to the glass by pressing the cut edges with a rag and burnishing the edges with a fingernail.

❖ Before each frosting, test the amount of white in the glaze by applying and dabbing on a piece of scrap glass. If the design calls for several tones, keep and compare successive tests.

❖ Dab the paint evenly. Go over each area first horizontally and then vertically with the cloth. Make a last pass with a section of the cloth that is already moist with glaze, to avoid bare spots.

❖ Let dry for three or four days. Then clean unpainted parts and smears with a rag wet with alcohol.

❖ Stabilize frostings with a coat of water-soluble matte acrylic varnish (the only translucent product that you can use on dabbed paint) applied before removing masks.

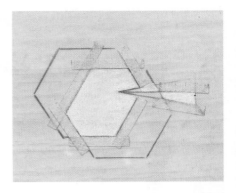

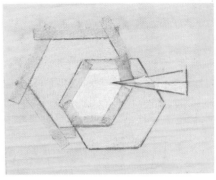

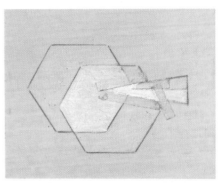

Detail of maskings

1

Multitoned logo

The initial tracing-paper design is used to cut masks, to position masks with reference to the design as seen through the glass, and, if necessary, to reproduce the same design on adjacent windows.

2

Classic design on glass door

The narow edging inside the panel was made by removing wet glaze with a ruler.

An example of faux glass engraving with masks is shown opposite. The size of this project necessitates the use of kraft wrapping paper for masking.

Basic Method

Unroll the paper on a table, and draw the design. Cut out, and mark the position of the layout on the back side of the glass. Cover the cutouts with dilute starch paste and position them on the side of the glass to be painted, following the guide marks on the opposite side of the glass. Use a wet sponge to smooth out folds and wrinkles, and tidy around the edges of the cutouts. Paint, dab, and let dry for a day. Then sponge the paper masks with warm water, and carefully peel off the scraps of soft paper.

FROSTED VERANDA WINDOWS

With a felt pen, trace the main lines of the layout, actual size, on the back (exterior) side of the glass: vertical uprights, semi-circular vaults, small horizontal and diagonal crosspieces.

On a strip of wrapping paper cut to the appropriate length, using a ruler and compasses, retrace the design from the glass.

Cut out the geometric elements to be masked, coat the backs with light and very liquid adhesive (water and a very little bit of powdered starch paste), and place them on the glass.

Repeat for the different plant silhouettes, after drawing them directly onto the stencil paper. Try to use all the available space. Affix to glass (1).

Frost by applying and dabbing paint over all the unmasked areas (2). Let dry.

Moisten the masking with a sponge and remove (3).

Frost the narrow interior remaining bands with an edging brush, and execute the hairline edging by removing paint with the shaft of a brush, using a ruler and a semicircular template for rounded parts.

Follow the directions for multitoned frosting (page 382) to render the interior sections of the plants. You will need several tones for the shadows (4).

1

2

3

4

*Frosted veranda
windows
View of finished
painting from the
exterior*

MAROUFLAGE

Marouflage is the technique of gluing a previously painted and decorated canvas onto a prepared surface. It is a useful procedure when you want to render elaborate and involved decoration on a movable canvas, placed temporarily on a wall, easel, or the floor, rather than working directly on a ceiling, casement, wainscotting panel, or column. You can enjoy the comfortable working conditions of your well-lit, well-equipped studio and the security of a canvas support that will not crack (not necessarily the case with ceilings with wooden joists, plastered surfaces, and jointed wood panels).

Canvas

The main types of canvas are:

❖ Cotton canvas. White and finely textured. Cotton canvas comes in various widths, up to 120 inches (230 cm).

❖ Linen canvas. Brown or beige in color, linen is stronger, finer, and considerably more expensive than cotton. It comes in several widths, up to 96 inches (400 cm).

❖ Synthetic, polyester canvas. With a fine textured surface, this material is best suited to marouflage because it is dimensionally stable. It comes in widths up to 144 inches (300 cm).

Commercially, these canvasses are available in different forms, from rolls of raw canvas to rather expensive pre-cut and stretched quadruple-primed, sanded, very smooth canvases. You may buy commercially prepared canvas or prepare it yourself. Depending on the fiber and weave, the degree of permanence you desire, the distance from which it will be seen, and other factors, choose from the following systems and supplies:

❖ Simple sizing with rabbit-skin glue and, depending on the ground desired, a white priming coat (rabbit-skin glue, zinc white), applied with a brush

❖ Acrylic or oil gesso primer, and, if desired, a coat of all-purpose acrylic gesso

❖ Oil prepriming and a coat of zinc white oil paint applied with a lath or brush

❖ Colored primer, alkyds, acrylic gesso, and so on

Note that some primers are porous and that oil-based primers are not suitable for acrylic designs.

Traditional Marouflage

The earliest marouflage was accomplished with the thick and viscous stagnant oil paint left at the bottom of paint containers, called *maroufle*. Canvasses were also affixed with glue made with rye, but this was more sensitive to water.

From around end of the nineteenth century, a paste made with white lead, boiled linseed oil, and whiting became the most common medium for marouflage. Ground zinc oxide in oil later replaced the highly toxic lead oxide.

Modern Marouflage

Today, for faithful restoration, we use zinc white ground in a bowl, softened with boiled linseed oil, a little turpentine, and dryer, and thickened with whiting to the consistency of a stiff cream. The technique requires some skill to apply the coating to the back of the canvas and to manipulate the canvas for correct placement.

When restoration of original work is not the object, white vinyl glues are the simplest and most frequently used adhesives. Vinyl glues, used for installing fabric wall coverings, are applied on the primed support with rollers, easily cleaned with hot water.

For special cases, consult the technical support staff of manufacturers of adhesives or your art-materials supplier. For example, for a temporary adhesive that can be easily removed there are special "peelable" glues. These require the prior application of a special primer.

Battle of Flowers at Nice
Oil on canvas, finished and marouflaged on rotunda ceiling. Extra canvas was cut off around the circumference of the gilded plaster molding.
(Henri Gervex, Salle Dorée, Le Train bleu, *buffet at Gare de Lyon, Paris*)

387

Basic Method

The support to be marouflaged must be nonporous and unabsorbent, so as not to take up even a little glue.

Ream out and fill cracks; cover rings, ink and rust stains, and any suspicious marks; fill irregularities, and sand to obtain a sleek, even surface.

If necessary, apply an alkyd primer to plaster, new wood, old water-based paints, or water-based caulking.

For marouflage with zinc oxide, apply a base coat of white satin-finish alkyd paint or prime the whole suface with the traditional oil and zinc-white coating.

For marouflage with vinyl glue, apply a white matte-finish (flat) alkyd or acrylic base coat.

Traditional Zinc-White Marouflage on a Vertical Panel

Draw a vertical axis in the center of the panel and on the back of the canvas, keeping everything square.

Roll the canvas (from the bottom, painted side in). With the roll laid flat on a worktable, thickly apply the adhesive to the back of the upper part with a brush or painting knife.

Position the top end of the canvas facing the panel, aligning the two vertical-axis lines. Start the marouflage at the center, going out toward the top and sides (1), getting rid of air bubbles and extra coating with a putty knife or marouflage knife covered with a soft rag or a chamois cloth dampened with water.

Tack the top and sides of the canvas in position temporarily or permanently, depending on the weight of the canvas. If it is very heavy, roll it on a rod, set it on spikes in two wooden slats as shown (2) while you marouflage.

Apply adhesive to the next section of the back of the canvas as necessary, depending on its length, and continue the marouflage, always working toward the bottom and sides of the canvas.

When the canvas is in place, check the adhesion of the sides, and remove air bubbles.

Cut off excess canvas around the edges of the panel, using a metal ruler and a craft knife. Deposit dirty scraps of zinc-white-covered canvas in a waste container designated for that purpose.

Carefully clean adhesive smears from edges and adjacent walls or moldings with a turpentine-soaked rag.

Note that the firmness of zinc-white marouflage can be increased by adding about six percent by volume of alkyd gloss varnish or boiled linseed oil. For the marouflage of delicate canvases, you can interpose a piece of sturdy paper between the support and the canvas to avoid direct contact. Check the fit of the guidelines on the canvas and the support before starting to glue.

Marouflage on a Wall

When the width of the decorated canvas is greater than its height, it may be unrolled horizontally. In this case draw two axes, horizontal and vertical, on the support, and the same axes on the back of the canvas (3).

Roll the canvas from each end toward the middle, so you have two cylinders that meet at the vertical axis. Unroll the canvas (and apply adhesive) one side at a time starting from the center. The marouflage starts at the vertical axis and moves out, first one side and then the other, ensuring that the horizontal axis lines coincide.

Marouflage on a Ceiling

This operation requires more resources, in terms of people, scaffolding, support boards, and jacks (4).

Draw two axes, as before, and position as for a wall, starting at the center. Depending on the weight of the canvas, you may want to use two rods for rolling the canvas to help you manipulate and keep the rolls straight (see 2 and 4).

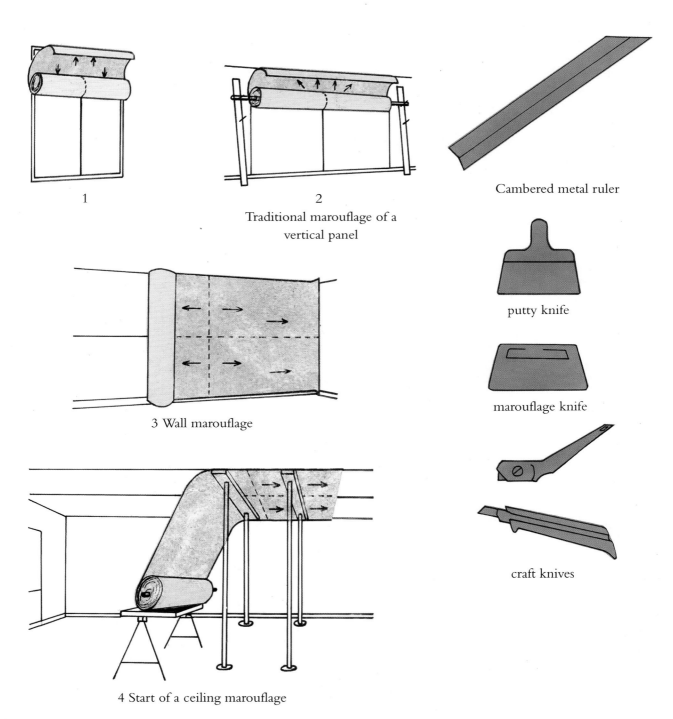

1

2
Traditional marouflage of a
vertical panel

Cambered metal ruler

putty knife

marouflage knife

craft knives

3 Wall marouflage

4 Start of a ceiling marouflage

389

Marouflage with Vinyl Adhesive
on a Door Panel

First apply adhesive around the borders with a lath and then coat the rest of the surface with a roller. Let the adhesive set for five to ten minutes (follow the manufacturer's directions).

When the painted design is complete and the protective finish coat is dry (1, opposite), draw the vertical axes for alignment on the panel and the back of the canvas.

Apply adhesive to the panel and let it thicken.

Roll up the canvas and position the top, lining up the two axes.

Unroll and marouflage, working from the middle to the sides.

Using a marouflage knife, press the edges of the canvas to fit it to the edges of the molding; then cut with scissors or knife to clean up curves and corners (2).

Trim the canvas, and clean adhesive smears around the panel with a sponge (3).

Marouflage of a painted canvas on a door panel

1
The incomplete canvas on an easel (with guidelines just visible top and bottom)

2
The canvas being marouflaged, after surplus fabric has been removed

3
The canvas completely marouflaged and trimmed

PAINTED CANVAS UNDER GLASS

This old technique consists of affixing a painted canvas under thick glass with a special glue; the transparent glass gives the painting stability and a brilliant shine. The evolution of the technique was related to that of wooden storefronts: very sensitive to bad weather, they increasingly became composed of glass. Between 1850 and 1930, signpainters commissioned to make signs, emblems, and ornaments employed the technique of canvas under glass for their best clients.

In Paris and elsewhere you can still see richly decorated old window displays on the front and sides (and sometimes in the interior, on ceilings) of buildings, from the old painting studios.

Other than for restoration of old storefronts, the technique can be used today for glass-topped tables, for decorative panels, and for personal or commercial signs or plaques (logos, initials, coats of arms, and so on).

You will need a sealed and primed cotton canvas, with a tight, smooth weave. Painting canvas is recommended. The dimensions should correspond to the glass under which it will be placed, plus about 1½ inches (4 cm) extra all around. (The canvas used for display windows at the height of the method's popularity was "moleskin," a cotton canvas prepared by soaking in gesso and natural resins; this is no longer available.)

Buy the glass cut to the exact dimensions you need. Glass from ¼ inch to ⅜ inch (6 to 8 cm) thick is typical. When you order, you must specify the kind of edge you want: simple cut edges if the sides of the panel will not be visible, or beveled edges of various kinds, if the sides will be visible. If the edges are not polished by your supplier, tape them while you are working with the glass to prevent injury.

If the glass is to be attached to a metal base with screws or studs (to make a table, for example) consider the placement of the holes in relation to the design.

For display windows, the glass is inserted in the hollow wood frame of the door, independent of the door structure. Once positioned and wedged in, it is held in place with a molding. Order glass that is slightly smaller than the opening, therefore, to leave sufficient play for installation.

Detail of display windows
The subject matter of the paintings under the glass relates to the business

Painted canvas
The painting, to be placed under glass, includes a
faux-relief frame with gold leaf highlights
(Atelier Christian Lachassagne)

Basic Method

Cut the canvas and prime on both sides with a heavy coat of alkyd or zinc white. Prime one side first, let dry, and do the other the next day. Use a plastic dropcloth beneath to keep the canvas from sticking to the work surface.

Give the side to be decorated an initial coat of satin-finish alkyd paint (one or several medium colors, depending on the colors of the planned design).

The last coat consists of the painting itself (in oils or alkyds and glazes). You can use tube or waterproof liquid acrylics, or water-based glaze, but these then need to be protected by a finish coat of oil glaze.

To prepare the special adhesive, wrap rock sugar crystals in a cloth and pound with a mallet. Pour the rough powder into a gum arabic solution in the proportions of 2 to 1 by volume. (Gum arabic is available premixed, in bottles, or in powdered form for making your own solution). Mix in a clean jar, and stir several times a day to help dissolve the sugar without lumps.

When you are ready to start, position the decorated canvas face up´ on the glass and, once you have it centered exactly, trim the surplus cloth from the sides only. Mark the two other trimming cuts on the back with a pencil. Remove the canvas.

Carefully clean both sides of the glass, ensuring that the side on which you will marouflage is spotless. Lightly degrease the painted canvas (with dilute detergent), so the adhesive can bond securely.

Apply the adhesive liberally on the painting and on the glass, with a flat bristle varnish brush.

With the glass lying flat, position the canvas painting side down and adjust it, aligning the side edges. Marouflage with a marouflage knife; remove excess glue, working from the center to the edges. Have a sponge and hot water handy to clean smears and the edges. It is helpful to place small weighted boards around the sides to ensure good contact with the adhesive.

Two or three hours later, check the marouflage and remove any wrinkles, using the marouflage knife. Cut off the extra canvas top and bottom.

Let dry and protect the back of the canvas with one or two finish coats of satin or gloss alkyd paint. A dark color is customary.

You can protect display windows or other exterior projects that are exposed to humidity by gluing aluminum foil (historically, tin on gilding size) to the back, folding over at the edges of the glass. The finish coats, however, are still required.

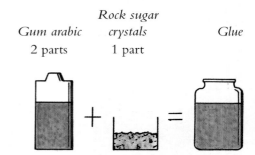

Gum arabic
2 parts

Rock sugar
crystals
1 part

Glue

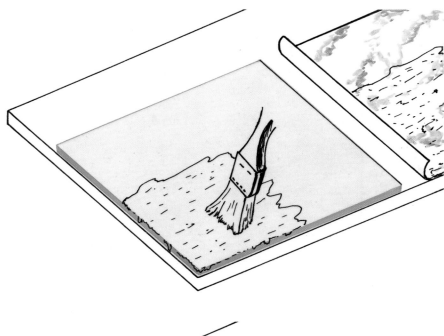

Apply the adhesive to the glass and the painted side of the canvas. Coat the painting thoroughly, working the adhesive into any relief

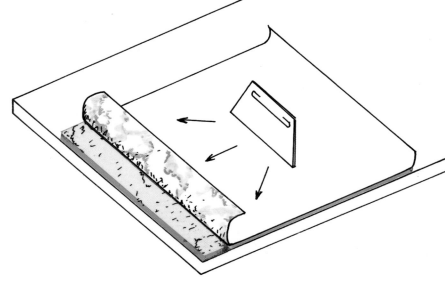

Marouflage, drawing the knife forcefully over the canvas several times to leave only the minimum amount of glue

Trim the edges and clean with a wrung out sponge to avoid dampening the edge of the canvas

The choice of an appropriate design for marouflage is a matter of personal taste. Note, however, that the deep shiny final appearance of work under glass suits decorative better than "artistic" painting; it is also more effective to use colors such as black, royal blue, sky blue, emerald green, bronze green, orange, crimson, gold, silver, copper, sand (and ivory, for small areas). Avoid white, light grays and beiges, and other pale colors.

Prepare for an elaborate design with color studies, and a layout or stencil, depending on how you plan to transfer the design.

LOW TABLE

This table has wood-graining and cloudy lacquerwork.

Base coat: one or two coats of satin-finish ivory (white + a little yellow ochre + a few drops of chrome white and vermilion)

Divide the canvas into four quadrants with a pencil, and render bookmatched light-colored shimmering wood grain with a glaze lightly tinted raw sienna.

Let dry and isolate with a coat of dilute matte-finish alkyd paint. Transfer the layout in pencil, using a stencil of half the design and turning it over to get the other half.

Apply a coat of blue satin-finish paint around the design, masking as necessary and edging with a pointed sable.

To render the cloudy effect use a darker blue glaze on the blue ground. Dab over this glaze with a rag. Remove the masking and clean any glaze marks from the yellow ground.

Render some flowers and leaves with differently tinted (but not opaque) glazes, to resemble the colored wood used in marquetry.

Let dry. Center the canvas on the glass, and carefully trim excess canvas from the long sides before gluing.

Detail
The blue coat has been applied

Detail
The second blue coat and the coloration of the flowers

Low table
The finished canvas, with a blue frame, under glass

LOW OVAL TABLE

This table is faux marquetry with marble and porphyry. Refer to chapter 3 for the marbles.

Base coat: black satin-finish, painted roughly around the central motif

From a preliminary layout, transfer the outlines of the oval and inner star to a prepared canvas.

Marble (with tube oils and glaze), as described for Portoro marble. Note the four different directions of the veining.

Apply a coat of black satin paint to the central star motif. The borders need not be precise.

Masking the center axis of each arm of the star, marble one-half of each arm, and then the other half, with a veined gray stone and a gray breccia respectively. Remember to let the first work dry before proceeding with the second operation.

Using the layout, transfer the final outside border of the star with a pencil.

Mask the outside edges and apply a bluish coat.

Using a sponge, marble to resemble blue granite.

Remove the masking, and apply a salmon-pink coat to the four fan-shaped sections.

Mask and marble to resemble pink porphyry.

Using a ruler, add the borders with bronze powder around the star when the marbling is complete, masking to protect the marbling.

When the canvas is quite dry, make guidelines on the back and on the glass, affix to the glass, and trim.

DECORATIVE PANEL WITH FRAME

A coat of arms with antique gold and green bronze.

Tranfer the design to the canvas, give each part the appropriate base coat, and mark the layout without rigorously observing the borders. Paint the black base last, to get clean, well-defined edges in one operation.

Crown and Volutes
Base coat: gold bronze, with an isolating coat of copal varnish.

Shade with oil glaze (raw sienna and burnt umber).

Helmet
Base coat: metallized gray

After rendering the gray marbles, mask each arm of the star to protect during stippling

When the marbling is complete, edge them neatly with gold bronze

Paint with two tones (aluminum bronze powder and black) and shade with black oil glaze. The stable bronze does not need to be isolated.

Unicorn
Paint with verdigris (bluish green), shade with raw sienna and raw umber glaze.

Shield
Paint with pale green, complemented with stippled gold bronze.

Low oval table
The front of the painted canvas, trimmed, under glass
33 in × 24½ cm (84 cm × 62 cm)

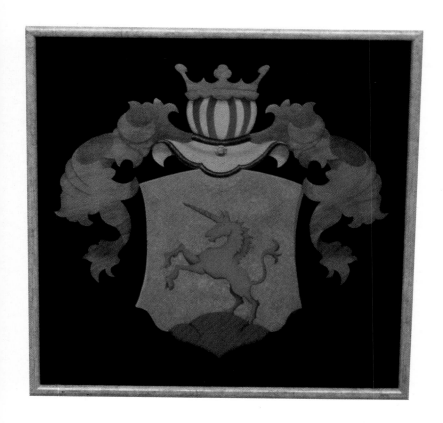

Decorative panel
Finished canvas marouflaged under glass, in an
antiqued gold frame
23½ in × 22½ in (60 cm × 58 cm)

MONOCHROMES

Harmonies in monochrome are made using several different values of a single color ranging from light to dark. The range of tones is obtained by adding progressively more white to an existing "parent" color (concentrated color, tube color, or ready-made paint). This is a simple exercise called *color modulation,* illustrated on page 402.

You can create the parent color by mixing several colors to reproduce an existing color, to produce a monochrome in exact harmony with a pre-existing sample. This, however, is more difficult work (see page 404).

Using a known parent color, however, allows you to create a scale of harmonious tones and has other advantages:

❖ You can prepare, as needed, a new quantity of paint in a given shade, simply by adding the appropriate amount of white.

❖ You can use reserved parent color to retouch a finished work later without straying from its tonal harmony.

The monochrome technique allows you to produce relief effects with the use of three judiciously chosen tones: a general base tone, a light tone for highlights, and a dark tone for shadows. A fourth intermediate tone can also be used. The top illustration opposite shows a monochrome relief.

GRISAILLE

The special monochrome work called *grisaille* is most spectacular. It is imitation, with different values of gray *(gris,* in French), of the shallow stone sculpture called bas relief.

Besides the grays used to render shaded stone or carved light-colored marble, striking grisaille effects are obtained, in classical ornamentation, with monochrome tonal scales from restrained colors—umbers and siennas, grayish-greens and gray-blues.

Monochrome decoration on interior panel with gathered-ribbon design in dusty rose on paneling

Allegory in ceiling cornice
Grisaille by Émile Levy
(Napoleon III Gallery, Louvre)

COLOR MODULATION

To produce a parent tint, either use a single colorant (concentrated color, colored paint, tube paint) directly (when the resulting scale corresponds to what you want) or prepare the parent color yourself, from various colorants (when you cannot match the desired color scale with a commercially available color).

Modulation from a Single Colorant

There are several ways to obtain the modulation:

Progressively shade white paint with a concentrated paint colorant (universal tint). This method is recommended for making modulations of light and middle tones. Since most of the paint volume comes from the white, obtaining dark tones would require the use of a great deal of colorant.

Progressively shade white paint with a ready-made colored paint (of the same type). This simple method sets no limits on proportions.

Progressively tint a ready-made colored paint with white paint (of the same type). This method is best for making scales of middle and dark tones, since white is not the main component. Always keep some base paint in reserve before adding white.

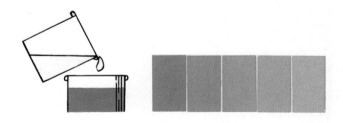

Judge the "distance" between tones of succeeding tints by checking the swatches against one another while wet, using a narrow painting knife held vertically under good light.

Monochrome frieze
Four tones from a single colorant, including the base
coat and sponged glaze

Decoration on a toy box: five tones from a ready-
made bronze-green paint, chosen from a chart
13 in × 13 in (32 cm × 32 cm)

The various elements that serve as a reference for color harmony in interior design (floor coverings, upholstery, and so on) often are of composite tones. To copy these faithfully demands careful color mixing, The parent mix, once synthesized, becomes precious, allowing the creation of a scale of always harmonious tones.

Modulation from Several Colorants

First, try to imitate exactly the tone of the sample by mixing a small quantity of white with carefully chosen base colorants (or ready-made paints, following the preceding instructions).

Compare the successive results of your work to the model, and save a bit of the final satisfactory mix on a knife.

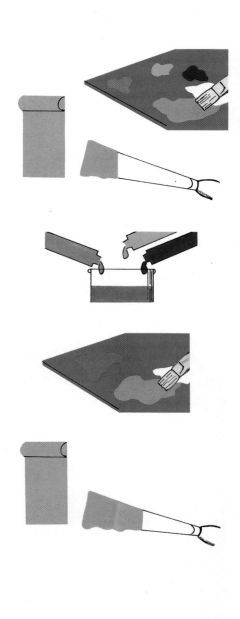

Start mixing the parent color by pouring quantities of each of the paints you used into a container, taking into consideration the rough proportions from which you obtained the desired color.

Test different mixtures of the parent color and white, and modify your proportions to match the tone on the knife.

A final comparison will confirm the match with the parent color, which you can now use to make a modulation scale by adding varying amounts of white.

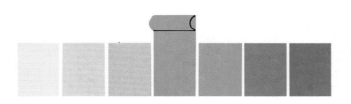

Monochrome harmony on paneling

Traditional multitoned painting, with one tone referring back to the background color of the wall covering. One subtle touch of ochre in the molding, recalling the leaves in the floral pattern, sets off the moldings and warms the blue-gray monochrome.

Different Glazes from a Single Coloration

In addition to harmonies based on flat tints of a homogeneous paint, you can produce harmonious monochromes with glazes of the same color but different intensities. This method, although applicable only in limited cases, is easy and useful to put into practice. For example:

❖ Following a sample, strongly color an oil glaze with pigment or tube colors and use this base mix to tint clear glaze, using more or less of the mix, as desired. This glaze can be used for two days; for more extended storage, prepare the same base color with only tube oil colors, and add to glaze when you are ready to use it.

❖ Make a normal parent color with acrylic colors (again following a sample), and mix with water-based glaze. Always test each glaze on a control surface before using it.

You can imitate colored freestone by applying three glazes of the same origin to a divided base, stone by stone, for a unified whole, as illustrated.

When you use patinas on walls, paneling, and furniture, more or less covering (opaque) glazes from the same scale allow you to accentuate chosen elements. In the example opposite, a base mix of three acrylic colors (raw sienna, burnt sienna, red ochre) yielded a light glaze for edging, a deeper-colored glaze for the panel, and a still more opaque glaze for the dado (which had a different base coat).

A yellow-green oil glaze, matching the fabric, is used in the subtle shading of the white moldings, the translucent edging of the moldings, and the stippled green baseboard.

In interior design the use of two well-chosen monochrome scales is most satisfying: choosing two complementary colors prevents the possible monotony of a single monochrome, and also suggests possible colors for other decorative elements in the room.

Glazed monochrome

*A sample panel to suggest materials and colors in harmony with
a fabric. It includes pinkish beige patinas (smoothed, sponged,
and rag-rolled) of three intensities from a single base color; and
a complementary yellow-green glaze in three intensities, from a
different single base color.*

Parent colors made from solvent- or water-soluble paints must be kept in a closed container; small quantities will thicken quickly and become unusable.

Parent colors made to approximate a sample color must be produced in sufficient quantity to cover the needs of the work, as well as possible retouching after its completion, to avoid having to make a new batch that might not exactly match.

Some paints (such as matte and satin alkyds) darken when they dry. It is thus advisable to check the color of the paint when dry with a test stroke before starting the final work. This allows you to judge and to anticipate, in the space of two or three hours, the tonal discrepancy, and to adjust the amount of white added to compensate as needed.

To gauge the difference between two tones, compare them wet, side by side. Comparing a wet color with a dry color frequently leads to mistakes (the dry color always being darker). Similarly, when making up a new batch of a color you need more of, use the unused wet paint as a sample.

In matching colors, you must also take into account the rule of contrasts, which causes us to perceive differences of light and dark greater than their actual values.

Note that sometimes it is helpful to add a drop of black, raw umber, or dark violet to the darkest tone of the monochrome for use in shadows, emphasis, and other effects when you retouch friezes, certain artwork, sculpture, and moldings. This addition must be done with care and preliminary testing, to avoid introducing any false note into the existing monochrome harmony. The addition is most useful for monochromes based on a very restrained parent color, like the mural opposite. Its tone scale is based on raw sienna. Some tones were very lightly warmed with a drop of chrome orange, others strengthened with a very little bit of raw umber and violet.

For this kind of work, it is advantageous, after establishing your range of samples, to make the four or five tones immediately and store them in different containers. This ensures harmony even if several hands work on the project, and keeps the paint fresh for several days.

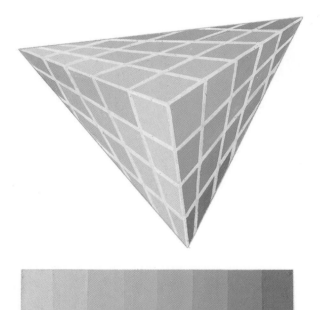

You can produce a regular tonal gradation by adding successively greater amounts of the base color to a given amount of white (with a small container as the unit of proportion).

The eight tones of green are obtained as follows:

* ❖ *one volume of white to one measure of green for tone number 1*
* ❖ *one volume of white to two measures of green for tone number 2*
* ❖ *one volume of white to three measures of green for tone number 3, and so on*

The position of each tone on the pyramid was determined with an initial numbered model. Studying a set of samples allowed placement of the two extremes of light and dark.

Contemporary monochrome mural
Panorama
114 in × 138 in (2.90 m × 3.50 m)
(P Amblard, IPEDEC entry hall)

FAUX PANELS AND SIMPLE DECORATION ON FLUSH DOORS

To make the flush doors of a contemporary home more decorative, without elaborate and costly trompe l'œil graining, moldings, and ornament, with different paint tones you can paint faux panels or other simple decorative elements. The plain two square yards (meters) of a flush door make an ideal support for classical carpentry elements, such as molded frames, raised panels, curved crosspieces, stained glass.

These elements can also be applied to furniture doors (cupboards, wardrobes) and walls, for faux wainscotting. The following projects detail easy techniques, all using masking tapes to produce sharp distinctions between painted tones.

The basic principles are these:

❖ Prepare each door with satin-finish paint based on a parent color, from which you can make small quantities of the other necessary monochrome tones. The resulting ensemble will have a more professional quality.

❖ Make an initial model (to one-tenth scale, for example) to plan the correct proportions of the shapes. Start by defining the width of the stiles. This width will vary, depending on the width of the door itself and the general style or character of the room.

❖ To make a sketch, start by marking off the stiles and then the rails. Before drawing the final layout, make erasable guidelines on the door.

Real woodwork on an elaborate traditional door

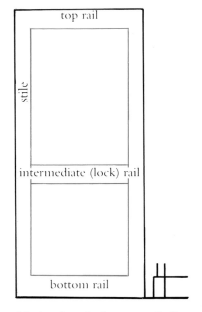

Notice that the bottom rail aligns with the adjacent baseboard

Some real door treatments

(Gardesa Doors)

(Husky Doors)

SIMPLE RECTILINEAR-PANEL DOORS

The trompe l'œil rendering of panels is based on painting precisely placed highlight and shadow. These are represented by edgings, mitered corners, rectilinear bands of various width, and stripes, and are colored in the same tonal scale as the base coat.

The following examples require a minimum of masking.

Example 1

Lay out the placement of moldings and the interior panel, thus also determining the faux raised panel and the panel surrounds.

Mask the two light moldings around half the perimeter, and apply the light tone.

Mask the dark moldings around the remaining perimeter, with their mitered corners, and apply the dark tone.

Render the light and dark borders around the raised panel, either with a brush or by masking at the same time as the above operations.

Example 2

Sketch the raised panel, and mask its interior.

On one half of the perimeter of the panel surround, apply the light tone along the length of the masked panel. Follow by stippling to grade the tone.

On the other half of the perimeter of the panel surround, apply the dark tone, with similar stippling afterward.

Render the moldings, in two operations as above, after double masking.

If you apply a light or dark tone over about a third of the width of the panel surround, and grade it by stippling, you can produce a curved effect (see page 416).

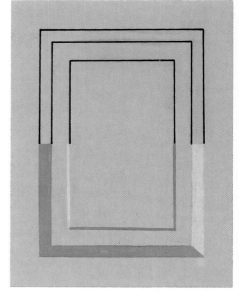

1

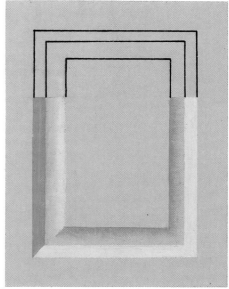

2

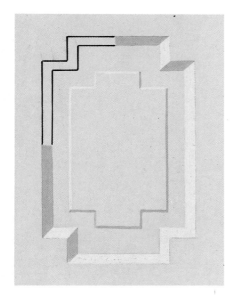

Two-tone panel with cut-in corners

Three-tone recessed panel

To obtain more contrast, as in this example,
paint the panel surrounds in a darker tone
than the base coat. Follow the pencil marks
for the edges, which will be covered when you
paint the moldings and the edges of the raised
panel.

EMBOSSED DOORS

These panels with their angular reliefs illustrate the results you can obtain with the careful use of light and shadow.

Very often, conventional oblique lighting (from the upper left) requires the use of three or four tones in addition to the base tone.

For neat work, paint nonadjacent opposing areas in one session, and the last tone(s) after you have masked the mitered corners and sharp angles on the dry finished parts.

In the two following examples the different tones, as well as their general base color, come from a single parent color (green, yellow ochre, and raw umber).

Example 1
Sketch the raised panel, and mask it.

Apply the nonadjacent lateral medium tones 2 and 3, bordering the pencil marks on the molded side (without masking).

Apply the light tone 1 and the dark tone 4, after masking the oblique cuts in the dry color, bordering the pencil marks on the molded side.

Render the moldings (in two steps, as above), after masking on each side along their delimiting markings.

Example 2
Sketch the design, and apply the lateral tone 2, masking only the left edge, bordering the other pencil marks.

Apply the lateral tone 3, masking only tone 2 and the right edge.

Apply tones 1 and 4 after masking all three ways.

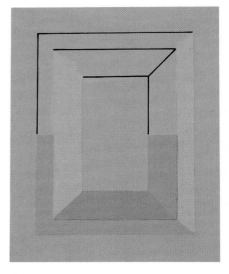

1

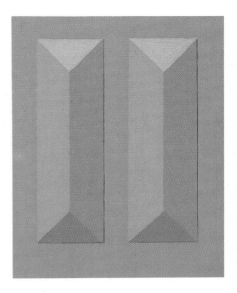

2

414

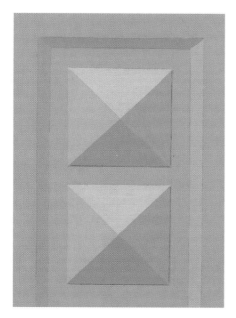

Four-tone diamond

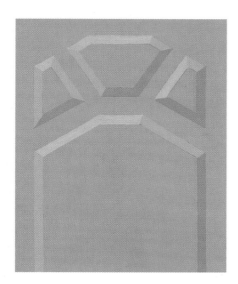

Three-tone arrangement

Louis XIII–style living-room door
82½ in × 32½ in (2.10 m × .83 m)

DOORS WITH CURVED PANELS

To render certain classical styles, and also some contemporary ones, it is necessary to reproduce curved, vaulted, and carved moldings and panels. Painting curves is an additional challenge.

For the following examples, in addition to freehand edging (practical only for experts), there are other suitable ways to paint curved parts. You can use:

❖ Special masking tapes that conform to the curves of the initial drawing

❖ Frisket film, reversed, allowing the cutting and transfer of curved designs to make a customized mask

❖ Heavy stencil paper (perhaps making a stencil in several parts, depending on the size of the design). This method may be best for the amateur, if the same curved element is repeated over one or several panels.

Whichever method you choose, be prepared to clean up edges with a small brush and to wipe away smears with a pointed brush handle covered with a soft white rag.

Shading the highlights and shadows of rounded forms is done by stippling around the boundaries of the paint applied to a particular area to soften and blend with the adjacent area. Use the tips of the bristles of a small spalter. This type of shading is facilitated by the use of a little bit of slightly more fluid paint applied with an artist's brush to the side you want to blend.

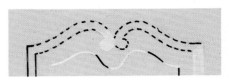

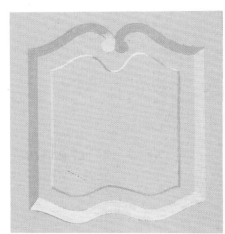

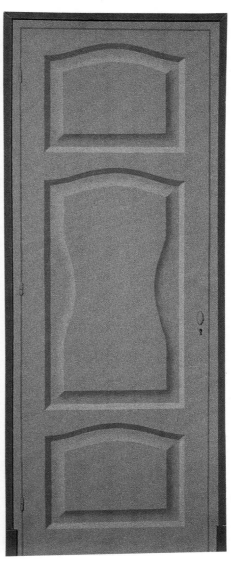

Paneled door painted in a range of wood tones

Door with curved raised panels

Panel with double raised panel

Bottom panel of painted furniture

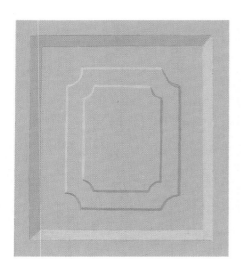

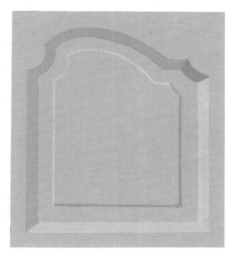

These different examples of painted panels and doors, not requiring expert skill, cannot compare to the elaborate faux moldings and ornament painted with glazes and patinas. Nevertheless, this simple and inexpensive trompe l'œil allows a free and easy change of decor to complement the colors of new furniture, wall coverings, carpets, upholstery. When choosing a color scheme, do not neglect the possibility of using two different colors on a single painted door (see the upper middle door, page 421).

Traditional forms

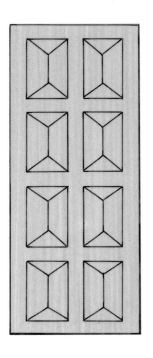
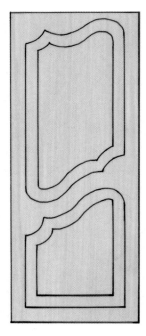

Contemporary forms

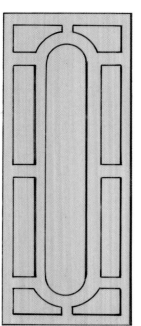
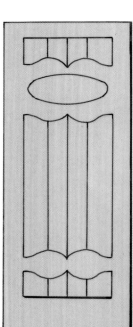

A variety of patterns

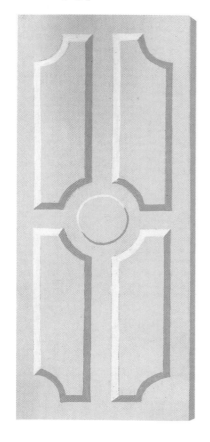

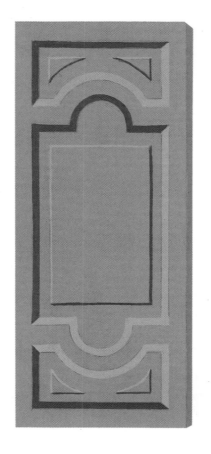

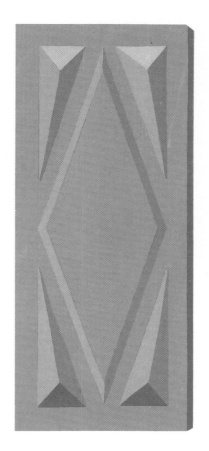

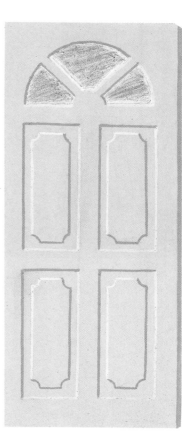

In addition to trompe l'œil door panels and different faux materials (see chapter 2), there are numerous other possibilities for decorating doors. Among them are:

❖ Stenciled motifs. This simple method allows you to create numerous compositions by repeating a motif at four corners, stenciling a central, upper, and lower ornament, making friezes, and so on (1)

❖ Edging and stripes—simple understated borders or elaborate interlocking bands

❖ Colored geometric forms

❖ Stylized, silhouetted, shaded painted forms

❖ Special themes appropriate to the placement of the decoration, such as a trellis at the entrance to a garden (2).

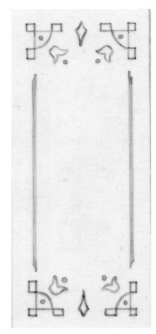

1   2

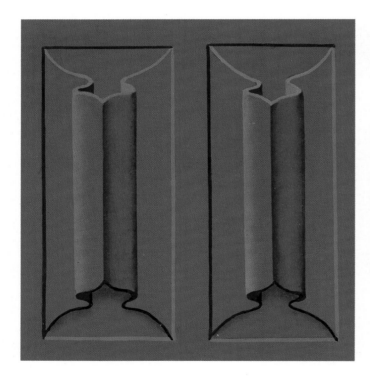

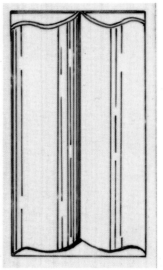
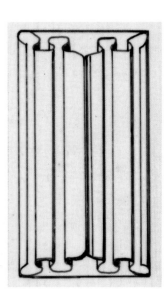

Napkin-fold panels

Characteristic of the Gothic style, this sculpted ornamentation with a medieval flavor goes well in rustic rooms. Render it on a wood-tone foundation (or better still, in faux oak) and other dark tones. Its form is inspired by the folded pelts covering old wooden chests.

A variety of patterns

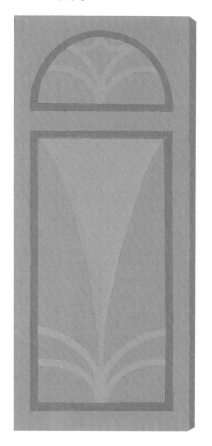
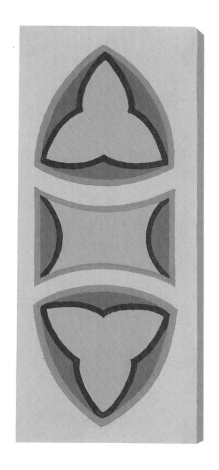

TRELLISWORK

Linked in France to the importance of park and garden art during the reign of Louis XIV, trelliswork remains an important decorative asset in the modern garden everywhere. Real trellises were—and are—made by assembling wooden laths into a latticework, the openings usually diamond-shaped or square, but also sometimes inspired by vaulting, doors, and various oblique elements. We copy these forms for interior and exterior painted wall decoration.

If diamond latticework, classical forms, symmetry, and the color green characterized the trellises of the early twentieth century, our tastes have evolved toward square lattices and more refined forms today. We shall start, however, with the traditional trellis.

DIAMOND TRELLISWORK

Trompe l'œil trelliswork calls for making a model, drawing a layout, masking, and reproducing the three-dimensionality of laths with light and shadow. The support should be sufficiently smooth to allow the use of masking tapes or edging brushes, or a combination of the two (depending on the skill of the renderer).

Making a Model

Depending on the complexity of the project, you may make a scale or same-size model on a colored base to determine the composition and form of the trelliswork, the sizes of the panels, the pattern and the color of the trelliswork.

Layout

Recommended dimensions for the diamonds:

❖ 10 × 6 inches (26 × 16 cm) width for standard trellises
❖ 14 × 9½ inches (36 × 24 cm) width for large-diamond trellises

Other proportions give very sharp diamonds. (See page 428 for square latticework.)

Draw the exterior edge of the panel.
Around the interior perimeter, draw the width of a single lath —about 1 inch (25 mm)—with a heavy line (1).

On these interior lines, make evenly spaced guide lines, which correspond to the tips of the diamonds, on each side of the panel. You must calculate the size of the panel to obtain whole and identical diamonds that will cover its entire length and width (2).

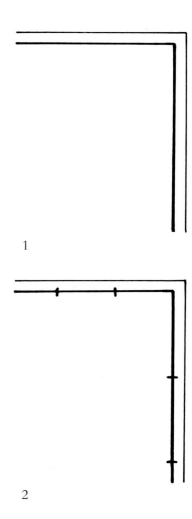

1

2

For example: a panel 55 inches (140 cm) wide, with diamonds of desired width 6 inches (16 cm)

1. 55/6 = 9.16 (140/16 = 8.75): nine diamonds will fit across.

2. 55/9 = 6.11 (140/9 = 15.55): allow 6.11 inches (15.55 cm) between guide marks to fit nine equal diamonds across the width.

3. Use the same process to obtain the height of the diamonds, figuring on a height of about 10 inches (26 cm).

Connect the guide marks with diagonal lines (using pencil for shorter spans, a chalkline for longer ones) to render the axes of the lattice (3).

Check the geometry of this initial layout (be sure the diamonds are symmetrical), and use a piece of cardboard as a template to mark the width of each lath on both sides of its axis (4).

Using a straightedge, draw the latticework. Remember that it has width, depth, and light and shadow depending on the desired three-dimensional effect.

Most edging of imitation trelliswork is done with a straight-edge and masking tapes. Always try to place masks as efficiently as possible, to save time and effort.

Real trelliswork

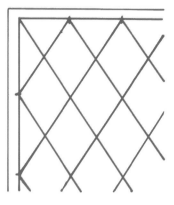

3

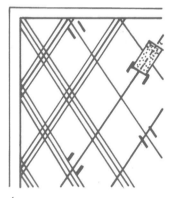

4

LATHS: DEPTH AND SHADOW

Relief with Partial Shading (1, opposite)

Lay out the whole lattice structure, as described on the preceding page.

Paint all the laths going in one direction, after masking both edges.

Paint all the laths going in the opposite direction, after masking.

Apply partial shadowing. Use a cutout piece of cardboard as a stencil, if desired, as shown in the detail opposite. Blend the shadows on one side, or leave unblended.

Relief with Discontinuous Depth (2, opposite)

The layout in place, draw the edges of the laths going in one direction, including their depth, which will be painted, and the boundary between the two.

Tape along the outer lines, and paint all the laths. Use the boundary line as a guide, and do not be concerned if the paint goes over the boundary line (see detail opposite).

Draw the depth of the laths, parallel to the first depth lines.

Mask on both sides and paint the depth strips thus marked off.

Draw the laths going in the opposite direction, edging their borders with two maskings, and paint. This operation covers, and so makes discontinuous, the depth strips of the previous set of laths.

Relief with Continuous Depth (3, opposite)

Lay out and paint first the laths that are without depth. Render the laths that do have depth as above.

Variations

With two different thicknesses

With discontinuous shadow

With continuous shadow and highlighted edges

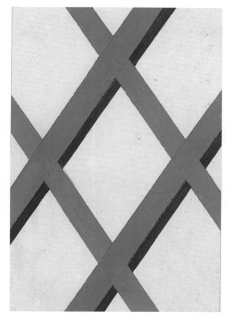

1. Relief with partial shadowing, unblended and blended

2. Relief with discontinuous depth

3. Relief with continuous depth

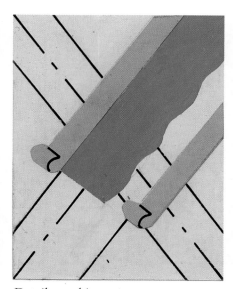

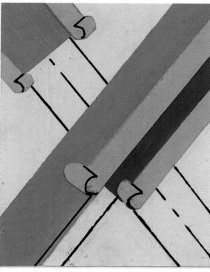

Detail: shadow stencil

Detail: masking

Detail: masking

When you imitate classical diamond trellises, work from the real form of the different elements, to give fidelity to the trompe l'œil. The main elements that give form to trelliswork include panels, pilasters, pediments, friezes, arches, doors, bays, and transoms.

While real trellises are usually dark green or white, other colors can also be used.

Color variations

Elements of diamond trelliswork

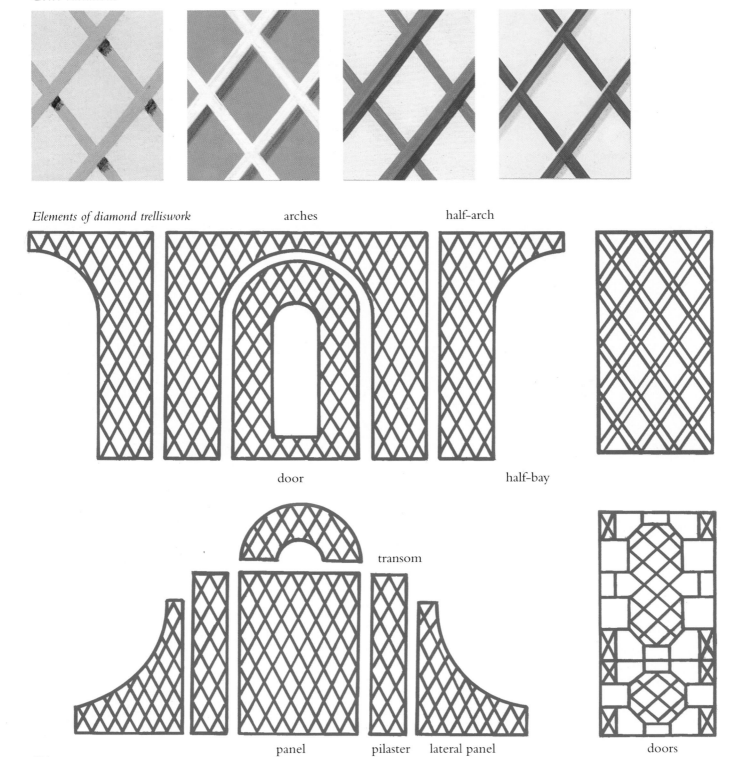

arches   half-arch

door   half-bay

transom

panel   pilaster   lateral panel   doors

*Trelliswork on jasper background with
grained cove and baseboard moldings*

SQUARE TRELLISWORK

Square trellises are usually constructed on a 6 × 6 inch (16 × 16 cm) grid for the axes of the laths, which are about 1 inch (25 mm) wide. It is therefore desirable that the widths and heights of the panels you render all be multiples of 6 inches (16 cm) or thereabouts, so the grid pattern can be complete and unbroken.

Shadow variations

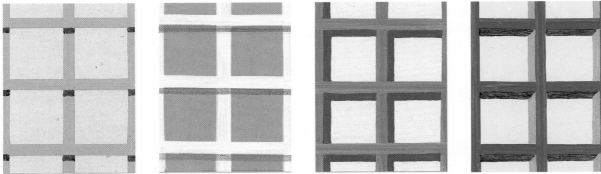

Elements of square trelliswork

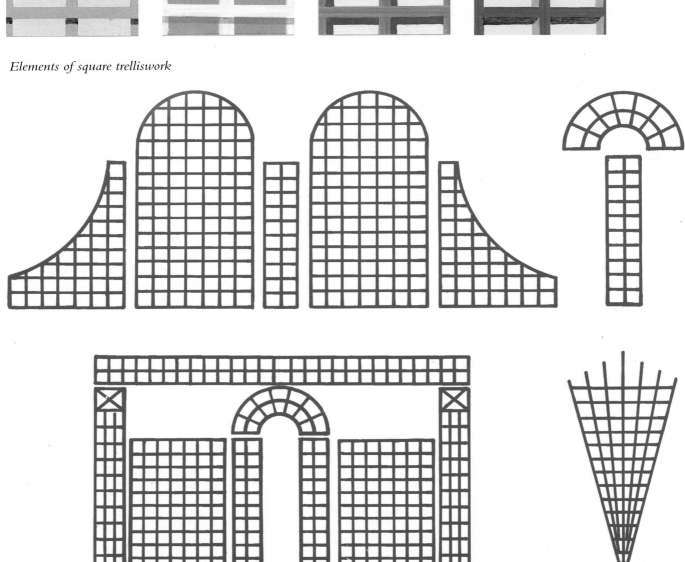

Contemporary mural with sky and distant landscape

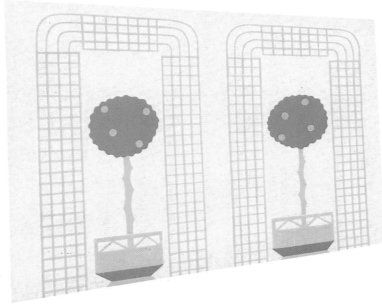

Sketch for a veranda design

Of all the elements of real trelliswork, the most difficult to render are vaulted doors and arches, because of their curves.
Studying and incorporating these forms, however, is what
makes trompe l'œil trelliswork most interesting.

Traditional mural
Vaulted trellis on a painted background with sky and stonework

FAUX STONEWORK WITH REAL RELIEF

Raw stone in interiors gives a rustic character, reminiscent of some rural houses, castles, and historic buildings (1).

Colored differently depending on the region from which they were quarried, raw stones are also characterized by a particular arrangement, and the resulting particular look of the facing.

Freestone, with its geometric arrangement and regular joints, goes well with many different styles of interiors. It can be used in arches or flat arches above bays and sculpted areas (2).

Imitating stonework with only flat colored paints lacks realism in the absence of real reliefs (save those decors seen from afar). It is thus worthwhile to be able to imitate stone with real reliefs; these must be shown off by surrounding light, strengthening the resemblance to real stone. You can find among contemporary construction material, however, a wide range of molded stones, manufactured in different blocks or tablets that are easily manipulated and affixed (3, 4). Thus, for durable large scale work you can use any of the various solid real materials, with a comparable execution time.

Imitating stone with relief is best used for smaller surfaces, for special color and relief, for shapes not commercially available, or for temporary applications (theater sets, exposition stands, etc.).

As described in chapter 2, there are three general categories of stone from which you can choose: *freestone,* with rather light beige tones, a uniform granular relief, and narrow rectilinear joints yielding a geometric arrangement of rectangular stones; this option suits large surfaces (5, opposite); *ashlar,* which presents rough-hewn stones of variable color arranged evenly in horizontal rows (6) and *rubble masonry,* which can be light or dark colored, with marked relief, and is laid irregularly (7).

1

Real arrangement of random ashlar

2

Real arrangement of freestone

3

Real stone facing

4

Real stone facing

5

Freestone

6

Coursed ashlar

7

Rubble masonry

FAUX FREESTONE WITH RELIEF

This imitation renders fine-grained rectangular stones with raked joints; it is often rendered without relief (with painted surfaces and painted edging for jointwork, as described in chapter 2), without giving the full effect of the material.

Basic Method

On a smooth white background, lay out the placement of the stones (horizontal rows, vertical joints, etc.), and mask the joints with narrrow masking tape.

Using a paint roller, apply a colored textured paint (stone-toned flat acrylic or alkyd paint, or paint thickened with about a third part of texturing powder). You can stipple it with the patina brush instead of rolling it on (1, opposite). Do not use matte enamel paints, which will not yield the desired relief.

Before the paint dries, remove the tape. Paint the joints with an edging brush, after shading with colored glaze or vinyl-based varnish.

(Note: For more detailed information on the layout and execution of trompe l'œil stonework, see chapter 2.)

After the usual preparation of the surface, apply a white flat acrylic undercoat (as described in chapter 1) or a similar product for giving tooth recommended by the manufacturers of the textured paint.

Lightly draw the arrangement of the stones, and apply masking tapes, about ¼ inch to ⅜ inch (8 to 10 mm) in width, over the joints; an erasable drawing may help you avoid having to repaint the joints in the end.

Cover the whole with a fine stone-toned textured paint, with a paint roller (more or less full, depending on the desired relief). You can also modify the relief by scraping horizontally with a putty knife.

Since the textured paint dries rapidly, apply it in sections, from top to bottom, keeping the paint from the joints.

Pull off the tapes before the paint dries, and remove any smudges near the joints.

Finish by painting the joints with the edging brush (in matte white, ochre, or light gray) (2 opposite).

1
*Thick matte paint, with final
shading of fluid vinyl varnish*

2
*Textured paint, with final shad-
ing of vinyl varnish*

*Fanciful freestone
Thick white acrylic paint, mottled with sponged acrylic
color, and raked joints rendered by masking*

*Brick œil-de-boeuf
Textured paint with light stone-by-stone coloration, and
off-white joints*

ASHLAR MASONRY WITH RELIEF

This arrangement is characterized by stones placed in horizontal alignment, with staggered vertical joints (although different placements are possible).

Basic Method

On a smooth light background, sketch the horizontal lines that determine the courses, or rows of stones (these can be of constant or variable height). Then draw the outline of each stone with a pencil, and use a knife to spread a thick coating to form each stone.

When the relief is dry, give it one or two coats of paint. You can give them different colorations for extra decorative effect. Finish by rendering the mortar joints in a different color.

Three Formulas for the Relief Coat

❖ Mix separately equal volumes of premixed gesso and powdered gesso; then mix them together in a container. Apply the mixture over a flat alkyd undercoat. This gives medium reliefs, of about $\frac{1}{32}$ to $\frac{3}{16}$ inch (1 to 5 millimeters).

❖ Mix powdered gesso with water (plus $\frac{1}{5}$ volume of plaster), depending on the relief desired). Because this mixture is porous, finish with two coats of paint.

❖ A reliable mixture for relief comes from mixing wall grout. This coating is very hard, provides a good bond, and allows reliefs from around $\frac{1}{32}$ to 1 inch (1 to 25 mm). See facing examples.

After the usual preparation of the support, apply a white acrylic undercoat.

Draw the horizontal courses.

Pencil in the form of the stones, aiming for a good fit, and good stagger of vertical joints.

Apply the coating, stone by stone, and model the reliefs (stippling them in part or wholly with a patina brush or a wet sponge, or shape with a spatula, a crumpled rough rag, or a painting knife.

When the relief is dry, clean the loose particles from the joints with a small knife.

Apply two coats of tinted acrylic paint, and edge the joints in a different tone.

Note: As before, shading and coloration can be worked in before rendering the joints, with an acrylic glaze, or a clear or tinted vinyl-based varnish.

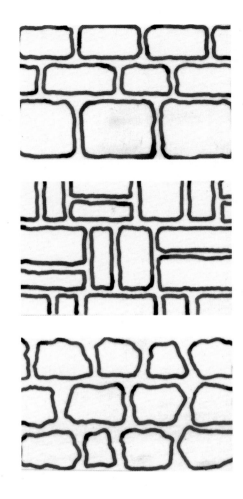

Relief stonework with colored joints

Arrangement of cut-off corner and perimeter of bay on interior wall in rustic textured paint.

Development of ashlar wall

The coloration was executed in a single operation, with partial applications of a yellow tone (raw sienna with a drop of raw umber) and a gray tone (raw umber with a drop of black), blended more or less in different places.

RUBBLE MASONRY WITH RELIEF

This arrangement of stone places no constraints on layout, but requires a discerning eye for the accord of the various shapes.

Basic Method

The stones are placed in similar fashion to ashlar masonry, but not in courses. Accentuate the stones with the relief coating and use colored glazes to finish the work.

If you want to render stonework, it is important to consider the many examples of masonry available as models, and to keep a photographic record of the different types of arrangement and colorations you see.

For all relief stonework you can render a special decorative effect by lightly coloring the relief coating during preparation (using, for example, ochre-color universal colorant) and afterward apply a somewhat stronger acrylic glaze. Sand the crests of reliefs (1, opposite).

If you prefer a less strong relief for the stones, you can obtain a "fluffy" look by thickening textured paint with filler powder, and, after applying the coating with a knife, stippling the whole of the stone with a wet natural sponge.

For all stone arrangements drawn freehand, you can make preliminary sketches with colored chalk, and use that, if satisfactory.

The faux stonework chimney opposite is executed by first studying the chosen arrangement (and, perhaps, making a chalk sketch), then pencilling in the outlines of the stones.

Apply the coating, using a grout mixture, stone by stone, modeling each as desired.

After the relief dries, clean loose particles out of the joints (a wood chisel can be helpful here).

Finish with two coats of paint, colored glazes, and, finally, render the mortar joints.

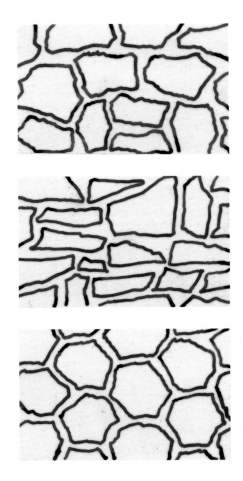

1

Development of raw stone

The final coat of vinyl varnish, applied over the whole, eliminates the porousness of the reliefs bared by sanding, and allows a partial shading before the joints are painted.

2

Chimney hood

Irregular stones, shaped with a knife, with patina in a related tone applied before the painting of the joints.

GLASS PAINTING

The technique of painting on the back of glass, which takes advantage of the brilliance and protection afforded by the glass, was developed and practiced by signpainters, for signs, logos, and storefronts. It is useful for simple decorative work that does not require detailed ornamentation—otherwise the work would more easily and more quickly be accomplished on canvas, as described earlier in this chapter.

Decorations painted on glass are used for:

❖ coffee-table glass

❖ framed decorative panels

❖ customized panels for decorative use (signs, logos, insignia, and the like)

The technique presents two main difficulties. First, the design must be reversed on the back of the glass, so that it will be seen as intended through the transparent front of the glass. For example, an inscription must be rendered with the (reversed) letters going from right to left. This necessitates a full-scale preliminary drawing, whether on tracing paper or a stencil, either eventually reversed. Perhaps a greater inconvenience is the need to paint in reverse order, starting with what would normally come last and finishing with what would normally come first. Thus, when you render relief, the shadows and highlights need to be correctly placed *before* the base colors. For an imitation of wood, final reglazing to grain will take place *before* the general veining that determines the figure, and the initial base coat is painted last (save perhaps for the flogging of the base, if necessary).

It is important, if your design is relatively complex, to make a full-scale colored rendering in addition to tracing paper sketches, including shadows and highlights, hatching, detailing, and edging, so these elements can be placed correctly on the glass at the proper stage of execution. After a bit of practice you may be able to skip rendering some materials.

As noted in the discussion of designing painted canvases under glass, be sure to choose appropriate colors and themes.

For glass painting we use tube oil paints, alkyd, or acrylic paints.

The following projects assume a preliminary tracing-paper model with all the motifs of the decoration, or a stencil with which to transfer them to the glass.

Window of an old tavern

Decoration painted on glass in yellow-gold and cream tones. The veins of the leaves were rendered before the leaves themselves.

Floral design
With internal illumination at night (Pharmacy, Seine-Saint-Denis, Paris)

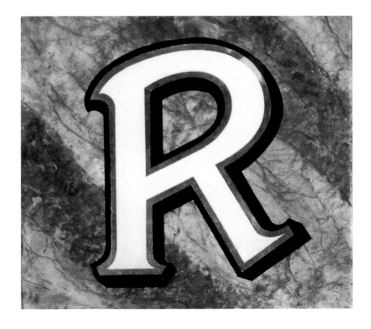

Initial

Detail, with gold leaf border. The background is imitation marble, rendered last and in the reverse of the usual order, starting with main veining.

SIMPLE DECORATIONS USING FLAT COLORS

These consist of isolated painted elements (figures, braids, and so on) and final paint over the whole work, for background (1, opposite).

Paint the main figure with a brush, following a tracing-paper design through the glass, or using a stencil.

If there are braids, paint them freehand with a brush, or with the help of masking tapes.

Apply the "base" paint over the whole, using satin-finish enamel.

COMPLEX DECORATIONS USING FLAT COLORS

For more complex decoration, paint the outlines of the elements represented (along with edging, braids, interlaces, etc.), and then paint the multicolored base, along the adjacent edges of these outlines (2, opposite).

Paint the outlines of the floral figures with a sable brush, using tracing paper or stencils.

Fill in the flowers and leaves in colored paint, bordering the outlines without precisely edging.

Apply the background colors, using the previously delineated edge between the perimeter and the curved central panel.

COMPLEX DECORATIONS

Shadows and highlights come first, followed by glaze and, finally, "base" coat, to produce the desired material effect (3, opposite).

Paint the highlights and shadows. Follow the tracing paper layout visible through the glass, and a color layout.

Paint the ornament itself, in a flat color, edging it carefully following the tracing paper outline, or extending the paint out to the previously painted shadows and highlights.

Render the wood grain in two operations, successively masking half and half again of the four sections of the base.

Apply the base-coat tone of warm wood (yellow ochre + a little white + a drop of chrome yellow + a drop of cadmium orange).

Work in progress on the reverse side   *Finished work seen from the front*

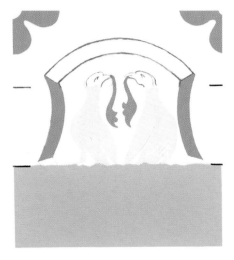

1

2

3

DECORATIVE PANEL WITH FRAME

A gold-tone silhouetted motif on a black background.

Draw the design on tracing paper (full scale).

Place the inverted tracing paper on the glass, front to front.

Paint the edging (with bronze powder in glaze or bronzing varnish with a sable brush, following the outlines from the tracing paper through the glass.

Clean any smudges made while edging, and apply the black foundation with one or two coats of satin or gloss black enamel to render the background opaque.

Decorative panel with frame

SIGN FOR A PHARMACY

It is absolutely necessary to execute the steps for this design in the specified order:

1. The brown outline of the snake and the beige edges of the two apothecary jars.
2. The yellow marking off the upper borders of the central container.
3. The pale green paint of the snake's body.
4. The light glaze shading the two apothecary jars.
5. The ochre glaze over the middle container, stippled.
6. The inscriptions on the jars, following the reversed lettering of the tracing-paper drawing (1).
7. The background colors, yellow and ivory, of the three shaded vessels.
8. The green edgings of the cross and the jar pedestals (2).
9. The strong green of the cross and pedestals, flogged with the flogger to grain.
10. The medium green base of the cross and pedestals.
11. The red-brown background glaze, with granite and jasper textures, over the rest of the design, without special attention to boundaries (3).
12. The brick-colored background paint.
13. The finish coat in a neutral tone.

With its depth and brilliance, a black background accentuates gold tones. The frame is added.

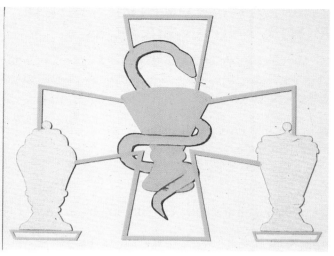

1
Sign for a pharmacy
Front view, with shading and inscription on side jars, and the finished central container painted on reverse

2
Reverse, with ivory jar backgrounds, and green edging for cross and pedestals

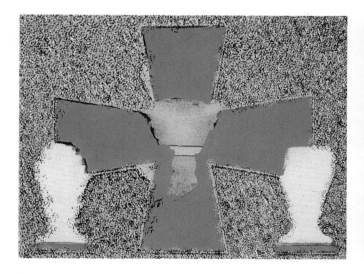

3
Reverse, with unedged green background, and the two tones (one light, one dark) stippled with a sponge to resemble granite

Finished work seen from the front. The third, middle, tone of the granite was obtained by applying the final brick-colored coat, partially visible through the other two tones

TRAY WITH SYMMETRIC FLORAL MOTIFS AND ARABESQUES

Rendering this design with extremely careful preliminary linework makes it possible to execute the following coloration without precise edging.

Using a sable brush with sienna, trace the linework of the motifs and arabesques through the glass.

Render the gold-yellow edging around the petals.

Color the motifs in graded emerald, area by area.

Add the orange hatching and tips on the petals.

Paint the petals pale orange.

Apply a dark green glaze over the whole, and remove glaze with a sponge slightly moistened with turpentine.

Apply the background coat in medium green (from the same scale as the emerald).

Protect with finish coat.

Checklist of Procedures

❖ Before each operation, be sure that the glass is clean, and if needed use a white rag and denatured alcohol.

❖ Before applying paints and glazes, or working them, test on a piece of glass to preview the result.

❖ To avoid unplanned see-through to other colors, check the opacity of painted layers by holding a piece of colored paper under the glass. If a second coat is necessary, its edging can be less precise.

❖ For very detailed work such as lettering, transfer the outlines directly onto the paint side of the glass with a stencil (by using a pounce bag and the initial tracing paper drawing). The thickness of the glass can cause distortion of the design underneath.

❖ All work painted on glass needs to be protected from wear, scratching, and air pollution by one or two coats of satin or gloss enamel paint. The customary finish is dark and neutral in tone.

The linework

The graded green and retouched petals, seen from the front (through the glass)

The work seen from the other side. The flower on the right has not yet received the background coat

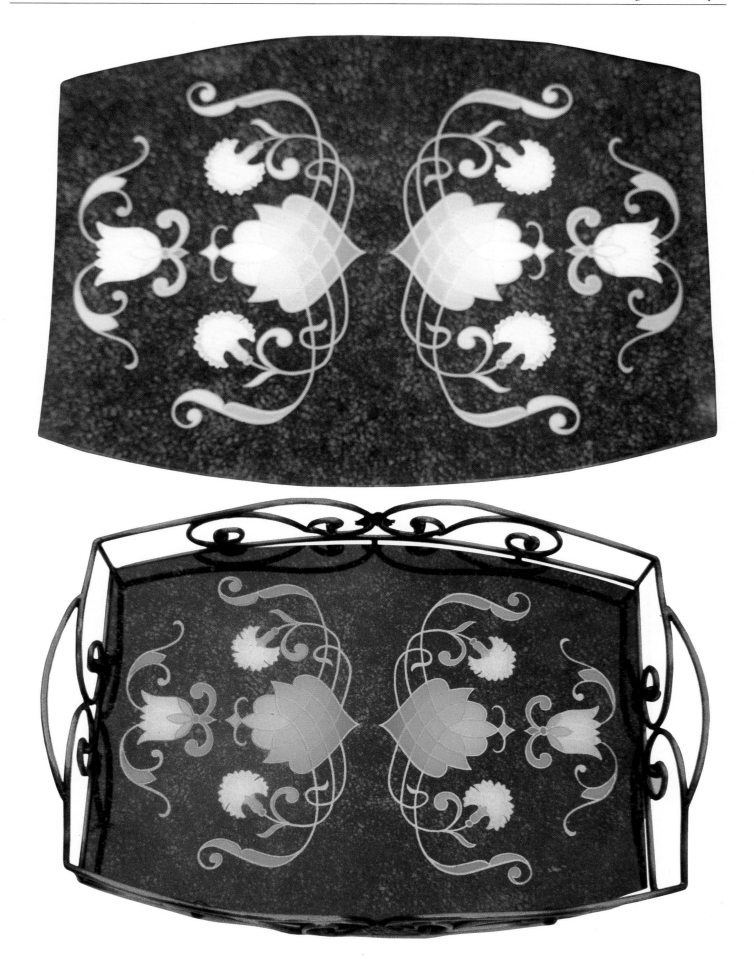

FAUX LACQUERWARE

Real Asian lacquerwork calls for a lengthy series of meticulous operations, from attaching cloth to wood, through numerous priming coats, engraving, inlay of jewels and giltwork, painted decoration, to many sandings and coats of varnish. The result is exceptional decoration—a brilliantly intense, flawless polish; that is to say, lacquer. Lacquerware from China, where the technique originated, gained a following as professionals the world over sought, through different techniques, to obtain the same results.

Today lacquerware panels, furniture, and screens are rendered in the traditional manual style only by a few studios; more often lacquerware is industrially produced with mechanical applications of the various coats of paint and synthetic varnish.

As with stained glass or etched glass, real lacquerwork is not for the amateur. The object of this section is to show how best to imitate lacquerwork, despite the impossibility of doing justice to the real thing.

Real lacquerwork is characterized by conventionally colored plain or jasper-textured backgrounds, *chinoiserie* themes and designs, and a perfectly finished high-gloss surface of varnish.

While the first two characteristics are accessible to painters and skilled amateurs, the finish is difficult to obtain. We offer a quick formula that gives a medium gloss, but without grain.

The following technique allows you to get the look of Asian lacquerware on different supports: jewelry boxes, decorative panels, screens, furniture doors, and other objects. Remember, though, that the results cannot approach the real thing.

Basic Method

After a primer appropriate to the chosen support, apply a foundation of two coats of satin-finish alkyd enamel. You may leave this base plain or give it a jasper finish (see chapter 2); then paint your design on it.

Give the work a gloss finish as described on page 452.

Real lacquerware

Top of a low table
Traditional Chinese lacquerware, gold on black base

Side panel of a piece of furniture
Polychrome decoration on brown base,
inspired by Asian lacquerware

Detail from a wardrobe
Gold decoration on amber base

Example 1

Base coat: satin black

Transfer the design from tracing paper, using a pencil, to the base coat.

Paint the different elements with bronze powder (rich gold or green gold) and oil glaze (thicker for flat coverage, thinner for parts to be blended).

Apply the varnish finish (see page 452).

Example 2

Transfer the design from tracing paper, using a pencil, to a base earlier painted in satin orange ochre.

Paint the different elements with burnt sienna, burnt umber, and oil glaze, more or less strongly for main outlines or secondary details.

Partially reglaze with the same colors.

Apply the different colors for leaves, flowers, and their edging.

Apply the varnish finish (see page 452).

Making an initial model (and a succeeding tracing-paper layout or stencil) presupposes a good bit of research on Eastern art, indispensable for rendering the traditional subjects: mountains and peaks, islands and islets, trees, pagodas, bridges, boats, dragons, flowers, figures, and so forth.

Base-coat colors can be plain, jasper-textured, or highlighted with bronze powder. Real Chinese lacquerwork uses only combinations of four natural pigments that do not interfere with the natural polymerization process of lacquering. Listed first here are the original tones. Each of the base-coat colors is followed by some recommended colors for decorating thereupon, but you can also use, in concert with these, modulated scales of the base-coat color, pink tones for flowers, dark bronzes ("old penny," verdigris), ivory, or mother-of-pearl.

- ❖ Black + gold, yellow, orange, raw sienna, burnt sienna
- ❖ Red + black, garnet, yellow oxide, burnt sienna, green
- ❖ Ochre yellow + burnt umber, raw umber, orange, gray-green, black
- ❖ Bronze green + gold, yellow, orange, yellow oxide, raw sienna
- ❖ Amber + gold, burnt umber, yellow, orange, moss green
- ❖ Red tortoiseshell + gold, yellow, orange, burnt umber, gray-green, black
- ❖ Brown + gold, yellow, orange, green, black
- ❖ Garnet + gold or copper, yellow oxide, orange
- ❖ Raw umber + gold, lemon, yellow oxide, orange, raw sienna, moss green
- ❖ Tobacco + gold, yellow, orange, burnt sienna, burnt umber, gray-green
- ❖ Orange ochre + gold, yellow, orange, burnt sienna, burnt umber, moss green
- ❖ Turquoise blue + gold or silver, yellow oxide, raw sienna, raw umber, black.

Example 1

Example 2

To minimize the difficulties of priming and varnishing faux lacquerwork for the amateur who has not mastered the art of making a perfectly level surface—skills more familiar to the professional painter—here are some suggestions.

New supports (smooth plastic-laminated wood, preprimed panels, or fiberboard) for a decorative panel, screen:

- Clean off scuff marks and dirt with turpentine.

- Apply a primer to give the surface tooth.

- Level irregularities, if necessary, with filler, especially on raw edges.

- Apply two base coats of satin-finish alkyd enamel.

- Apply a colored oil glaze over the whole surface for a jasper-, granite-, or sponged texture, or use one of the gold bronzes shown on the preceding page. These optional textures should be covered with a fluid coat of satin finish to seal the glaze.

- Transfer the design, with tracing paper or stencil.

- Paint the different decorative elements with a smooth, uniform application of oil or acrylic.

- Render the final gloss, as described below.

Old supports (already painted or finished furniture, paneling, jewelry boxes, etc.):

- Remove the old paint or finish with medium grain (320-grit, for example) wet sandpaper, wearing away old coats to get down to a smooth foundation.

- Apply the appropriate primer to give tooth to the new coat.

- Fill in irregularities, if necessary, with a gesso, spackle, or other filler and proceed as above.

The Final Gloss

In place of the traditional varnishing, use:

- Furniture polish (cream) or an automobile polishing paste, applied with an aerosol or on a rag, with final burnishing with a wool rag; this method gives a smooth brilliant satin reflection

- Water-soluble acrylic gloss varnish, applied with a brush, gives a shinier reflection, but is not as smooth. Acrylic polishes for vinyl tile floors, polished with a rag, are also possibilities.

- For a more meticulous finish, apply two coats of satin alkyd varnish, and lightly sand with fine sandpaper (600-grit, for example), followed with a coat of acrylic varnish.

Panel with turquoise base coat

The sky is ragged whitish patina, the details mainly raw sienna and yellow oxide.

Chinese-style details

FAUX STAINED GLASS

Traditional stained glass is an assemblage of pieces of colored glass set in grooved lead cames, forming a decorative composition held in place with metal brackets or masonry crosspieces. Glass artists usually use antique hand-blown glass, but all kinds of glass—plate, etched, textured, even safety glass—are also used for contemporary work. Beyond the many tones of the glass itself, the technique of painting glass allows the creation of real paintings in light, obtained by successive strokes, which, after firing, are permanently colored. This ancient technique, like grisaille, is about light and shadow. It goes with all styles, from the classic to the modern.

The starting point for real stained glass is the cartoon, a full-scale color model, allowing the cutting of glass corresponding to each colored shape. These represent the differently colored pieces of glass. After a first provisional assembly, the glass is colored and baked and inserted in the cames, which are then soldered together.

By using colored adhesive film (like that used to imitate engraved glass), we can also imitate the colored glass of stained glass. Manipulating these films and applying them requires some know-how, and careful consideration of the manufacturer's directions.

Our technique employs special colored varnishes and adhesive lead or lead substitute (for the cames) on glass.

Real stained glass

Detail of stained glass composed of tinted textured glass (Restoration studio, France Vitrail)

Classical painted stained glass
The paint is applied to the rectangular panes

Modern stained glass
Grisaille, built in entry hall (France Vitrail)

Basic Method

The design is rendered on paper or tracing paper, with lines marking off the different colored parts and the final placement of the cames. The color layout may be complete or partial, only to determine the range of colors to be applied. The colors are applied to the glass with special colored varnishes that are soluble in turpentine. These quick-drying varnishes are very translucent and come in a variety of colors. The adhesive came strips are added, following the lines of the drawing positioned underneath the glass.

In painted stained glass there are several levels of difficulty:

* Simple stained glass, realized with a rectangular or diamond frame system, possibly with a simple geometric arrangement, with two or three colors of painted glass. The stained glass effect is heightened if you use all the diagonals of the rectangle to make an interior diamond frame, underlined by the coloration.

* More elaborate geometric motifs, symmetrical arrangements, etc., with straight and curved lines. When making your model, plan to place the cames to complement and emphasize the main lines. Symmetrical motifs can be reproduced from a quarter- or half-model.

* Colored compositions with painted details, shadings, etc., as for a painting. Again, carefully consider the placement of the cames to approximate the look and the logic of stained glass.

"Stained glass" colors are colored finishes with pleasing transparency, but they dry quickly; thus, when planning, it is necessary to limit the size of each area (the largest should not be larger than a postcard). With each application, you must quickly spread the color, even it out by brushing it one direction and smoothing in the other direction. Use flat artists' paint brushes (with synthetic bristles), soft to the touch, or synthetic sable-style brushes.

Most stained glass colors can be overlaid, but this dilutes some colors. To avoid this problem, isolate the first coat with alcohol-based clear copal varnish.

If you render painted details in glaze or tube oils, you also need an isolating coat of copal varnish.

In every case, including the testing and sampling of colors, make extra samples of glass, and save them to overlay on other possible tests the next day.

There are different ways of rendering the final lead came edging:

* Adhesive lead tapes (in several widths); these best approximate the look of stained glass; they are ideal for straight lines, and with a little skill can be adapted to curves.

* Special tube pastes, allowing the edging of the most sinuous areas with a rounded band similar to lead.

* Metallic gray paint, which can be substituted in the case of pieces that are backlit or seen from a distance; this technique consists of applying a painted edging to the outlines of the colored regions with the following mix: satin varnish, aluminum powder (white bronze), tinted with a little black oil paint.

SIMPLE GEOMETRIC STAINED GLASS
(1, opposite)

Render the geometric layout on paper, and place it beneath the glass.

Apply the colored finishes one by one to the appropriate areas, using a sable brush for sharp corners.

Let dry for a day, and position the came bands.

DECORATIVE COMPOSITION WITH CURVES (2, opposite)

Render the general design on paper (transferred with tracing paper), and place it beneath the glass.

Apply the colors one by one; numbering the different tones on the paper helps the correct painting of each area.

Place the came bands in studied arrangement, giving priority to the main lines.

LANDSCAPE (3, opposite)

Render the general design on paper, taking care to consider the possible division to set off each element, and place it beneath the glass.

Apply the colors, after testing them on a scrap piece of glass.

Paint the details and shading, in unpainted areas and over the previous colors.

Position the came bands.

1

Simple geometric design, glass door panel

2

Geometric composition
Uneven tones on interior panel

3

Landscape on glass bay
in an entry hall

The faux stained glass shown here is appropriate principally for furniture with glass doors, false niches (with internal lighting), display cases and cabinets, and modern glass doors, transoms, and windows.

WINDOW (below, opposite)

Lay out the design to full scale and make a duplicate of this drawing on tracing paper. When the duplicate is reversed, place the two sections underneath the windows so you need work with each color only once.

Color the light-yellow rectangles, and then the medium-yellow rectangles, following the layout underneath.

Paint and edge the curves of the plant stems.

Apply the came bands on the decorated side and on the reverse.

All of the decorative techniques we have discussed spring from and rely upon old practices, most dating from the end of the nineteenth century. While they adapt easily to contemporary styles and surroundings, they lend a traditional, "retrospective" character that everyone will appreciate.

To nourish your imagination and your familiarity with these traditions in architecture and the decorative arts, become a student of the subject matter and the design elements that you will interpret and imitate. Go to museums and visit historic buildings. Collect photographs of decorated ceilings and walls, sculpture, arrangements of stone, majestic drapery, artistic woodwork to form a personal archive that you can draw from for any project and to broaden your repertoire of decorative techniques.

Detail from real painted stained glass

This piece is rendered in the style of Mucha. The curved cames require the use of outlining with a "ring color," to give the appearance of relief.
(Atelier France Vitrail)

Faux stained glass on casement window

The adhesive lead bands make the panes on the interior of the window; the horizontal bands span the vertical ones, with no cutting. On the exterior side, the painted bands, hardly visible except from very close, replaced the lead.

459

CREDITS & ACKNOWLEDGMENTS

Colotheque/Artephot: 306 (© Colotheque/Artephot); JF Faroualt: 327, 330–331, 342 (top), 344–347, 349, 353, 359, 363, 375; Giraudon: 317 (© Giraudon); Yannick Guégan: 25, 318, 319, 320, 321, 323, 324, 325, 326, 328, 329, 336, 337, 343, 348, 350, 354, 355, 356, 360, 361, 362, 363, 369; JP Haudry: 362, 368; Hoepffner: 26–35, 37–97; Hoffner: 397; Jeanbor: 36, 234–272, 274–305, 309–312, 322, 332–335, 338–339, 342 (bottom), 351–352, 357–358, 364–366, 370–373; Pierrre Manu: 273; Oronoz: 316 (© Archives Photeb); Scala: 308 (© Scala), 313 (© Archives Photeb), 315 (© Archives Photeb); Eileen Tweedy: 314 (©Archives Photeb).

Mme Ambonville, pharmacist, 93130 Noisy-Le-Sec (441 right); M. Amblard, IPEDEC professor, 93500 Pantin (409); M. and Mme Bonte, France Vitrail International, 92000 Nanterre (379 top, 455 top and lower right, 459); Chambres d'agriculture, Messrs. Dupont and Goupilleau, avenue George-V, 75008 Paris (423); M. Chazal, *Le Train Bleu*, Gare de Lyon, 75012 Paris (387); Ets Heude, avenue Chanzy, 93320 Pavillons-sous-Bois (392); M. and Mme Heurtrier, 07260 Rosieres (449); M. Lachassagne, fine-art painter, 93220 Gagny (393 lower right); Ets Leroy, rue Popincourt, 75011 Paris (393 upper left); M. Mazarguil, *Chez Georges*, boulevard Pereire, 75015 Paris (379 bottom); M. Payelle, Service de la Communication, the Louvre, 75001 (401 bottom); Portes Gardesa, 29016 Cortemaggiore, Italy (411 top); Portes Husky, M. Dupin, 44270 Machecoul (411 bottom).

W. W. Norton & Company gratefully acknowledges the following for their invaluable assistance with technical aspects of the translation:

Nicola Vigini, Vigini & Associates, 619 Western Avenue, Box 15, Seattle WA 98104 (206 682 4868)

Phoenix Miller, Miller Wagenaar Workshops in the Decorative Arts, 346 N. Justine, Chicago IL 60607 (312 563 9999)

Sepp Leaf Products, 381 Park Avenue South, New York NY 10016 (212 683 2840)

For further information about courses, contact
Yannick Guégan
Institut Guégan
Ecole de Peinture Decorative et de Trompe l'œil
61 Rue d'Hoëdic
44420 Quimiac Mesquer
France

(33) 40 42 56 07; FAX (33) 40 42 66 29

SOURCES OF SUPPLY

Some of the specialized materials we use in our work may be difficult to find. Always try your local art supply dealer first, then larger companies, many of which sell by mail-order, such as those listed below. For items you cannot locate, contact the French companies listed, which are the most specialized and best known in our profession in France.

FRANCE

Ets. Cleton
41, rue Saint-Sabin
75011 Paris, France
(33 1) 47 00 10 41

La Règle d'Or
10, rue Gassendi
75014 Paris, France
(33 1) 43 00 06 05

Hache Calippe et Cie.
7, rue Brézin
75014 Paris, France
(33 1) 45 40 60 82

Rougier et Plé
13, 15 Bd. des Filles du Calvaire
75003 Paris, France
(33 1) 42 72 82 90

USA

Dick Blick Art Materials
P.O. Box 1267
Galesburg IL 61402-1267
800 447 8192

Janovic/Plaza
30-35 Thomson Avenue
Long Island City NY 11101
800 772 4381

Johnson Paint Company
355 Newbury Street
Boston MA 02114
617 536 4838

Pearl Paint
308 Canal Street
New York NY 10013-2572
800 451-7327

Pratt & Lambert Inc.
101 Prospect Avenue
Cleveland OH 44115
800 BUY PRATT

Sepp Leaf Products, Inc.
381 Park Avenue South
New York NY 10016
212 683 2840

Daniel Smith
4150 First Avenue South, P.O. Box 84268
Seattle WA 98124-5568
800 426 6740

UK

Green & Stone Ltd
259 King's Road
London SW3 5EL
207 352 0837

F A Heffer & Co Ltd
24 The Pavement
London SW4 0JA
207 622 6871

John T Keep & Sons Ltd
Croyden Road
Beckenham Kent
208 658 7723

John Myland Ltd
80 Norwood High Street
London SE27 9NW
208 670 9161

Simpsons Paints Ltd
122-124 Broadley Street
London NW8 8BB
207 723 6657

Lewis Ward & Co.
128 Fortune Green Road
London NW6 1DN
207 794 3130

GLOSSARY

AIRBRUSH. A small tool, shaped like a pen or a gun, used to project fluid paint with compressed air, allowing quick shading and, with masking, rendering of moldings and ornaments.

BADGER BLENDER. A brush made from badger hairs or other hair dyed to resemble badger, used for softening or blending.

BASE COAT. The layer(s) of undiluted opaque paint applied to a primed support, directly preceding the decoration. We usually apply *two* coats to ensure adequate coverage and opacity), but we refer to these in the singular.

BEDS. Somewhat oblique bands, usually straight and parallel, but sometimes ribbon-shaped, of varying width and tone, marking off areas of marble. Rendering the beds is one of the first steps in imitating marble.

BOOKMATCH. To match the grains or patterns (as of pieces of wood or marble) in apparent mirror-image for decorative effect.

BRECCIA. Stone composed of fragments in a fine-grained bed or matrix. Large breccias are composed of large, often angular stones embedded in limestone (such as French Grand Antique). Little breccias are composed of a multitude of small, variously colored pebbles, the largest of which are about two inches (5 cm) on a side, and the smallest of which resemble grains.

BROCADE. Fabric produced by a weaving process in which raised motifs are formed with supplementary weft thread (often silk, gold, or silver) in a base fabric.

BROCATELLE. A superb marble, and also a richly brocaded silk fabric.

BRONZE (BRONZING) POWDERS. Metallic powders, simulating copper, zinc, tin, aluminum, and other metals, in different colors: pale gold, rich gold, silver (white), copper (red), etc. They are applied with bronzing varnish or in oil glazes. In oil glazes, they require a protective finish.

CALICO. Light printed cotton fabric.

CARTOON. A preparatory design or drawing used as a model by painters and weavers.

CASCADE. In drapery, a piece of fabric hung for its decorative "fall." *See also* Festoon.

CHAIN. A pattern of marble veining in the form of interlocked rings (as in Campan, Griotte, Portoro).

CHALKLINE. White braided cord, covered with powder (chalk, whiting, pigment), that is stretched between two points and "snapped" to aid in drawing long straight lines.

CHIQUETEUR. A round, squirrel-hair specialty brush used for stippling.

COTTON. Fiber from the cotton plant, used to make the fabric of the same name.

DABBING. Term used to describe the decorative technique (similar in method to stippling, but for a different effect) used to imitate the frosted look of engraved glass: liquid white paint is applied with a piece of rolled-up cotton.

DAMASK. Wool or silk fabric with a monochrome matte design on a satiny background, obtained through the play of the weaves.

EDGE. To make straight, even brushstrokes (with an edging brush and ruler, freehand, or with an airbrush), to render faux moldings, stone joints, and borders, as of motifs or lettering. Edges may be soft (blended) or sharp (unblended).

EFFLORESCENCE. A whitish powder, sometimes found on the surface of masonry, caused by the deposit of soluble salts carried through or onto the surface by moisture.

FESTOON. In drapery, a piece of fabric hung between two points. *See also* Cascade.

FIGURE. Term employed to designate the general and particular pattern of markings of wood derived from the way it is cut.

FISSURES. Fine cracks in stone.

FLAT COLOR. Uniform application of paint, without relief or nuancing; for example, for geometric motifs.

FLOGGER. A brush with very long bristles used to simulate wood grain.

FLOGGING. A technique used to render wood grain and pores by "drumming" or "slapping" the surface with a long-bristled brush.

GILDING SIZE. Adhesive for metallic leaf, available either as twelve-hour or "quick" size.

GLAZE, OIL. A paint or mixture of products (turpentine, linseed oil, dryer), more or less strongly colored, that is sufficiently transparent for the paint layer beneath to show through.

GLAZE, WATER-BASED. A very dilute water-based solution colored with powdered pigment, tube or liquid acrylic, that is sufficiently transparent for the paint layer beneath to show through.

GLAZE, UNCOLORED. Glaze that contains liquid ingredients without any colorant.

GLAZING. Process of applying glaze, either oil or water-based, to all or part of a surface.

GOLD AND METAL LEAF. Gold, silver, brass, copper, and aluminum beaten into thin, square sheets. The thinnest and most fragile of these is genuine gold. Gold is usually alloyed with silver and/or copper to produce different colors. Gold and silver leaf are available in three forms: 1) books in which 25 sheets are sandwiched between tissues, 2) transfer or patent leaf in which gold is mounted on tissues, 3) rolls or ribbons in which sheets of gold are mounted continuously on a roll of paper. Brass (also called Dutch metal or composition leaf), copper, and aluminum leaf are available only in the book and roll forms.

GRADE. Within a decoration, a continuous, gradual color transition.

GRAIN. Arrangement of the fibers in wood.

GRAINING BRUSH. Hog-bristle brush used to make a pattern of wood grain on a large scale.

GRISAILLE. Decoration in monochrome (tones of a single color), especially gray.

HEMP. Fiber from the stem of a plant, which makes a strong thread.

ISOLATE. To apply a finish or an oil glaze to preserve or seal a surface, in preparation for future operations.

JASPERING. Term used to describe the technique of producing a decorative patina or effect resembling fine- or coarse-grained jasper or granite by applying paint or glaze of different colors on a painted base coat, generally by stippling with a sponge.

KNOT. The sinuous rounded shape produced by wood fibers at the junction between branch and trunk.

LAMPAS. Silk upholstery fabric, ornamented with large relief decorative motifs from a separate weave than that of the base.

LAYOUT. The basic plan or arrangement of a design.

LINEN. Fiber from a blue-flowered herbaceous plant, isolated from the stem by retting (soaking in water or drying in air) and used to make the fabric of the same name.

LIQUID ACRYLIC. Premixed fluid acrylics, often intended for use in airbrushes, which we use for water-based glazes.

MAROUFLAGE. An old artisanal technique of gluing a canvas to a support, such as a wall or ceiling.

MOIRÉ. Visual effect of different tones used to render certain linear patterns in marble or undulations in wood grain to achieve nuance and depth.

MONOCHROME. A special color harmony resulting from the use of only a single scale of tones.

MUSLIN. Light, supple, transparent fabric that is not very tightly woven.

PIGMENT. Coloring material in the form of a powder that is mixed in a given medium to yield a chosen tone. Early painters fashioned their own pigments (by grinding minerals and other natural substances); today, a wide range of natural and synthetic pigments is commercially available.

PLUME. The rounded, more or less regular marking (depending on the type of wood), in the shape of a whorl or vee, yielded by flat-sawing wood.

POUNCING. Use of a perforated stencil dusted using a "pounce bag" (a small porous pocket of fabric filled with a fine pigment scuh as talc or yellow ochre) in order to transfer a design to a support. The stencil may be made by laying out the desired design on sturdy tracing paper and pricking holes along the contours of the design with a heavy needle held in a cork.

PRIMER. The layer of paint, usually white, under the base coat, used to provide a nonporous and opaque surface for painting.

PROTECTION. The final stage of decorative painting, in which the decoration is secured against wear and deterioration with a layer of varnish.

RAY. The pattern of markings resulting from quarter-sawing wood (cutting across the growth rings).

REGLAZES. Applications of succeeding layers of glaze over an original layer.

REMOVAL. The process of lifting (wiping off) wet paint or glaze, with sponge, brush, rag, or finger, for example in rendering marble, wood shimmer, and certain patinas.

RETOUCH. To give more importance, emphasis, or detail to a painted element.

RINGS. Term that designates the forms, more or less round, that mark certain marbles (for example, Campan, Griotte) and, in wood, the pattern created by annual growth.

RONDIN. A small soft-haired specialty brush similar to a stencil brush.

SABLES. Brushes made from very high quality sable hairs, used for precise work (retouching, ornamentation, lettering).

SANDPAPER. Abrasive used for smoothing supports and removing previously applied finishes. Wet-dry sandpaper is designed for use with water, minimizing scoring of the support. A sponge is used to keep the surface wet, and to rinse at the end. Sandpaper comes in different grits, from coarse (number 60) to fine (number 600 and up).

SATIN. Fine, soft, brilliant fabric, in silk, wool, cotton, or synthetic fiber.

SILK. Fiber secreted as a fine, shiny thread by various worms and spiders. Silk fabric is made from the thread of the silkworm.

SOFTEN. To blend a color or brush marks by lightly smoothing, partially or wholly, generally with a badger blender.

SPALTER. A flat brush used in decorative painting, most notably for making undulations in wet glaze.

SPATTER. To make small spots of light- or dark-colored paint or glaze, often with the bristles of a toothbrush, for example to imitate the pores and cavities of stone. Spattering with turpentine on oil yields bare spots.

SPONGE. Natural (marine) or synthetic porous material, used to remove glaze from or apply it to a painted surface, in broader or finer irregular spots, depending on whether the tight fine cellular parts or the more open pores of the sponge are used.

SPONGING. Applying or removing paint or glaze with a sponge.

STENCIL. Device, made of sturdy paper or card, for the accurate transfer of a design. *See also* Pouncing.

STIPPLING. Term used to describe the technique, used to produce a fine regular or irregular pattern of marks, by repeated dabbing motions made perpendicular to the support, in order to achieve a desired texture either by *removing* paint or glaze (for example, softening patinas with a stippling brush) or, in certain cases, by *adding* touches of paint or glaze (for example, rendering jasper or granite with a sponge or *chiqueteur*).

TEMPLATE. Model cut from a sturdy material, such as cardboard, allowing the speedy duplication of repetitive designs by following the lines of the template with a pencil or other tool.

VEIN. To render the long, narrow, sinuous, colored marks produced in marble by geological transformations and in wood by growth pattern, usually with a fine pointed brush.

VELVET. Fabric with short pile on one side, with very tightly woven erect pile on the other. There are many types of velvet, according to the fabrication process and material used: silk velvet, synthetic velvet, uncut velvet, cut velvet, velvet with relief motifs, etc.

WOOL. Thick fiber, soft and curly, from the fleece of sheep or other animals, used to make fabric.

INDEX